"Mary Beth has given all who grieve and are bound by guilt the ability to SEE freedom and embrace truth. She makes the deepest places of our being easier to embrace and grasp. I felt like I was looking at my own heart exposed on the pages of this book."

Denise Jonas, mother of the Jonas Brothers

"Every now and then a book comes along that is not only great. It's a gift. An extravagant gift. This is one of those books."

Beth Moore

"There is something silencing about sitting beside and looking into the eyes of a person who has walked through the valley of the shadow of death. But when that person tells you that the Lord God was there with them, in the darkness, your empathy turns to hope, even joy. It is one of the treasures of the kingdom of God that we as followers of Christ get to enjoy, His intimate, personalized comfort in the midst of our nightmare. Mary Beth has opened the doors of her stories to us, telling the secret ways that God personally comforted her and her family, so that our deepest fears may be overcome with hope. And that we can all walk in a deeper trust that God is good . . . all the time."

Toby (TobyMac) and Amanda McKeehan

"What a book! With a balanced combination of heart-wrenching honesty and absolute grace, Mary Beth shares her 'severe mercy.' She writes as she speaks, in a comfortable, conversational, connecting way. I couldn't help but sense God's presence in every sentence. This wonderful family helps us SEE."

Mary Graham, president, Women of Faith

"Having been through grief ourselves, it was so refreshing to hear how someone truly feels in such a time of unexplainable heartbreak. When the world is telling us to suffer alone in despair and hopelessness, the Chapmans are fixing their eyes on Christ and faithfully walking each step clinging to the Lord and the hope we have in the promises in His Word."

Bart (of Mercy Me) and Shannon Millard

Choosing to SEE

God Bless You!

Choosing to SEE

A JOURNEY *of* STRUGGLE *and* HOPE

Mary Beth Chapman

with ELLEN VAUGHN

R
Revell
a division of Baker Publishing Group
Grand Rapids, Michigan

Published by Revell
a division of Baker Publishing Group
P.O. Box 6287, Grand Rapids, MI 49516-6287
www.revellbooks.com

Library of Congress Cataloging-in-Publication Data
Chapman, Mary Beth.
    Choosing to see : a journey of struggle and hope / Mary Beth Chapman with Ellen Vaughn.
       p.   cm.
    ISBN 978-0-8007-1991-3 (cloth) — ISBN 978-0-8007-1992-0 (international trade paper edition)
    1. Chapman, Mary Beth. 2. Christian biography—United States. 3. Suffering—Religious aspects—Christianity. I. Vaughn, Ellen Santilli. II. Title.
BR1725.C443A3 2010
270.092—dc22
   [B]   2010021147

Unless otherwise indicated, Scripture is taken from the Holy Bible, New International Verson®. NIV®. Copyright © 1973, 1978, 1984 by Biblica.™ Used by permission of Zondervan. All rights reserved worldwide. www.zondervan.com.

Scripture marked ESV is taken from The Holy Bible, English Standard Version, copyright © 2001 by Crossway Bibles, a division of Good News Publishers. Used by permission. All rights reserved.

Published in association with Creative Trust, Inc., Literary Division, 5141 Virginia Way, Suite 320, Brentwood, TN 37027, www.creativetrust.com.

10   11   12   13   14   15   16   7   6   5   4   3   2   1

In loving memory of
Maria Sue Chunxi Chapman

Mommy misses you so much. Your time with us was too short, but there is only One who holds all of time and eternity in His hands, and we trust Him. My prayer is that Mommy's tears will continue to water the seeds of your life, and that all who read this story will be pointed to the One who holds you in His arms until I can. I miss your slobber and your laughter and the way you always made me pinky promise to come back and check on you "like in three minutes" after I tucked you in. You are definitely the "Silliest Goober I know."

I love you; to infinity . . . and beyond!

Dedicated to
Will Franklin

You have been entrusted with an incredible pain! I'm so sorry. I wish as your mom I could take it away, but I know God has a plan for you to steward this story well and to minister to others through your suffering. You are my hero, as well as Maria's . . . she loved you so much, as do I!

Shaoey

The day you became my daughter changed my life forever! Love took me in, and everything changed. Thanks for telling me on your own you wanted me to write this book. I love everything about you and am so proud of you!

Stevey Joy

Since the night you danced without Maria at the recital just nine days after she went to heaven, I've been so proud of your courage. I know that Maria is with you in your heart because Jesus is, and Maria is with Jesus! I love you. Thanks for kissing Mommy's tears.

Emily and Tanner

October 4, 2008, the day you two were married, was a beautiful picture of the love of the Father. That we could celebrate while still missing Maria so desperately was truly a gift. I believe it was a taste of the spring that will truly come out of this hard winter season. Tanner, thanks for loving not only Emily, but our entire family selflessly during such a dark time.

Caleb and Julia

Caleb, when Will Franklin needed you most, you were there to hold him. God was with you and the strength He gave you was perfect! I know this is a story of great struggle that you will treasure as you allow Jesus to heal your heart. Julia, thanks for being right by Caleb's side. You love him so well.

I'm so thankful that on May 10, 2009, you became my daughter-in-law. Another sign that spring is continuing to bloom.

Steven

To my best friend and at times, worst enemy if we were to be honest: there are no words . . . I love you when we are on the same side and when we find ourselves on different sides. Thanks for being my biggest fan and cheerleader during this process. You believe more in me than I believe in myself. The foreword you so graciously wrote made me smile. It was way generous and kind. (That may have something to do with the fact that I sleep with you!) The words are proof that your love for me has been unwavering. Navigating our lives has not been for the faint of heart, and your heart has been that of a warrior, valiantly protecting his own family from an enemy who seeks to devour and destroy. God is good, even when things seem bad.

Contents

Contents

Foreword

Steven Curtis Chapman

I'm going to start off with a little secret that you who hold this book in your hands are about to discover. Don't worry—I'm not going to give anything away and you don't need any "spoiler alerts." For many years I've been known as "the writer" of the Steven Curtis/Mary Beth Chapman duo. And while I've been known to pen a song or two, and maybe even a book or two (with a whole lot of help, believe me!), here's the real, honest-to-goodness truth: *Mary Beth Chapman is a way better writer than Steven Curtis* . . . don't tell anybody. No, actually, please tell everybody! The world needs to know, and I'm proud to be the first to tell them.

When my wife reads this, I can picture her shaking her head and saying, "He's just trying to be nice and encouraging." But I am truly amazed at the way my wife is able to communicate what's in her heart with such honesty and transparency. (Not to mention that she can write in thirty minutes what would take me about three days!)

When Mary Beth's blogs posted on my website began getting attention and someone first mentioned that she should write a book, I began cheering her on in that direction. Because I realized that one of the last things my wife ever planned or had the time to do was write a book, I cheered cautiously. But I knew if it was something God wanted her to do, it would speak powerfully and profoundly into the hearts of readers. She has a rare and beautiful gift to bare the pain, confusion, and questions that stir in her soul with a deep and raw honesty, and yet do it in such an inviting way. She also has a natural ability to have you laughing one moment and weeping the next as she takes you on the journey into her heart and life.

That's what this book is about . . . a journey. Mary Beth's journey, to be sure, but also the journey of faith that each of us who follow the unseen God is on. At the time this book is being written, I have had the incredible privilege of walking beside Mary Beth on her journey for twenty-six years. She has had enough twists and turns, surprises (wonderful and terrible), and peaks and valleys to fill several lifetimes . . . and she still looks amazing! (Hey, just look at the cover . . . hubba hubba!)

For a while this book carried the working title of *Mary Beth vs. God*, which I still think would have been a very appropriate title. By her own confession, she has had a lifetime of watching God overwrite her plans with His story. Sometimes the result has been wonderful, and sometimes it has been devastating. Sometimes she's been a willing participant, and sometimes she's gone "kicking and screaming." But in every case the process has been difficult at best. I've watched my wife wrestle with the providence of God in as real and honest a way as anyone I've ever known. And there has certainly been much to wrestle with. Great depths of pain and sorrow have marked the journey that my precious wife has traveled, and that is what has brought about the writing of this book.

I must also say a heartfelt thank you to the wonderfully gifted Ellen Vaughn for taking the journey alongside Mary Beth in the writing process. Her skillful pen and tender heart have been vital to making this book a reality.

I was reading a book recently by our dear friend Dan Allender. He talked about how for many Christians, sorrow and pain are seldom embraced by those experiencing it but rather "often denied or swept under the spiritual rug of 'God's sovereignty'" (*The Healing Path*, WaterBrook Press, 2000). Well, I can say that *this* book is written by someone who is deeply committed to *not* sweeping the pain or struggle under any such rug. While I know my wife to fully and desperately believe and trust in the sovereignty of God, I also know her—as you will come to know her in these pages—as one who is determined to be honest about the struggle. And I believe you will, along with me, be much richer for it.

Finally, I want to say that this book and the hours Mary Beth has given to create it are part of a "sacred trust" that our family believes we were given on May 21, 2008, when our Maria was carried to heaven in the arms of Jesus. While it is very intentionally not a book primarily about our loss or grief, it is out of deep desire to see our God turn for good what Satan meant for evil (Gen. 50:20) that my precious wife has been willing to retake the difficult journey in writing it. A tremendous price has been paid to create the book you hold in your hands . . . it is a treasure. As her husband, I'm proud beyond words of her courage. And I sincerely believe you will be, as I am, very grateful that Mary Beth has invited us into her journey as she is choosing to SEE.

Soli Deo Gloria.

May 2010

Prologue

Beth Moore

I've never been one to have meaningful dreams. Goodness knows it's not from lack of trying. In the course of a forty-year relationship with God, I can't think of many supernatural manifestations I knew He was capable of giving His children that I haven't blatantly requested at one time or another. The way I saw it, what was the harm in asking? Couldn't we all use some wonders from time to time? I figured God could always say no. And, by and large, He did. It became clear to me along the way, if not downright humorous, that God saw me in the category of people who were safer—both to themselves and others—sticking primarily with Scripture. That's the way He most often reveals Himself to me. The Word has been my glorious wonder and an open Bible the center stage where I've watched Him perform and felt measures of His presence that were sometimes so strong, they were painful. Those are the moments I live for. I've heard other followers of Christ who seemed of sound mind and doctrine testify to experiences and giftings that I had no biblical grounds to deny. He just normally did things a different way with me.

He still does. But something out of the blue happened to me several months ago. Something exceptional. Something I knew instinctively didn't even belong to me. I had a dream for somebody else. I was not a participant in the unfolding scene. I was only there to watch.

In my dream, I was backstage at an event center behind the usual black curtains. I could hear and feel the crowd in the seating area and knew that the event, whatever it was, had not yet begun. I did not feel anxious in my dream, as if I were about to go onto the platform. I was carefree and calm, like someone only there to observe. The gray concrete floor backstage was just like those I've seen numerous times. Thick black cables were gaff-taped to the floor in bunches. Men wearing headphones were huddled over the soundboard. Somebody else was adjusting the lights.

That's when I saw Mary Beth come around the corner. I instantly knew she was the one going onto that platform, but she was not going out there alone. She was going out with Maria, who was just to her right in a twirly skirt and a white, tucked-in blouse with a single ruffled collar. Her coal black hair was swept back in a matching headband with a chunk of her long bangs escaping and falling forward into her eyes. Mary Beth was trying to hold on tightly to Maria's hand as the child sped in front of her and nearly pulled her over. One of the men backstage stopped Mary Beth to brief her and, all the while, Maria squirmed, giggled, turned, and kicked out her wiry little tan legs until her mother, typical of all who have an active charge, was nearly twisted into a pretzel. I could hear Maria laughing and I could see Mary Beth smiling.

I felt myself smiling back and all the while staring, perplexed at my own frozenness. I sat completely still, as if one little twitch would make it all disappear. And then I woke up. My eyes sprung open, but otherwise I did not move a single muscle. My heart pounded and I felt butterflies in my stomach like something extraordinary had happened. I've had thousands of vivid dreams in the course of a long lifetime, but this was unlike any of the others. This one meant something. I was certain of that. This time God gave it to me. I was also certain of that. It was a tremendous departure for me, and even in those first few moments of alertness, I believed I knew a measure of what it meant. Part of my friend Mary Beth's joy was going to be restored after the tragic loss of her darling Maria by telling her story as God Himself would unfold it. Her own healing would come in many ways as she ministered her pain and her hope. As she moved forward by faith with fresh vision, the memories of

Maria's playfulness and the echoes of laughter over her antics would little by little eclipse the images from the day of the accident. And I knew one more thing.

I knew Maria was alive. Very, very much alive. Many of us believe in life after death by faith and by creed, but what shook me to the bone was that I also had the rare occasion to know it by sight. The thought never occurred to me that Maria had morphed into an attending angel of some kind or, worse yet, an unsettled apparition walking around holding Mary Beth's hand until she was whole again. I knew in that moment that her happy, playful presence right next to Mary Beth in the dream was symbolic. She is joyous and whole and beautiful in God's presence, but the Chapmans would again recover the gladness she'd ushered into their lives as they poured their fragrant, expensive offering before God, drop by heavy drop.

I knew I had to tell Mary Beth, but I wasn't sure how to approach a subject so tender, where even angels should fear to tread. As God would time it, her birthday offered me the perfect opportunity to touch base and ask her if we could talk soon. I still have the text conversation on my cell phone, and I delighted to discover that it was recorded right under several other texts she and I had exchanged over getting fresh highlights. I do dearly love being a woman. Here's how the door opened to an encounter of titanic proportions for us both.

Me to Mary Beth:
   Happy birthday, my darling sister! I am at a conference this weekend but I want to talk soon. I had a dream about you. I never have had a prophetic or meaningful dream but I had the strangest feeling this time. It was short but if it confirms something God is already telling you, it would be worth me sharing it with you. I love you and am honored to sojourn with you.

Several minutes later, Mary Beth back to me:
   Thank you so very much! So strange that you've had a dream . . . I'm anxious to hear as God has stirred and is doing so much . . . if only you knew . . . Let's talk soon. I am so humbled to call you friend. Please pray for me as I come to your mind and I will you. Looking forward to a chat!

A few days later, while I was on the way home from work, I got the courage to bring up her number on my cell and hit *send*. Steven grabbed her phone and answered it, "Mary Beth's personal secretary, may I help you?" We laughed and teased back and forth a bit, then he handed her the line and the conversation ensued.

"Mary Beth, as I told you in the text, I had a dream. And I don't have dreams. Not the kind that mean anything, anyway. I mean, God has never spoken to me in a dream before in my entire life. But I think He did this time."

I was hedging. Not sure how to say it. I could hardly make the word "Maria" come out of my mouth because, after decades of interacting with women, I knew that the name of every lost child is sacred to the grieving mother. A person is wise to use it with great care and caution because the stab of pain it will invariably cause had better be worth it. I awkwardly made my way through the dream with a completely silent partner on the other end. When I finished telling her about it, I realized how brief it really was. It could only have lasted a few seconds but, when I had it, it seemed like everything moved in slow motion over the course of a half hour.

"And that was it. My dream. Mary Beth, it was so real. I'm so sorry. I know it hurts, but I so hope God means it for some measure of healing . . ."

Then she bawled. And I nearly bawled with her. When Mary Beth began to tell me with tears that, just prior to the night I received it, she had specifically asked God to let her see Maria in a dream, I had to pull the car over and park. My chin fell to the ground. God hit me with such a sense of awe that I could hardly form words, yet I had a knowing in my heart that I will never be able to understand.

"Mary Beth, God allowed me, another mom, to have the dream for you. I think He knew that if He'd given it to you so early in your healing, you might wish you could just stay asleep. He wants you to know He heard you and that He even gave you what you asked, just through a means that might bless and do no harm in the long run."

It was as sacred a moment as I've ever shared with another woman. As it turned out, God did indeed use the dream to confirm what He'd already been saying to her. I knew that would be the determining factor for its legitimacy. I don't believe God often cold-calls His children through others. He's mostly a one-on-one kind of communicator with people who are apt to listen. Usually He employs others to confirm what He's already been telling us or preparing us for. Mary Beth and I pledged to talk soon, then we hung up the phone, both, I feel sure, overcome emotionally. I have had many wonderful moments with God through the years when, for whatever reason, He'd grant a sudden revelation of His majesty, mercy, or love. These are times when, even for a few seconds, the veil almost seems to thin. I can't think of many other times in my life, however, when I was more overcome with God's flagrant tender mercies. All I could say on the way home was, "O, God! O, God! You, God! I can't believe You just did that, God!"

Stunned, I pulled up into my driveway and walked into the kitchen to a happy husband who greeted me with the usual, "Hey, Baby! Had a good day?"

"Uh, yes. You are not going to believe what just happened."

True to form, my rugged husband cried. An unbelieving onlooker could reason that, to have a God who cared enough to orchestrate something like the timing of that dream, we'd have a God who'd never let such a tragedy happen to start with. These are places where God exercises His sovereign right to retain mystery. We cannot fathom the intricacies of the divine plan. But make no mistake, when we are in the driest desert, we can receive the manna to make it all the way to the other side where trees bud again and children laugh. God sometimes delivers us from evils we never see. Other times He parts raging oceans before our very eyes. Still other times He says, "When you pass through the waters, I will be with you; and when you pass through the rivers they will not sweep over you. . . . Do not be afraid, for I am with you; I will bring your children from the east and gather you from the west" (Isa. 43:2, 5).

April 27, 2010

1

Winter

It was the day the world went wrong.

"Beauty Will Rise"
Words and music by Steven Curtis Chapman

In the bleak midwinter frosty wind made moan,
earth stood hard as iron, water like a stone

Christina Rossetti

The sky was a bright, springtime blue that day. We were planning a wedding and a graduation. We were happy.

It was May 21, 2008. It didn't look like winter—yet.

We were the parents of six beautiful children, blessed beyond our dreams. Our twenty-three-year-old daughter, Emily, had become engaged four days earlier. Just the night before, we had bought her wedding dress. I had brought it home to show Emily's three little sisters from China. Shaoey was eight, Stevey Joy was five, and Maria had just turned five a week earlier. They shrieked about the lacy white gown and all started talking at once about being flower girls at her wedding.

On this particular Wednesday afternoon, Emily was at work, and Steven and I had converted the dining room table into Wedding Central. We had phones, laptops, calendars, and notepads spread all over the table. Caleb, our eighteen-year-old, was to graduate high school in a few days; he was messing around with his guitar in our music room. Will, who was seventeen, had driven over to his school to try out for a play. The three little girls were running in and out of the house, playing together like a thousand other afternoons.

Maria ran up to me, breathless. "Mommy!" she said. "I can't get Cinderella Barbie's gloves on her! Can you do it for me?"

"Sure," I said. Maria climbed up on my lap. She was sticky and sweet as usual. She sat for a second while I tried to scoot the tiny, elbow-length white gloves onto Cinderella Barbie's rubbery little hands. It was hard; no wonder Maria hadn't been able to do it.

Maria got impatient. There was fun to be had. She scooted off my lap and ran away giggling. As Steven and I continued to talk, I used my fingernails and tugged, eventually succeeding with the gloves.

"Hey, Maria!" I yelled. "I got Cinderella's gloves on her!"

There was no answer, and I assumed that the girls had gone outside to their playground. They loved to climb on the monkey bars, swing, and pretend they were "the Chapman Sisters," a famous musical group.

Steven took a call on his cell phone and walked out on our front porch to get better reception. He saw Will arriving home and watched as Will slowly turned his old Land Cruiser into the driveway, which winds past the house to the garage in back, near the playground. I was sitting at the table, writing a list.

Then everything changed forever.

I realized I was hearing odd sounds outside—not just the yelling of happy play but screams and commotion. I bolted into the kitchen to head outside just as Shaoey ran up the back steps and met me there.

"Mom!" she yelled. "Will's hit Maria with the car!"

I flew outside. Will was near the garage, holding his little sister in his arms. There was a lot of blood, on both of them.

"Maria!" Will was crying. "Maria! Wake up!"

2

Not My Plan

Love of God is pure when joy and suffering inspire an *equal* degree of gratitude.

Simone Weil

Obviously, I never planned to write this book.

No mom can come up with words to express the ripping pain of losing a child . . . and no words can do justice to the mysteries of God in the midst of tragedy.

When people ask how we are doing, the first thing I always say is, "I want Maria back. I want my son Will Franklin not to have this as a chapter in his story. I want my children to be healthy, my family secure. I don't really care whose life has been touched or changed because of our loss!"

That is the heart of a mother who lost a daughter and is determined not to lose another child. I believe God can handle my heart, my questions, and my anger. It's okay to want Maria back. It's okay to be angry. The question is, what do I do with it all? What do I do with God? In the midst of such heartbreak, do I really believe that *all* things work together for good for those who love Him and are called according to His purpose?

The answer to that question has come at a great cost. It has been agonizing to choose to see God at work through the tears of losing my daughter. I have, however, experienced the kindness, sweetness, faithfulness, and redemptive heart of God. I believe none of my tears have been wasted.

So here I am, putting down these words one by one, because God has surprised me over the long days since Maria went to heaven. I have come face to face with evil and what part it plays in our lives, past, present, and future. I am realizing, though, that God is God, and He is purposeful in destroying what evil intends for harm. He is surprising me in *good* ways beyond what can be measured on this earth! I am *living* what I once only read in Genesis 50:20–21, where Joseph tells his brothers, "You intended to harm me, but God intended it for good to accomplish what is now being done, the saving of many lives. So then, don't be afraid. I will provide for you and your children . . . "

Even in this free fall of pain, I've landed on a solid foundation and my faith has held . . . on most days. I have learned that God is good . . . always. Hope is real. I have found—even in the awful pain of tears and grief so intense you think it will kill you—that my family and I can *do* hard. We'll never get over our loss, but we're getting through it. And so I have prayed that our journey through the shadows of loss might be of some help to those who have experienced similar pain . . . that our stewardship of this story would comfort many.

But I need to be clear. This book isn't just about the spring day when Steven and I lost our precious Maria Sue in a terrible accident. It's about a story . . . a story God is writing. All along the way, He has changed my story in ways I didn't like. I've had whole chapters added and deleted and strange plot twists that I never saw coming.

The truth is, I was born with a plan. I wanted life to be safe and predictable. My plan was to marry someone with a nice nine-to-five schedule and have a tidy, organized life—everything under control.

Absolutely none of that came true!

And if it had—if I had lived the life I thought I wanted—I know I wouldn't have experienced the grace or the miracles of God in the ways that I have. What I've found is that it's in the most unlikely times and places of hurt and chaos that God gives us a profound sense of His presence and the real light of His hope in the dark places.

So this book isn't so much about me and Steven, as broken and crazy as we are. It's about God . . . and how He can comfort, carry, and change us on our journey, no matter how hard it is.

My husband has always been considered the creative, public side of our marriage. Everyone loves him and people assume that I'm a lot like him.

I'm not.

Steven is an extrovert who gets his energy from being around people. He loves to speak—and speak—and speak—in front of large groups. I am an introvert who loves to nest at home with my kids. If I'm invited to speak in front of a gathering of people, I get so nervous I feel like I'm going to pass out.

Steven is an optimist; I tend to be more melancholy. To him the glass is half-full; to me the same glass is half-empty. He is overflowing with great expectations; I'm sure that if things can possibly go wrong, they probably will.

Steven would never think of pulling a practical joke; it's not nice. I laugh and get all excited just *thinking* about playing jokes on my friends. It's like a love language to me! The other night I took Shaoey and Stevey Joy, and we headed over to my daughter-in-law's house. My son Caleb was out of town, playing a show, and I knew Julia had a friend over to spend the night.

We parked our van, snuck around the back of the house, and proceeded to scratch on the window screens and knock on the walls. I could hear Julia and her friend running around in panic, and then it got real quiet. I decided we should go around to the front and knock on the door so they would know it was us.

When my sweet Julia opened the door, she had tears on her face and the phone in her hand. I heard her tell the 911 dispatcher through her tears, "Oh, never mind . . . it's just my mother-in-law!"

I promised I'd never do it again, and I think she still loves me!

Anyway, it's obvious that Steven and I are very different, kind of like Tarzan and Jane, but we'll get to that a little later.

As long as I can remember, and throughout my twenty-five-year marriage to Steven, I've held on to certain expectations about life. But Jesus has always loved me enough to show me that even when I push my own ideas and expectations, He is there to guide me back to green pastures. He has shepherded me through the mountainous terrain of my stubbornness, shame, depression, and inadequacy and brought me gently back to the lushness of His love. He loves us enough to never let us go . . . even when it feels like He has.

It wasn't like I wanted a life that was unreasonable or questionable. My plans had to do with a Christ-centered ministry, an easy marriage, a peaceful and orderly home, constructive growth rather than shattered dreams, protection rather than fires . . . all good things. Still, God has turned my life, my expectations, and even some of my dreams completely upside down so many times.

I hope that in these pages you'll find a friend for your own journey . . . whether you're in a good place, or in a place that's hard, sad, mad, or desperately hopeless. In the midst of it all, God really is with us and for us. I have found that even during those times when the path is darkest, He leaves little bits of evidence all along the way—bread crumbs of grace—that can give me what I need to take the next step. But I can only find them if I choose to SEE.

3

Coloring inside the Lines

You cannot amputate your history from your destiny. . . . My past is something Jesus takes hold of and makes into a destiny. That's called redemption.

Beth Moore

Where I grew up, nothing ever changed. My dad, Jim Chapman (yes, I was a Chapman even before I met Steven), worked at International Harvester. My mother, Phyllis, was a stay-at-home mom who was so stay-at-home that she didn't even have a driver's license until after I got mine.

Mom's nickname, at least among us kids, was "Supervac"—not a speck of dust ever dared settle on the baseboards of our perfectly ordered home. My dad used to tell us to keep moving around, because if we stopped in one place too long, Mom might throw us out with the trash.

Most of the kids I knew from kindergarten graduated with me from high school. Everybody was white. I never knew of anyone who got divorced. I assumed everyone else's house was just like ours: our parents rarely fought or talked about anything unpleasant in front of us, although I'm sure they had their moments in private. Many things that presented great opportunities for discussion were often swept under the rug, where there was plenty of room because no dust would ever be found there.

I grew up wanting to do everything right. I wanted somehow to be, well, perfect . . . as if that were possible.

I was the youngest of three children, with a sister seven years older and a brother nine years older. Every morning during the summers, I'd hop on my glittered purple Huffy with bright plastic flowers stuck all over a fake wicker basket on the front, and I'd pedal off with friends. We'd ride all over the neighborhood and through a path in the woods, which came out at our elementary school. We'd play Barbies, ride to the ball fields and buy shoelace licorice, and have big water fights until the fire department blew their siren at noon.

At that signal, all us kids would race home to eat bologna, mustard, and potato chip sandwiches for lunch—I loved crunching the chips in the soft white bread—and then get back on our bikes and go off to play until dark. We weren't afraid of bad things happening. We had never heard of kidnappers. Our lives were safe and fun.

My dad was a handyman who could fix anything. He changed the oil in our car every three thousand miles, like clockwork. We Chapmans knew there was a place for everything and everything should be in its place. From the time I was little, I knew how to work hard and put things in order, so I pushed myself to excel and make my hard-working parents proud of me.

We went to church Sunday mornings, Sunday evenings, and Wednesday nights. I still remember the flannel boards of Sunday school—all those felt animals lined up on the ramp to Noah's ark, or Joseph and Mary and baby Jesus in the manger, or Moses parting the Red Sea. I went to youth camp every summer, walked the aisle, and got saved. Again.

I was always confused. Did you get saved again when you felt like you'd drifted away from God . . . or was it a rededication . . . or what? I'm not sure whether it was the church, my work ethic, or a little bit of both, but I ended up thinking that the one thing that could change in my changeless world was my eternal destiny.

Our church taught that you could lose your salvation . . . and so you never quite knew where you stood with God. I don't remember ever hearing the concept of grace. A relationship with God was all about working hard and being as good as you could possibly be.

Once when I was about nine years old, I was coloring in my bright pink bedroom with its variegated pink shag carpet and matching bedspread and curtains. I loved my room. My bed was always perfectly made, which was a challenge, since I had about a hundred stuffed animals that had to be placed on the spread in a certain sequence. I also raked my shag carpet, starting at the far corner and going all the way out the door, so that all the strands stood precisely on end, looking like no one had ever stepped on it.

Anyway, one day I was coloring a giant Holly Hobby picture in my bedroom, and I was doing my best to stay inside the lines and make it as beautiful as I could. I was in the zone, trying my hardest. It looked perfect . . . until I made one little mistake.

The more I tried to fix it, the worse it got. I felt desperate. It wasn't perfect anymore. I started crying and felt this rage well up inside of me. Before I knew what was happening, I was ripping my picture into tiny shreds. Then I ran to my bike and rode as fast and as hard as I could. I didn't even know where I was going. It was frustrating not to be perfect.

I couldn't live up to the expectations that I had for myself . . . and I knew that God must be disappointed with me too.

My grandfather wasn't perfect either, but in my young eyes he came close. He was a leader in our church, and I was amazed by how much Scripture he had memorized. I would sit next to him in church, sucking on a cherry candy my grandmother had given me and watching as Grandpa took sermon notes.

Once he got bored with a sermon. Never one to waste time or be unproductive, Grandpa pulled out a sheet of paper and began to write. When he finished, he handed it to me and whispered, "Here, check me. See if I got it right."

It was the whole chapter of Isaiah 53. Grandpa was strictly a King James man, so for a little girl it took a while to maneuver my way through the "thees" and "thous," but in the end there were no mistakes. Perfect. Word for word.

When I got older, I'd sit with my grandfather and we'd drink Cokes from the bottle and eat Ritz crackers with cheddar cheese while we talked about theology. I had lots of questions, and by now I was brave enough to push my grandpa on our church's stand on issues that I either disagreed with or misunderstood.

"Grandpa," I'd say, "so how does it work? Let's say there's a guy who's a Christian, and he's doing great, walking along the road one day, and then he sees this pretty girl with a great figure ride by on her bike. He can't help it, this lustful thought pops in his head . . . and then, bam! He gets hit by a bus. Are you telling me that he'd go to hell because he died with an unconfessed sin in his heart?"

I don't even remember what my grandfather said when I asked him this. But the point is, by the time I was a teenager I was pretty upset about the idea that you could lose your salvation. One false move, I thought, and I could end up on the outside of the pearly gates looking in, wondering what went wrong.

You get the picture: I grew up very works oriented, with the idea that Christians don't sin, they have "faults." I wasn't quite sure where the line was between people who sinned and people who simply had faults. As someone who likes to know the score, I became confused. I knew I had a relationship with God, but at what point did the big, far-off God in the sky get mad enough or disappointed enough to look at my faults and see them as sins? And if they were sins, was I really saved to begin with?

With my perfectionist personality, always trying my hardest to be good enough, I was setting myself up for huge disappointments. When bad things happened, was God so disappointed with me that He didn't care anymore? I always had questions like this in my mind, and without the reality of grace, I just couldn't wrap my arms around the Jesus who supposedly lived in the heart.

Looking back, I'm not sure if this works orientation is what my church really taught, or if this was how I perceived it. I did desire a relationship with Christ. Every summer when I'd go to youth camp, I'd get fired up about Jesus and my relationship with Him. I'd always get saved again, or at least rededicate my life to God. I wanted to do it all just right. I'd read the Bible and pray and journal about Jesus . . . for a while. Then I'd go back to school, the fervor would fade, and I'd backslide, sin, have faults, or whatever the word was, and the cycle would start all over again. I couldn't be what I thought a Christian should look like.

I loved my church friends, but I also had other friends at school. I wanted everyone to like me, and if conforming to peer pressure was the way for that to happen, I'd allow myself to be pressured from time to time. So I was a good girl who got good grades, but also a fun-loving girl who had an adventurous spirit and would hang with the wild crowd from time to time.

As a child I'd always been a bit heavy, thanks to my grandmother's cherry pie and my mother's homemade sourdough bread dripping with lots of butter. I hated shopping for clothes. At Sears, back in the day, if you were a thick boy, you were considered "husky"; if you were a thick girl, you were considered, yes, "chubby"!

My grandmother called me her little butterball. The kids at school called me Chubby Chapman. I was a big fan of justice—so if something seemed unfair, I wasn't shy about voicing my opinion. I hated how the popular kids would pick on people like me. I'd always stick up for the underdog.

Then, during the summer between my freshman and sophomore years, when I was fifteen, I grew about three inches and lost about twenty-five pounds. Everything on my body shifted around in some pretty amazing ways. All of a sudden, the people who had teased me wanted to be my friends. Boys who had called me "el Chubbo" the year before were asking me out on dates. I found great pleasure in turning them down.

During my summers growing up, I spent most of my time at a family swim and athletic club. My brother was the coach of my swim team, and as soon as I was old enough (about the same time as my physical metamorphosis) I was certified as a lifeguard.

So there I was, tanned, bleached blond, with a deep dimple and straight white teeth, thanks to my parents' splurge on braces when I was younger. I loved the pool smells of chlorine, baby oil mixed with iodine (for that great, oh-so-natural orange hue), and Coppertone lotion. I loved sitting up in the lifeguard stand, flipping my whistle on its cord around my index finger, in charge and lovin' life!

During the summers, camp meetings would come to town. There were big revivals every night, with special choirs and singing groups and youth events. One night I went to a church service with the intention of staying for a youth meeting, and a man at the entrance stopped me. He looked about 112 years old, and he said, "Excuse me, young lady, but you are not welcome here dressed like that!"

"Excuse me?" I asked.

"You're not welcome here!" he repeated, grabbing hold of my upper arm. "Not with what you're wearing!"

I looked down at myself. The one-piece culottes outfit, red with white stripes, complemented my nice suntan, but it was *not* inappropriate! It wasn't too short or cut too low . . . definitely not over the line of any reasonable dress code.

Part of me was ready to cry; the other part was mad at the injustice of it all.

"Isn't this a church service?" I asked the Grandpa Inquisitor. "What if I was a person who didn't know Christ and desperately needed to be saved, and you turned me away and told me I wasn't welcome because of what I was *wearing*?"

All he did was tell me to leave. "You are not welcome here!"

I turned away, tears rolling down my cheeks, and got into my car. My dad, brother, and sister had a Southern gospel group and they were singing in a small church nearby. I drove there . . . and the pastor, my parents, my siblings, and the small congregation all told me I was welcome with whatever I was wearing, and anyway, I looked just fine.

You would think that with my upbringing and the support of my parents and grandparents, I would have felt healthy and secure with who I was.

But I didn't. There was a hurricane of stuff going on inside of me: my hard-working perfectionism, my desire to be well liked by everyone, my body-image issues of having been a chubby preadolescent and now a pretty teenager.

As time went on I continued to engage with the church kids, while at the same time pushing some of the boundaries with kids in my high school. I continued my battle with the theological questions of God that started so long ago with my grandpa.

Does God love me only when I make good choices? Does He love me even then? Would I ever be worthy enough for a relationship with the God of the universe?

The answer I kept hearing inside of me was "no." I couldn't color perfectly inside the lines of what I thought God expected of me. I couldn't do it right. Grace was not a word I understood, and I had no concept that I was created in the image of God. The Enemy of my soul whispered to me that I could never be good enough, that I just wasn't worth God's attention and love.

Around this time I fell victim to a predator who manipulated my naivete for his pleasure. He used me and left me with a deep emotional wound. My trust was broken. I was more shattered than that torn-up Holly Hobby picture. Feeling lonely and scared, I tried fixing it myself by stuffing the guilt and shame deeper and deeper inside.

All these years later, I am still dealing with this pain. It has scarred all of my closest relationships, especially with my very patient husband. Those closest to me have seen the effects that evil and shame can bring.

Now I understand that the blame is not mine to own. But when I was a sixteen-year-old girl, I lived in a swirl of confusion, trying to figure out where God was when I needed

> If we want to grow in faith we must be open to listening to our own stories, perhaps familiar or forgotten, where we have not mined the rich deposit of God's presence. With better eyes and ears we will sense how God has worked to redeem even our most tragic experiences.
>
> Dan Allender

Him most. I couldn't work hard enough or be good enough to escape the reality of my damaged soul. I was driven to avoid, at all costs, the shame that was deep inside. I felt like nothing I did really mattered anymore.

By my senior year of high school, I didn't know where I would go, or if I would go, to college. I had taken some college level classes and had a high GPA, thanks to my work ethic and academic abilities. As a young girl I'd dreamed of going to Anderson University, but I knew that wasn't on my parents' radar. It would be a financial stretch.

But my dad had suggested that nursing would be a great option for me. Since Anderson had a solid nursing program, he and my mom made whatever contacts and calls they could. They helped me take out student loans to finance the part that they couldn't . . .

and the next thing I knew I was accepted at Anderson and on my way to Indiana. One of the last things my mom said to me was, "If you're going to Anderson just to meet someone and marry him, can you please do it your freshman year so we don't have to spend all this money?"

My plan was to avoid any situations that could potentially set me up for further pain. Dating wasn't on my priority list. I would work hard, study hard, and graduate with honors. The hazy future after that would reward me with a great job, and I'd eventually marry the most reliable, consistent man I could find . . . an accountant! He would work nine to five, except during tax season; we'd have two weeks off in the summers for vacation. He would be organized and predictable. He would change the oil in my car and keep everything working properly. Life would be orderly and secure.

I told my mom that I had a plan, and I certainly wasn't going to do some crazy thing like fall in love, get married, and drop out.

But sometimes God's plans are a little—or a lot—different from ours.

4

Tarzan and Jane

Deep in the jungle up in the trees in Indiana, 1983
Living on pizza and too little sleep
Just me and my animal friends
Then in the distance I saw through the leaves
A creature of beauty like none I had ever seen
The trouble started when you smiled at me
And our two worlds came crashing together
And a true love story began

I am Tarzan you are Jane
I am night and you are the day
We're like sunshine and rain
We're so different from each other
You are woman, I am man
You are the sea and I am the land
And I would not be who I am if I didn't have you

"We Belong Together (Tarzan and Jane)"
Words and music by Steven Curtis Chapman

As I started college at Anderson, I was pretty disillusioned about a lot of things. I felt lonely and unworthy of God's love. I wanted so badly to trust Jesus, but trust had been stolen from me. So I desperately needed a fresh start as I turned a new page in my school calendar and in my spiritual life.

The great thing was that I would be rooming with a good friend, Dondeena, and we were both excited about the Christian community on campus. In spite of my disillusionment, I really did want a fresh beginning. I rededicated my life to Christ, and something down deep felt it was different this time, as opposed to my annual rededications when I was growing up. Back then my relationship with God was fear and performance driven. But now I was longing for an authentic closeness with Jesus.

I would find out much later that what I was hungry for was grace. But I didn't even have a word for it when I was starting college.

Dondeena and I both prayed and asked Jesus to walk with us and to breathe fresh life into our souls. Then, before classes started, we decided to go to the annual freshman orientation concert. The band was this guy named Steve Chapman, his brother Herbie, and a friend, Brent Henderson. They played contemporary Christian music with a definite country twang.

Steve did most of the talking—later this would come as no surprise to me—and was obviously the leader of the band. He had a perfect mullet (business in the front, party in the back), a big smile, cowboy boots, and a green guitar. Since I was from Ohio, anyone from south of there was considered a hillbilly, and this mullet guy, who went by Steve back then, seemed to fit the bill. But Steve had written most of the music, and it was really good. And he was pretty amazing on the guitar. I didn't register his last name. Dondeena and I giggled our way through the concert, making jokes about the country boys.

A few days later I was checking my mail, and there was a letter in the box for Steve Chapman. Then it clicked . . . *Oh yeah*, I thought, *isn't that funny? That mullet guy with the band must be my mailbox buddy since we have the same last name.* I didn't give it much thought.

Classes started, and one day I was walking toward the main campus when Steve and his friend Greg, who I had met earlier at a freshman orientation event, came walking toward me. I had my tan and my white teeth and my Farrah Fawcett hair, and I guess I was looking cute in my denim jacket all decked out with Precious Moments pins. Steve nudged Greg to introduce us.

Greg wanted to ask me out himself, so he told Steve, "Oh, uh, you wouldn't be interested in *her*, ew, she's a big partier!"

But Steve wasn't put off by Greg's sneaky little lie. A few days later, I was walking past Steve's dorm and he must have seen me through his window. He came tearing out of the dorm, no shoes on, so the closer he got to me, the more autumn leaves got stuck all over his socks.

We talked for a while, laughing and picking the leaves off his socks, and something clicked between us. All of a sudden, Steve Chapman didn't seem so hillbilly anymore.

One night, a bunch of us were having chicken fights in the dorm. Steve and I liked each other, but we hadn't gone on our first official date—which would be to a gourmet meal at Red Lobster—yet. That would come later.

At any rate, I was up on Steve's shoulders, and we were trying to beat all the other chicken fighters, and I was laughing so hard that I knew I was going to pee my pants. I always did growing up when I laughed too hard. My poor bladder couldn't take much more; it was going to give way.

"Put me down!" I yelled at Steve. "Please!"

"Not yet!" he yelled. "We're winning!"

"You've got to put me down!" I yelled. "If you don't, you're gonna be sorry. I'm telling you the truth, I have a weak bladder, and I am going to wet my pants!"

"No!" Steve yelled, laughing. "You won't wet your pants while you're on my shoulders."

At that I laughed more, and you can guess what happened next. He put me down. Quickly.

We had both started our school year determined to focus on our studies and stay unencumbered by major dating relationships. So we spent the first several weeks of our friendship regularly reminding each other, "I really like you, but I don't want to get serious."

But we were spending every moment we could in each other's presence . . . studying, talking, sharing meals, and walking to every class together. Within six weeks we were declaring our love and were thinking about spending the rest of our lives together.

We had bared much of our souls to each other, but I still had not told him about the pain and shame I had carried around since high school. I wanted to be completely honest with Steve, but I'd shoved all that to another part of my brain and locked the door.

Then, on a Friday before our school's homecoming, Steve and I spent a fall afternoon together at a park, lying on a blanket, looking up at the sky, talking about anything and everything. It was a beautiful day for talking . . . and kissing . . . and eventually we found ourselves with our feelings and hormones in overdrive. While we didn't have sex, we had gotten carried away physically, and Steve was upset with himself when we pulled into the parking place at his dorm that night.

"We need to talk about something," he said. "I've made a commitment to save myself for the girl I'm going to marry, and today I know I let things go too far. I'm sorry and I really want us to set some boundaries so that we honor each other. Do you feel the same?"

I couldn't look at him. I turned away and stared out the window, tears rolling down my cheeks.

"I do feel the same way," I said. "Now."

"What do you mean, 'now'?" he asked.

"I wanted to save myself for marriage, but some things happened during high school and it hasn't exactly worked out that way," I said.

These were devastating words for Steve to hear. He got really upset, and it killed me to be with this person I loved and wanted to marry, and feeling like I might lose him because of the harm I'd experienced in the past.

"I'm sorry, but I just don't know what to do with all of this," he said. "I need to go somewhere alone and try to figure some things out."

There was nothing I could say. I slowly got out of Steve's white Cutlass, and I had barely shut the door when the car reversed, pulled out of the parking lot, and drove away. I watched the taillights get smaller and smaller in the distance.

I decided I needed to go find Herbie.

Steve's older brother Herbie was and still is one of the sweetest, funniest people I know. I knew that Herbie would help me. I couldn't stand the fact that I had hurt Steve, and in a very untypical way, given my family's usual way of dealing with things—stuff it down and wait until morning—I felt like I had to try to talk things through and set them right, even if it took all night.

I ran to the dorm room that Steve and Herbie shared, crying.

Herbie opened the door, looking confused at first, then concerned.

"Herbie!" I yelled. "I've really upset your brother, and you've got to help me find him!"

Herbie took me to one of Steve's usual spots where he would go to be alone. Sure enough, there was Steve in the white Cutlass, just sitting in the driver's seat, pounding the steering wheel, praying and sobbing.

"I don't know what to say," he said to me. "My parents have prayed for my spouse-to-be ever since they came to faith, and I've always prayed, 'God, prepare me for the one you have for me, and prepare her for me.' And if I'm completely honest, I mainly hoped for two things: that my future wife would have a great figure and that she would be a virgin!"

Staring at Steve through my own tears, part of my brain thought, *You prayed that? Isn't that kind of hard to find in the same person?*

But then we cried together and I told him how much I cared for him and how very sorry I was that I had hurt him. Steve ended up feeling more compassion than anger as we talked about how alone I had felt, unable to go to anyone to share what I was going through. We talked about our future and how we would "start new" with God's forgiveness. We cried and prayed some more . . . and somewhere, through that long night, we came to a place of peace.

A few months later, during spring break at his parents' house in Paducah, Kentucky, Steve took me to a park gazebo. He sat me up on the railing and asked me to marry him.

I quickly said yes and laughed. Back then we had a game we would play with each other. Steve would ask me a hundred times a day to marry him, and as fast as I could, I would answer yes.

I thought this was like any of those other times. But then, as I put my hand on his chest to jump down off the railing, I could feel his heart thumping wildly.

This was the real proposal!

Out from behind his back came a little red jeweler's box. I started crying.

"Yes!" I sobbed.

"Aren't you going to open the box?" he asked.

Steve had just gotten a royalty check for a song he'd written that had been recorded by the Imperials . . . and so he had splurged and bought me a $900 ring. I cried some more, we kissed, and then we began to plan our future together.

He'd been told that he needed to be in Nashville to further his chances in the music industry, and so we decided together that I'd drop out of Anderson and he'd enroll at Belmont University. I had already realized that nursing school was not for me—since it involved vomit and bedpans. And my parents were kind enough to understand how I felt . . . particularly since I was moving on and they wouldn't have to pay for three more years of college.

Steve and I got married at my home church in Ohio on October 13, 1984. The reception was in the church hall, with nuts, mints, ham and chicken salad and pimento cheese triangles my mother had made, and a lovely cake with a Precious Moments bride and groom perched on top.

They looked a little more confident about their future than we did.

We had a grand total of fifty dollars in our bank account and no time for a honeymoon, so we spent our wedding night at a Clarion hotel in Cincinnati. We thought it would be cool since it had a rotating restaurant on the top. Then we went to the Cincinnati Zoo, where the zoo staff let us in for free since our green Ford Pinto was still covered in sticky gobs of shaving cream, bedraggled streamers, and a "Just Married" sign.

While this is a lovely zoo, I don't necessarily recommend it for a honeymoon. It was pouring rain that day, and all the animals were hiding in their habitats, depressed. As we strolled in the rain, we realized we were about as far apart in personality as two people could be. We cried together on the drive back to Nashville. The wedding was over, and reality was upon us.

We had known some of this while we were dating, of course, but dating is the Land of Magical Thinking. Once we had moved to the Land of Matrimony, we realized that Tigger had married Eeyore. Steve's bouncy-bouncy, glass-half-full perspective was now linked till death do us part with my glass-half-empty, "Oh bother" outlook, and rarely the twain would meet.

I was nineteen years old. I'd been consumed by the fun of planning the wedding, and now, in the wet zoo, reality hit. I realized that although I was in love with this man, now "real life" was starting, and all I had to look forward to was working hard to put my bouncy, blond husband through school.

He was confident that all would be well. I totally believed in him and knew he was great. I was his biggest cheerleader. But sometimes life felt scary and bleak. Sometimes my hopes for the future were thin and gray, barely holding, just like Eeyore's tacked-on tail.

5

When the Puppy Eats
Your Birth Control Pills

God moves in a mysterious way His wonders to perform.

William Cowper

We had fifty dollars in the bank, a green Ford Pinto, and we were livin' on love.

We found a dingy, three-hundred-square-foot apartment in not the greatest part of town. The price was right, and I scoured the apartment with Clorox bleach until it was spotless.

Steven was a full-time student at Belmont University. He had auditioned for a college group called the Belmont Reasons. They told him he wasn't good enough to be a vocalist, but they wanted him to play guitar. He also continued working on his writing and developing as an artist at Benson Records.

I got a job at what was then Westside Hospital. I was secretary to the comptroller. I loved reconciling numbers, admittances, and whatever else could be neatly added or subtracted and come out equal in our accounting records.

I was beginning to realize, more and more, that musicians are nothing like accountants. They are more . . . abstract. Two plus two doesn't necessarily equal four, if you know what I mean. Musicians operate out of a place in the brain that I'm pretty sure I don't have.

I was very organized and punctual. To me, "on time" meant you needed to be at least ten to fifteen minutes early. Steven thought that thirty minutes late was fashionable and acceptable . . . even for scheduled appointments. It made me crazy! He seemed to march to the beat of his own drum, and I was beginning to feel that the world was supposed to fall in line with that rhythm. I felt frustrated and angry at his carefree, Tigger attitude.

We both loved Jesus, and we both wanted a Christ-centered marriage. But I thought—in my twenty-year-old Eeyore maturity—that this sure wasn't going to be easy, to die to myself and take up my cross and live with the most self-centered man on the entire planet!

I was working eight to five, and was in an efficient, regular routine. Steven was an artist accustomed to staying up late with bursts of creativity, which couldn't be scheduled. We were working toward a common goal, but nobody could frustrate me like that man!

I couldn't communicate the way Steven could. (Believe me, I still can't!) He was frustrated and was trying to fix me. I didn't think I needed fixing.

When we would fight, he'd quote Scripture at me (he would later admit that this was a huge mistake). So he'd say things about how we couldn't let the sun go down on our anger, and I would say "Oh, yeah? Watch this!" And I'd lie down and fall instantly asleep.

After all, when I was growing up that was how we dealt with conflict. We avoided unpleasant conversations, and then in the morning it would be a new day and a fresh start. I would only realize later how much bitterness and resentment was building up inside of me.

One winter night, it was snowing outside and we'd gotten into an argument inside, no doubt about our calendar and our schedules. I was furious and just wanted out of my three-hundred-square-foot apartment. I got up, leaving Steven behind, and walked out the door.

"Where are you going?" he yelled.

"I am walking to Ohio!" I yelled.

Crying, I made my way down to the sidewalk, walking to Ohio. I felt something nearby, and there was Steven, driving slowly beside me . . . in *my* green Pinto, I might add. I kept walking. He kept driving.

"Get in the car," he said. "I'll drive you to Ohio, if you need to go home to your parents!"

Somehow we made it back to our own little home that night.

It was at this point in our lives that we met Geoff and Jan Moore, who would become lifelong friends. Geoff had recorded one of Steven's songs as a demo to be pitched to other artists. When I met Jan later, we became instant friends. We'd spend hours at their condo, visiting and dreaming about the future.

When I had interviewed at Westside Hospital, the last thing my future boss said before he hired me was, "Now, you're not going to get pregnant anytime soon, are you?"

"Of course not," I said. I had a plan. "I just turned twenty years old, and we aren't going to start a family for a long time."

The only baby we had was our puppy, Peso, who was officially a Pekalhasaapsopoo. We'd gotten her from a shelter, a little ball of Pekinese, Lhasa apso, and poodle fluff. She was also teething, and chewed everything.

My grandmother had given me some old, old bedroom furniture. We had painted it an ugly blue. I left my birth control pills on the little blue table next to my side of the bed. They were in a blister pack, but that didn't stop our puppy. Peso chewed up the whole thing, cardboard, plastic, and pills, and then moved on to whatever else she could ingest.

I called the vet and explained what had happened. "It shouldn't hurt her," he said. "But she may be a bit moody."

I went to the pharmacy the next day, got another pack of birth control medication, and didn't think much about it. After all, I thought, I'd only missed one pill due to Peso's little snack.

Did you know that missing just one itty-bitty pill can cause pregnancy?

There we were, six months into Holy Headlock. No money. A moody dog. A happy Tigger bouncing around writing great songs, not worrying about much because God was gonna work it all out.

And Eeyore, the main breadwinner—that would be me—gradually growing great with child . . . and fear.

I had to tell my boss. That in itself was scary. I had promised I wasn't going to have a baby so soon, and here I was, pregnant. He was a great boss, but he also could throw a phone across the room, and we didn't have cell phones back then.

To my surprise, when I met with him he just said a few words under his breath and then said, "Let me guess, you're not coming back to work when the baby is born, right?" Well, the $250 I made every week was about the only source of income that we had. I told him I didn't want to, but that I might have to.

During all this time, Steven had signed a development deal with Benson Records. This meant that he would continue to write songs for them and they would eventually develop him as a recording artist. It looked as though there might be a beginning to his ministry/career, and just in time, as our little Chapman would be arriving soon.

Then, when I was five months pregnant, we were standing in the parking lot of the record company. We just happened to run into the executive who was working with Steven. He told us that Benson had been sold to a big company in New York. "And all of the main executives," he continued, "including me, have been let go. Don't worry, everything will be just fine."

We didn't see him again for years.

Now we were realizing that Steven's contract could potentially keep him involved for about fifteen years . . . in a company where all the people who knew him had been fired. He was in limbo.

When Steven originally signed this contract, we didn't have the money for an attorney. We had earnestly prayed, asking God to do what He wanted with Steven's career, read the fine print as well as we could, and signed away. All was well until that day in the parking lot.

What we didn't realize was that by God's providence Steven had a "key man" clause in his contract. This essentially meant that if any of the main people who were directly responsible for signing him and working with him were let go, then his contract was considered null and void. These kinds of contracts don't exist today because of all the changes in the music business. But thanks to God's provision for us, we found out we were not contractually bound to Benson for years to come.

What a relief!

Still, things weren't looking so great, as far as a planner like me was concerned. Let's see, I was working to put Steven through school and help pay the bills while he developed as an artist. Now I was five months pregnant, and the recording company had been sold, so we had no recording contract, no future for me working, really, and pretty much a failed plan.

About this time, Steven decided not to go back to school in the fall so that he could concentrate more on doing concerts. He also went back to work at Opryland USA, a Nashville theme park where he'd worked in the summers. They quickly hired him back to do the Country Music USA show for three to five performances a day.

I'd waddle out there, very pregnant, and lie in the back row of the theater, singing right along while Steven impersonated various country greats. Little did I know that when I married Steven Curtis Chapman, I also married Lester Flatt, George Jones, Porter Wagoner, and an awesome clogger.

But down deep, I was afraid that clogging wasn't going to get us very far.

6

Smoke Signals

Love and learn that's what we will do
Love and learn through the flood and through the flame
This world will turn and the seasons will change
But there's nothing we can't get through
as long as we both hold on to
The hand of God and each other and
take a lifetime to love and learn

"Love and Learn"
Words and music by Steven Curtis Chapman

I had always wanted to be a stay-at-home mom. My childhood was full of memories of my mom always being there for us. Now my prayer was that God would make a way for me to do the same for our children.

The only problem was that we needed my salary from the hospital in order to do a few things like eat and live.

Eventually, Steven met Greg Nelson, who produced Sandi Patty at the time. Greg believed in Steven and his ability to communicate. He introduced him to Lorenz Creative Services and talked to a few record labels in town.

We were excited.

They all passed on Steven, saying they loved his writing but weren't interested in him as an artist.

We were crushed.

The Christian music business was going through cutbacks. White male artists were a dime a dozen, so the interest level was not high.

Greg sent Steven's stuff to a company based in California at the time, Sparrow Records. Billy Ray Hearn Sr., Sparrow's CEO, didn't want Steven as an artist. But he was interested in his writing.

Steven continued writing for Lorenz and working hard. To earn extra money he would stay up all night and do what he called $100 demos. These were other writers' songs that needed to be recorded so that they could be pitched to other artists to record. Steve would do the bass, vocals, keyboard, everything—and he got paid $100 a song.

Somehow, some of these demos ended up back out in California at Sparrow Records. Billy Ray Hearn Sr., who passed on Steven the first time, was walking past someone's office one day and heard Steven's voice.

"Who is that singing on that demo?" he asked. In the end, Billy Ray's interest led to a co-publishing deal in which half of the publishing went to Sparrow and half went to Lorenz Creative Services, with the idea that Sparrow would develop Steven as an artist.

Steven signed a contract with BMI—Broadcast Music, Inc.—which collects license fees on behalf of songwriters, composers, and music publishers, then distributes them as royalties when their works are performed. So Steven would get royalties each time one of his songs was played on the radio, in Muzak on an elevator, wherever.

Around the same time, EMI Music, the third largest music company in the world, bought Sparrow Records. EMI gave Steven a second chance to prove himself as an artist and agreed to give him an advance on royalties, which tapped out at $250 a week . . . the exact amount I had been earning but would soon have to stop due to our baby.

We saw this as God's direct provision, and we were so thankful. We had moved into a little townhouse that had an extra room to decorate as a nursery . . . and once the baby arrived I could stay at home, just like I had always wanted. After a bumpy start, I thought that my marriage, and my life, were finally settling down to the orderly plan I'd longed for all along.

On February 24, 1986, Emily Chapman entered the world by emergency C-section.

I had just turned twenty-one. I tried and tried, and Emily wouldn't, couldn't, nurse. It hurt, and she seemed mad all the time. I felt like a complete failure. I was constantly on the phone with the pediatrician, my mom, anybody's mom, even the La Leche League, trying to get nursing advice. I desperately wanted to be a low-key, calm mom, but I was full of anxiety because I was clearly doing something wrong.

Then I gave up, bought some formula, cuddled her, stuck a bottle in her mouth, and all was well.

That was fine for a while, but then Emily hit a stage where she'd scream from about 4:00 p.m. until about 8:00 p.m. every night. I would keep her in her little crank-up swing while I tried to fix dinner so I'd have it hot on the table when Steven got home. Emily would settle down, and then the swing would need to be cranked again. I'd turn the handle, it would make an awful noise, and Emily would startle, her little arms and legs straight out. Then she'd start screaming again, and the cycle would repeat.

My plan of having the peaceful, perfect baby just wasn't working out.

One spring afternoon when Emily was six weeks old, we went out with a real estate agent looking for an inexpensive house. When we came home there were fire trucks all over our development, and our little townhouse was full of ashes.

The bad news was that everything inside had been burned or scorched. The good news was that we didn't have much . . . and of course, that the three of us were safe. A neighbor had not seen us leave, and so she had told the firefighters that we were still in the townhouse. In its charred ruins, you could see the black marks of where the firefighter's hands had felt their way up the wall next to the stairs, through the bedroom, into the baby's crib, feeling along the surfaces in the heavy smoke, trying to find and rescue us.

As we stared at the ashes of our stuff, seeing those hand marks made me realize how much we could have lost.

Wonderful friends gave us their basement to live in. Our dear friends Geoff and Jan Moore showed up with clothes from their closets. My mom and dad arrived within five hours of when we called them. They had paint buckets, ladders, brushes, and work clothes, ready to help however they could. They weren't big on discussing life's deepest feelings, as I've said, but they were great at showing up to do whatever needed to be done.

My dad and I took all of Emily's bedding and blankets and clothes and little stuffed animals to the Laundromat. We couldn't afford to buy new things, so we had to wash everything over and over to get the smoke smell out. I remember sitting in front of the glass-front washer, watching the little stuffed animal faces going around and around. I felt like one of them, bouncing around in circles, pressed hard against the glass, subject to forces that were stronger than me.

My tidy, forward-motion plans just weren't coming true.

We were young. We had never heard of renters' insurance. The man who owned the building had insurance, of course, for the actual building itself, but he decided to sue us for damages to see if he could get anything from us. The fire happened on April 13, and the only money we had, all $2,200 of it, went to the IRS on April 15 to pay our taxes.

So when our landlord sent us a bill for $13,000 in damages, Steven and I just stared at each other, devastated. We had always prided ourselves on living within our means and staying debt free. All we had at this point was Emily and a paid-off Honda Civic. I'm not sure what this man thought he was going to get from us.

Again, friends came to the rescue. Someone in our church connected us with a great lawyer. He got the landlord to agree to a $2,000 settlement. We would pay the guy $50 a month—interest free—for what seemed like a very long time.

My parents were worn out. They were cleaning, painting, repairing, helping to take care of baby Emily, and going the extra mile for us. Unfortunately, I could see their resentment building up. I felt it too: where in the world were *Steven's* parents? They knew about our need, of course, but they hadn't come.

On the Sunday afternoon after the fire, we were at our friends' house doing more laundry, weary and frazzled. Our friends had gone out of town. We looked out the window to see Steven's mother and grandmother driving up to the house. They were both dressed up in their Sunday church clothes, while my parents were in work clothes, sweaty from toiling away on yet another fire-related project.

Steven's mom and grandmother came in, and conversation flowed awkwardly for a little while. There was obvious tension. My mom was exhausted from working so hard and taking care of me. She felt pretty teary and on the verge of a breakdown.

For my part, I was with my mom, feeling tired, teary, and hormonal. I had been letting bad feelings build up in me without talking with Steven about it all. It felt natural to gravitate toward my parents' side of things rather than my husband's. It didn't help that there stood my mother-in-law in her Sunday best like she was out for a Sunday drive—all the way from Paducah—just stopping by to give hugs and see her new grandbaby.

All this came to a head and went from tense to loud when someone asked where Steven's dad, Herb, was. Steven's mom, Judy, explained that Herb assumed that "no news was good news," and because he hadn't heard from Steven, they thought everything was taken care of. It caught her off guard that my mom, dad, and I might have wondered why they hadn't been here to help.

My mom was crying and talking, I was "commenting," Judy felt attacked and got mad at the absent Herb . . . it was a fiasco. My dad stood quietly behind my mom as if to support her, and he definitely didn't like how the whole thing was coming down. At one point, someone from my side of the family suggested they just take Emily and me and head back to Ohio. It felt as if Steven and I were being split right down the middle.

The Enemy was having a field day.

As the conversation escalated, Judy became more and more angry with her own husband. She began to think that Herb really should be with us all. She called him . . . and he said he'd buy us a new refrigerator! It was crazy.

Suddenly Steven walked into the middle of the room where all the fussing and feuding was spiraling out of control. He flung his hands in the air and shouted at the very top of his lungs, "Satan will not have my family!"

Absolute silence. We all just stopped and stared at him.

Well, we all eventually apologized and set things right. But there were issues at hand that should have served as warning flags for my future. I was having a hard time trusting, really trusting, my husband. I looked more to my dad to ride in on his white horse and save the day. I resented disorder and chaos in my life—and I blamed it on Steven.

Still, we had a lot going for us. We really loved each other, we really wanted Christ at the center of our marriage, and we were young and resilient. So we were able to recover from the fire, though perhaps we didn't really deal with some of the stuff we discovered in the midst of it. But we moved on to the next thing . . . which, happily, was the opportunity to buy our first home of our own.

It was the very property we had gone to look at on the day of the fire . . . and this princely estate was ours for the sum of $48,000. It was dingy, sort of creepy, had peeling paint, mold, and rot, and needed a huge hug.

I went to Lorenz Creative Services, the publishing company, EMI/Sparrow Records, the publishing and record company, BMI, the performance royalty company, and had letters written predicting the amount of income Steven would generate in the next few years.

Much to our surprise, the bank gave us the loan based on this forecasted income and our character. This was a huge compliment to Steven, demonstrating how hard he was working and how much promise he was showing to the companies that had invested in him.

Once we got settled in our little nest, I loved the routines I established. I did laundry on certain days, went to the grocery on certain days, did my cleaning on certain days, worked to promote Steven on certain days . . . it was wonderful.

The structure gave me a false sense of control that would not hold once our dreams eventually started coming true. As our family grew and Steven's success took off like a rocket, the wheels started coming off this nice illusion. So, ironically, even as everything in our lives would be spiraling up, my state of mind would spiral down.

But I'm getting a little ahead of my story.

7

"Ladies and Gentlemen, Please Welcome . . . Caleb!"

The father of a righteous man has great joy;
he who has a wise son delights in him.
May your father and mother be glad;
may she who gave you birth rejoice!
My son, give me your heart
and let your eyes keep to my ways.

Proverbs 23:24–26

On the days I had designated as "office" days, I would sit on the end of our bed as my chair. My desk was a piece of linoleum stapled to a rough old gardening table given to us by Steven's Grandpa Rudd. I'd contact churches to ask—well, beg—for them to have Steven for a concert, saying I was calling from "the office of Steven Curtis Chapman." And for all they knew, we were a pretty slick operation.

Steven's first record—yes, it was released in vinyl—came out in May of '87. It was called *First Hand*. His song "Weak Days" went to number two on the Contemporary Christian Music chart. We were optimistic that his career might be taking off.

Since Emily came bounding into our lives when we were still babies ourselves, we had a brilliant idea. Since we were so young, we should just go ahead and have our children now, so that later down the road we would be hip, young grandparents.

We didn't have Peso the pill eater any longer . . . but even so, we were pregnant pretty quickly. We were thrilled.

But while visiting my family in Ohio, I had a miscarriage. It was scary and sad . . . not what I would ever want to be part of my story.

I had to have an ultrasound to check things out. They wouldn't let Steven be with me, and as she was looking at the screen, the technician said, "I can't tell you were ever even pregnant!"

I'm sure she didn't mean to be cruel, but I sobbed, wanting so badly to have Steven by my side. We were twelve weeks along . . . and we believe that we indeed have a child in heaven, waiting to meet us there one day.

We eventually started trying again to get pregnant. This time I wasn't going to leave anything to chance. I went to the pharmacy and bought an ovulation predictor kit. I had to wait until my cycle was at a certain point and then start testing my urine to see when it would be optimal ovulation time.

Well, I arrived at that time . . . and Steven was out of town doing a concert nine hundred miles away.

I was all business. I called my husband and calmly informed him that it would be a wise decision to come home, *now*! He sensed the urgency but also knew that the kit predicted ovulation for up to seventy-two hours.

"Am I supposed to walk out on stage and tell my audience that I have to go home because you're ovulating?" he asked.

"Yes!" I said.

He didn't . . . but I was waiting at the airport when he came home, along with some close friends. They had offered to take Emily for us while we spent the evening, well, making up for lost time.

So, back to Home Sweet Home we went, knelt at the foot of our bed, and asked God to bless us with another child.

And nine months later, on October 2, 1989, Caleb Stevenson (Steven's son, get it?) Chapman was born.

8

I Will Be Here

Tomorrow morning if you wake up
And the sun does not appear
I, I will be here
If in the dark we lose sight of love
Hold my hand and have no fear
'Cause I, I will be here

I will be here when you feel like being quiet
When you need to speak your mind, I will listen
And I will be here when the laughter turns to crying
Through the winning, losing and trying, we'll be together
'Cause I will be here

Tomorrow morning if you wake up
And the future is unclear
I, I will be here
As sure as seasons are made for change
Our lifetimes are made for years
So I, I will be here

"I Will Be Here"
Words and music by Steven Curtis Chapman

One dark and stormy night, Steven's older brother Herb came rap, rap, rapping at our front door.

He was wet, upset, and told us that that Steven's parents were divorcing.

We were shocked . . . but it wasn't like it had come out of left field, really. There had been plenty of signs that all was not well with Herb and Judy.

Still, we never thought it would come to this. Steven's dad had assured him that they were just working through issues. He said that "divorce is not a word in our vocabulary."

So how had it entered their vocabulary?

We understood stress and hard times in a marriage . . . that was to be expected. Steven was praying for his parents constantly, even asking people during his concerts to join him in prayer for his mom and dad.

But as we continued to try to walk with Herb and Judy, we started hearing two distinctly different sides of the story. Steven started feeling like he was the parent-counselor to two adolescents. His parents had been his spiritual heroes, and now he was talking to them in pretty candid terms about unhealthy choices they'd been making and how they really needed to do whatever it took to save their marriage.

"Don't worry," his dad said in a phone call. "We've signed legal papers, but we're not divorcing. It's more of a legal separation. You know how lawyers are. We're just protecting ourselves."

We felt like it was just a matter of time before things slipped further down the slippery slope, and we were right. The next thing we knew, in spite of our daily prayers and earnest conversations with them, Steven's parents chose to divorce.

This was devastating for Steven. His parents had been spiritual models for him—and rightly so—after they came to faith in Jesus when he was about seven years old. They had modeled prayer, repentance, commitment to God's Word, connection to the body of Christ . . . all the right things.

Further, they had talked through divisive issues in their relationship when Steven was growing up, rather than just sweeping them under the carpet. They had done their best to not let the sun go down on their anger. Even though there were plenty of arguments, his parents usually ended up on their knees together, asking each other for forgiveness and asking God for strength. They had also counseled many other couples who were going through difficult times in their marriages. They loved serving God together in their church.

So it was pretty surreal for Steven to see them come to the point of divorce. Bit by bit, they had allowed the faith that had held them so tightly, and had saved them so radically, to lose its hold on their hearts. I believe they began to listen to the wrong voice in their heads; subtle lies influenced their decisions, and they couldn't see how irrational they were becoming.

In addition, they had lost their commitment to the accountability of their fellowship of believers. As a result of some church politics, the pastor who had been an integral part of their faith journey was asked to leave the church. This eventually led to bitterness, which Herb and Judy kept inside. They gradually slid away from fellowship. Once they were isolated and separated from the group, it was as if Satan had moved in like a lion, now able to take them down as individuals.

Aside from the terrible sadness we felt for Herb and Judy's pain, the hard thing was that we had consciously decided, early in our marriage, to model our relationship on theirs. If *their* relationship was failing, we now had to wrestle with questions about the foundations of our own marriage.

We had already struggled in our first turbulent years together, and now we realized that just saying "divorce isn't an option" wouldn't necessarily protect us. So we began seeking out godly counsel and putting what we called "preventative maintenance" into place.

We met with our pastor, with counselors, with whoever would meet with us to help us build our marriage as strong as possible. We told these people the truth about what we were feeling and how we were struggling, which was sometimes ugly and sad. We were honest and open because we knew it would only be by the grace of God that we could not just survive but grow. We did not want to be one of those Christian couples where everything seems perfect on the outside, and yet they're falling apart on the inside. We wanted to be real.

Steven has always responded to life's challenges and hurts through his music. Certainly this was the case with the pain of his parents' divorce. Their breakup was a wake-up call, a catalyst, to say to me that he would not leave me, that in spite of the difficulties we faced, whatever came, we would be together.

"I will be here," he promised, and those lyrics were a comfort, a commitment, and a lifeline that would prove vital on the road ahead. So on Mother's Day 1990, he sat me down. He played me a song, written to me, for me, to encourage me.

And it did.

I will be here, and you can cry on my shoulder
When the mirror tells us we're older, I will hold you
And I will be here to watch you grow in beauty
And tell you all the things you are to me
I will be here

I will be true to the promise I have made
To you and to the One who gave you to me

9

Crying in the Bathroom
at Chuck E. Cheese

"For I know the plans I have for you," declares
the LORD, "plans to prosper you and not to harm
you, plans to give you hope and a future."

Jeremiah 29:11

All had been well with Caleb's birth, but once he started taking bottles at home we had a problem. He spit up just about everything, and as he got a little older he moved on to projectile vomiting. We were amazed that this itty-bitty baby could hit a wall ten feet away.

I changed his formula about fifteen times and took him to the doctor repeatedly, and eventually we discovered he had a narrowing of the pylorus, the opening from the stomach into the small intestine. Normally, food passes easily from the stomach into the first part of the small intestine, but because of the blockage, Caleb's formula had nowhere to go but up, up, and away.

This condition is easily corrected by surgery . . . but if it's caught too late, babies can lose weight and eventually even starve to death.

Choosing to SEE

After the surgery, Caleb was on morphine for about twelve hours . . . and then, when he was finally alert, he looked at me and smiled. I gave him a tiny bit of formula, and then I knew from the look on his little face that all was going to be well. We still waited for the heave-ho of vomiting . . . but it never came.

When Caleb was five months old, chubby, happy, and healthy, my brother called me to announce that his wife Yolanda was pregnant with their third child, due on Valentine's Day. Then Steven's brother Herbie and his wife Sherri called to say that they were pregnant with their first child, due on . . . February 14th. We decided to all meet at Chuck E. Cheese to celebrate. The children could play for the afternoon, and we could all dine on fine pizza.

What my extended family didn't know was that my period was a few days late. Since I was always irregular, I didn't think much of it. But I did stop at Target on our way to the party and bought a pregnancy test. That way I could be sure that I had *nothing* to announce to the family.

At Chuck E. Cheese, I helped Steven get the kids settled at a table, and then I headed off to the bathroom with my little science experiment. In the distance I could hear the mayhem of the restaurant, but there in the bathroom stall it was just Mary Beth and God. I stared at the test-kit applicator. It turned positive a nanosecond after it met my urine.

I sat there, staring, not moving. Then the tears began to stream down my face.

"Oh, God!" I wept. "I shouldn't be upset. This is new life!"

Then I pictured baby Caleb, all plump and happy, just five months old.

"It was so hard to get pregnant after Emily, how did this happen?" I asked God. "I mean, I know how it happened, but . . . I'm not ready!"

I was afraid, elated, mad, sad, thrilled, and confused, all in one minute in that stall at Chuck E. Cheese.

The pain of my last C-section was fresh in my mind, and I still hadn't regained my strength after Caleb's medical issues and surgery. Steven's career was taking off, and that meant he was literally taking off, often away from home for long stretches of time. I knew that being pregnant was a great gift . . . but having another child so soon after Caleb was not my plan. What was God doing?

I emerged from the stall. I bolted through the ladies' room door, making a beeline for Steven. I could see him through the chaos of small children, balloons, and games.

As soon as our eyes met, Steven knew.

As I made my way toward him, a lady came up to me. "Aren't you Mary Beth Chapman?" she asked.

Thanks to Steven's growing career, he was starting to be recognized in public. But this lady wasn't connecting because of Steven.

"I think you used to work with my sister at Friendly's Ice Cream!" she continued.

Maybe she didn't see the tears streaming down my face.

"I'm sorry," I babbled to her. "I just did this pregnancy test in the bathroom, and I haven't told my husband yet, and he's right over there, and I'm a little discombobulated right now . . ."

"Oh!" said the lady, thinking she had just gotten a little too much information. She quickly made herself invisible. I barreled toward my husband and buried my head in his chest, weeping.

Little Emily Chapman looked up at me.

"Mommy!" she said. "Why are you crying?"

"Well," I said, trying to be an adult, "you know how there are sad tears, but there are also happy tears? Mommy just found out she's going to have another baby!"

Emily stood there, staring at me. She jammed her hands on her hips, then burst out, "What in the *world* are we gonna do with another baby?"

I lost it. "I don't know!" I wailed. "That's why I'm crying!"

When I look back to those Chuck E. Cheese days, I can see a lot more of the picture than I could then. Back then I was just putting one foot in front of the other—what else can you do?

Now I see my life at that time like a big weather map. There were high pressure systems building, then dramatic lows that would bring in thunderstorms. There were calm periods as well. But what was brewing was a perfect storm.

Once I accepted the fact that we were having another baby, my pregnancy was fine. As God would have it, Yolanda, Sherri, and I all had the same ob-gyn, and all three of us were due on Valentine's Day 1991. It was fun, but I'm sure the doctor thought it was also kind of weird.

We knew from an ultrasound that our new baby was a boy, and I was grateful. Since he and Caleb were going to be so close in age, it was great that they would have each other to do boy things together. I wanted to name him Levi Franklin; Steven wanted to name him Will Franklin.

The birth went well. I had a third C-section. Before they sewed me up and I went off to drug-induced la-la land, I was instructing Steven to make sure to mark the baby with a Sharpie so the hospital wouldn't mix him up with some other baby. (Can you tell I had control issues?)

"What about his name?" Steven asked, wondering just what he should write on this child.

"Oh," I said, loopy from drugs. "You see what name works best for him."

Even in my drug-induced state, though, I knew what would happen. Sure enough, I woke up and my son was named Will Franklin. My choice never had a chance.

So here we were, blessed in a million ways. Three healthy children under the age of five. Steven's growing success meant that we had been able to buy a beautiful piece of land in Franklin, and we were building a Victorian farmhouse with lots of room for the kids to play.

Steven's second album, 1988's *Real Life Conversations*, earned him four big hits, including the number one song "His Eyes," which also received the Contemporary Recorded Song of the Year award from the Gospel Music Association in 1989. That year, he also won a GMA award for Best Songwriter of the Year. Released later that year, his third album, *More to This Life*, contained four number-one hits and in 1990 earned him an unprecedented ten nominations at the GMA Awards. He won five. His next album, *For the Sake of the Call*, contained five number-one singles and earned him another slew of GMA awards and his first Grammy in the Best Pop Gospel Album category.

We couldn't believe all this was happening. We felt so grateful to God.

Steven was getting ready to release a new album, *The Great Adventure*, and would be doing big-venue concerts in just a few weeks. Our lives now included managers, booking agents, band members, crew, assistants, trucks, and tour buses.

My mom arrived to help take care of Emily and Caleb as I recovered from Will's birth. She cooked and of course cleaned, vacuumed, mopped, dusted, and set everything in order. I couldn't have made it without her. But every evening, about a half hour after dinner, my stomach would start hurting.

I ignored it; Steven was kicking off his "Great Adventure" concert tour with a seven-day rehearsal at Reunion Arena in Texas, and I was determined to get there for the opening night.

One night I woke up at about 3:00 a.m. The pain in my abdomen was nauseating and intense, radiating to my back. I literally had to crawl to my mother's room.

"Mom!" I whispered to her. "Wake up! I don't mean to alarm you, but if you don't get me to an emergency room, I'm gonna die!"

She flew out of bed, we called a friend to come stay with the kids, and Mom took me to the emergency room, where I had an ultrasound.

"Honey!" my doctor told me the next morning. "You've got a couple of *huge* gallstones!"

I didn't even know what those were, but the nice people at the hospital got them out of me with a little laser surgery. I hurt all over from the effects of that, and the, well, *gas* buildup from the procedure, but I was not a person to be stopped by mere physical agony. I flew off to Dallas that very weekend for the first show of "The Great Adventure" tour.

Again, we were blessed. And to everyone else we looked like a beautiful family of bouncy, blond children, a handsome, gifted husband soon to be a big celebrity, and the lovely wife with the big white smile. That would be me.

But there was something wrong with this happy picture, because the lovely celebrity wife, wrestling with dark tides inside, was about to have a breakdown. And I couldn't figure out why.

10

My Friend Prozac

When my spirit faints within me, you know my way!

Psalm 142:3 ESV

Save me, O God, for the waters have come up to my neck.
I sink in the miry depths, where there is no foothold.
I have come into the deep waters; the floods engulf me.

Psalm 69:1–2

People who don't know much about depression often think of it as great sadness, and while it is that, it is so much more. I was sad, mad, frustrated, fearful, reclusive, critical, overwhelmed, and hopeless. No one wants all these adjectives . . . and certainly no one wants to live with a person who's experiencing them.

And here was Steven, trying his best to understand, but because of his positive outlook on life, it was hard for him. I felt like he was just clueless to what was going on inside of me. We'd moved into a new house, I had three children under the age of five, and it was up to me to multitask my way through all kinds of challenges each day.

Meanwhile, Tigger the optimist was getting ready for his biggest tour to date. It would be full of ministry opportunities and happy fans who would applaud his performances and confirm how talented he was.

So as far as Steven's managers, promoters, and music team were concerned, the single focus was "The Great Adventure" tour. As it became more and more apparent that I was overwhelmed and hurting, managers said they could pull the plug on the tour at any point so Steven could care for his family. I knew that a lot of money had already been invested and spent to get this tour off the ground . . . and the way the business works, no matter what, this Great Adventure tour would happen. Therefore, Mary Beth needed to keep herself together.

But I couldn't.

Steven would come home from the recording studio or rehearsals to find me curled up in our bed crying. Emily had started kindergarten. I loved having little Caleb and Will at home . . . but then there were times when they were right under my feet while I'd furiously clean the house, pay bills, do laundry, and try to keep our domestic life afloat, while continuing to manage various business aspects of Steven's career.

Sometimes I would just stop, sit, and cry. Other days, I would actually crawl under my bed or in my closet. I was physically and emotionally depleted, and though I'm a real pull-yourself-up-by-your-bootstraps kind of person, I could not pull myself up and out of this any longer.

One day before Steven was to leave on the tour, we were out on the driveway talking with Steven's manager, Dan Raines. Dan was discussing plans that were taking me by surprise. I like to schedule things on the calendar, be prepared, take care of details, and not get caught by something unknown. I had asked over and over to be given as much information as possible.

But I was now hearing about all kinds of add-ons . . . more shows, television opportunities, interviews . . . things that would keep Steven out on the road longer than I'd been told. This was great for his career . . . but this latest batch of last-minute information sent me over the edge.

I started crying and couldn't stop. I was way beyond the point of caring who saw me. Complete breakdown. I wanted to die. Steven actually carried me into our house, me kicking and screaming all the way.

Dan was very wide-eyed but compassionate. He told us about a good friend in his small group from church who was a psychiatrist. "Maybe we ought to see about getting you an appointment," he told me when I was calm enough to hear anything.

I knew nothing about psychiatrists, except they were for crazy people. And that definitely wasn't me, even though I'd always felt half-crazy and now was flipping out in the driveway and hiding under the bed.

Actually, I had always been quite open to getting counseling help as Steven and I struggled with some of the difficulties in our marriage. We knew the value of having trained people walk through hard places with us.

So I met with the doctor. We talked for some time, and he said to me, "I don't know if you're familiar with the term 'clinical depression,' but I believe you've suffered from it for a long time."

I thought back to my high-performing childhood and the pain and shame of my adolescence. The doctor was right.

It was a relief to know that what I suffered from had a name. At the same time I felt guilty and ashamed. Like everything was my fault. I had no logical reason to be depressed. I had a wonderful, loving, faithful husband and healthy, great kids. We were financially blessed. I wasn't living in poverty, persecution, or pain. Why should I be depressed?

What I began to understand was that this was a medical condition. It wasn't logical. It wasn't a response to my environment. It had to do with my brain chemistry and coping mechanisms that I'd developed over a lifetime. I began to see that I'd carried this for years, that depression had been the filter through which I had experienced much of my adolescence and everything since.

It obviously had affected my marriage as well. And now, with the depression diagnosis, it felt like any problems or differences between Steven and me were automatically *my* fault, because, well, I was depressed. This dynamic meant that I now carried more guilt, thinking every difference between us was because I wasn't able to let go or lighten up, no matter how hard I tried. It often came down to this: Steven's fun and spontaneous outlook trumped Mary Beth's need for planning almost every time.

Depression also affected the way I reasoned, the way my brain itself perceived everyday life. While Steven might see a problem as an inconvenient obstacle he just had to figure out a way to bounce around, I saw problems as insurmountable mountains.

The doctor prescribed an antidepressant, which was the good news.

The bad news was that the Prozac took a few weeks to ramp up in my system and take effect. So there were many dark nights when I was battling intense emotions of fear and anger, and Steven was on the road. He'd call late at night, after his show, and I concentrated on putting on a brave, fake front.

It was so hard, because sleeping was the one time I was at peace, and he could usually only call after we were all in bed. I would try and tell him news and funny stories about the children. But I didn't want to talk. I just wanted to go back to sleep.

As I said, when I was first diagnosed I felt like I was to blame for everything and anything that had ever gone wrong. Later it would be important to discern ways that Steven's personality and patterns had also contributed to our conflict. We still had to do a ton of work to untangle issues in our marriage and why we both responded certain ways to certain situations. But it helped to know that we were normalizing my brain chemistry so I could perceive things better.

That was good.

But it was not enough, on its own, to really transform me. What I found is that my depression actually became an opportunity to acknowledge to God that He was literally my only hope. In the darkest, loneliest times in the middle of the night, I realized that Christ is truly all I have. I realized that everything else—*everything*—is fleeting.

If I put my security or peace of mind in my husband, children, or home, I would only continue to wrestle with life and how out of control it felt. I'd already seen how a home and possessions can burn, and I knew that no matter how precious a relationship with a loved one is, it can be lost in a moment of tragedy.

I also knew quite clearly that I couldn't rest my hope or security in how I looked or how productive I was, or anything else that had to do with my hardworking, churning, anxious personality. If my outlook was dependent on me and how together I was, I'd have no peace.

I know you've heard me say these words before
But every time I say I love you the words mean something more
I spoke them as a promise right from the start
I said death would be the only thing that could tear us apart
And now that you are standing on the edge of the unknown
I love you means I'll be with you wherever you must go

I will take a heart whose nature is to beat for me alone
And fill it up with you—make all your joy and pain my own
No matter how deep a valley you go through
I will go there with you
And I will give myself to love the way Love gave itself for me
And climb with you to mountaintops or swim a raging sea
To the place where one heart is made from two
I will go there with you

I see it in your tears—you wonder where you are
The wind is growing colder and the sky is growing dark
Though it's something neither of us understands
We can walk through this together if we hold each other's hand
I said for better or worse I'd be with you
So no matter where you're going I will go there too

I will take a heart whose nature is to beat for me alone
And fill it up with you—make all your joy and pain my own
No matter how deep a valley you go through
I will go there with you

I know sometimes I let you down
But I won't let you go—we'll always be together

"Go There With You"
Words and music by Steven Curtis Chapman

Depression became my friend, in a strange and painful way, a pushy friend I really did not want. But this strange friend made it so clear to me that I couldn't just buck up and *feel* better, or try harder and *do* better. I was helpless.

My husband could not fix me. My closest friends, who somehow loved me too, could not fix me. And Lord knows I could not fix myself. If I wanted to live in a different place than this dark cloud of fear, anger, and sadness, I had to realize that this burden was way too heavy to carry alone. God and God alone was the One who could take the depression and turn it into something teachable. All I had to do was the hardest thing possible for a person like me: I just had to be willing to give up control and give in to Him, and let Him use this cross in my life.

This was passive in the sense that I had to give up my will, but active in the sense of the action that required. It was also active in the sense that there was plenty of work I had to do if I wanted to get better.

But the first step, before my efforts, was to realize that the essential transformation inside of me would not come through my work, but as a gift of grace from God Himself.

When I was growing up in church, no one talked about this. My expectation then was that Christians were strong and victorious all the time. If someone was struggling with something, it was because his or her faith was not strong enough.

Now, thankfully, you hear a lot more in most Christian circles about brokenness. Most people I know are quite fond of the apostle Paul, not because he was a superachiever who spread the gospel throughout the known world, but because he realized that his pains and limitations were what kept him dependent on Christ. He knew he was a mess.

He said that we carry around the knowledge of Christ like a treasure in "jars of clay, to show that the surpassing power belongs to God and not to us. We are afflicted in every way, but not crushed; perplexed, but not driven to despair; persecuted, but not forsaken; struck down, but not destroyed; always carrying in the body the death of Jesus, so that the life of Jesus may also be manifested in our bodies" (2 Cor. 4:7–10 ESV).

I could relate with that.

The Prozac was not an instant fix-it kind of drug. It was medication, like high blood pressure medication. It treated my symptoms. As I started feeling better, I could then work on the root of the problem and begin to heal from things in the past. It helped me clearly think about how God's grace applied to me.

I believe that Steven's success, and the fact that it put both of us in the spotlight, was part of God's plan to glorify Himself through my struggles and inadequacies. I am the absolute least likely candidate in the world to be a "Christian celebrity wife." I've always wanted to be just like Beth Moore when I grow up . . . so wise in the Word, a prolific speaker, great hair, and in love with Jesus! Or Ruth Graham, married for a lifetime to Billy, spunky and beautifully graceful all at the same time. Or Mother Teresa, who simply lived love through her actions.

But God made me the way He did and gave me the story we're living. And even though I am not your usual candidate for celebrity wifedom, I believe it is all about showing off *His* glory. If a lot of people are watching our faith journey, our marriage, and our family because of Steven's musical success, then that's great, because it will help to shatter the illusion that Christians are supposed to be perfect.

People need to know that Christian leaders, singers, preachers, writers, whoever, are as cracked and broken as the next person. Maybe more so. Hopefully they are in positions of leadership, though, because they are serious about following Christ, and so people can see that real success in the kingdom of God is not about being strong and looking good and knowing all the right answers. It's about continually yielding oneself to Jesus and determining to take purposeful little steps of obedience, and the ragged reality that it's all about God and His grace at work in us.

I still have awfully dark days. I still take medication. I still see a counselor. I wish God would take my depression away. But so far He hasn't, and perhaps that is because He's using this as a way to keep me dependent on Him. I have to get my worth from Christ and Christ alone.

It's a journey. I recognize the dark tides that can push and pull me to places I don't want to go. So I anchor myself to the One who can take me where I do want to go.

I take a perverse pleasure in so many of the Psalms, and I am so absolutely grateful to God that He would include the wild writings of a guy like David, who clearly had his ups and downs. I can relate with the pain and great sweeps of melancholy in the Psalms. But I can also relate with the way David always returned to his hope in the Lord. His pain was real, but so was his hope. And in spite of being slightly crazy, David knew that the Lord God Himself knew him before he was born. He is the One who will cause our stories to ultimately end secure and well, right in His arms.

I was diagnosed with depression early in 1991. All these years later, I can see how the seeds of hope God planted then would need time to root and grow deeply into the faith that I have in the God of all comfort . . . so I would be able to withstand the terrible storms that would devastate our family in 2008.

11

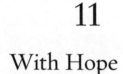

With Hope

> But we do not want you to be uninformed, broth-
> ers, about those who are asleep, that you may
> not grieve as others do who have no hope.
>
> *1 Thessalonians 4:13 ESV*

It was Friday evening, January 2, 1998. Steven and I had recently joined a small group of four or five other couples from our church, and all the families had gathered at the home of our friends Terri and Dan Coley. The University of Tennessee was playing in the national championship football game, and the adults were cheering and yelling at the TV while the kids were having a great time running around the Coleys' house.

I've always been a big fan of college sports, but by halftime I needed to go home as I was struggling with bad cramps. Being in my bed with a heating pad sounded like a great way to watch the second half of the game. Steven helped me gather up our kids, and we said goodbye and headed home.

Our friend Lori Mullican decided to leave at halftime as well. She had two little girls, Erin, eight, and Alex, five. She wanted to get them home to bed since they were going hiking with friends early the next morning. As Steven and I pulled out of the driveway, I saw

Lori getting her girls situated in the back seat, helping them with their seat belts.

Off we drove, trying to get home soon so we wouldn't miss much of the second half.

Lori hopped into her Honda Accord and headed down the same road we had taken a minute earlier. Her house was close by, so she didn't fasten her own safety belt.

Chatting with her girls, she headed down a road we all drove dozens of times each week . . . and the last thing she remembers about that night was approaching a familiar intersection. The traffic light was green.

What Lori doesn't remember is the seventeen-year-old driver of a truck approaching the same intersection. His eyes were on his rearview mirror, and he didn't see his light turn red. He never even slowed down and T-boned Lori's side of the car at full speed, right behind the driver's seat. Right where Erin was sitting.

The next thing Lori knew was that she was lying on a very hard bed. Every part of her hurt. She would later find out that she had a broken neck, abrasions, lacerations, and bruises everywhere. Ironically, not wearing her seat belt had saved her life; she had been thrown clear of the spinning car through the front driver's side window and so had been spared more serious injuries.

As she regained consciousness, though, all she cared about were her daughters. A nurse got her husband, Ray . . . and he told her that Alex had been leaking cerebral fluid through a crack in her skull, but she was alive. Then Ray had to do the hardest thing he had ever done: he told Lori that Erin did not make it.

When we got the phone call that night, I couldn't believe it. We prayed for this precious family. Then we agreed that Steven should go to the hospital to offer what comfort and prayer that he could. Being the "newbies" of the small group, we wrestled with how much to enter in, and we tried our best to support those who at the time were closest to the Mullicans.

When Steven arrived at Vanderbilt Children's Hospital and eventually was able to connect with Ray for a moment, Ray looked Steven right in the eyes. "We're not home yet," he said. It was the title to a song Steven had written a year or two before about the journey toward heaven.

This is not at all how
We thought it was supposed to be
We had so many plans for you
We had so many dreams
And now you've gone away
And left us with the memories of your smile
And nothing we can say
And nothing we can do
Can take away the pain
The pain of losing you, but . . .

We can cry with hope
We can say goodbye with hope
'Cause we know our goodbye is not the end, oh no
And we can grieve with hope
'Cause we believe with hope
There's a place where we'll see your face again
We'll see your face again

And never have I known
Anything so hard to understand
And never have I questioned more
The wisdom of God's plan
But through the cloud of tears
I see the Father smile and say well done
And I imagine you
Where you wanted most to be
Seeing all your dreams come true
'Cause now you're home
And now you're free, and . . .

We wait with hope
And we ache with hope
We hold on with hope
We let go with hope

"With Hope"
Words and music by Steven Curtis Chapman

They hugged and cried. Then Steven stayed and prayed as Ray and Lori needed to make decisions about Lori and Alex's medical treatments and organ donation for Erin.

Steven and I couldn't imagine such pain. Lori and Alex's physical injuries would slowly heal, but the emotional loss was devastating.

As they made preparations for the funeral, Ray and Lori asked Steven to sing "Not Home Yet," the song that Ray and Steven talked about in the emergency room that night.

Alex got out of the hospital an hour before her sister's funeral. Lori had been discharged as well. Alex couldn't understand what had happened, and she internalized the pain of her older sister's death. For years to come she would struggle in school and bottle up intense frustration and guilt.

As Steven and Ray spent time together over the months that followed, Steven was moved to write the Mullicans a more personal song about their grief journey. He took a tape of Erin singing "Jesus Loves Me" and incorporated it into the beginning of his song "With Hope," which was recorded on his *Speechless* CD. It's a testimony to a family that we watched grieve with the hope of a living Comforter, a brave family who daily confirmed through their pain and tears that they would see their little girl again.

Since we were new to the small group, I didn't know Lori very well yet. I had no words for her. I couldn't even imagine losing a child so suddenly . . . and on top of that being injured and worried about her other daughter.

But I wanted to do what I could. Over time I started going over to Lori's house and just hanging out with her. She showed me a recent picture of her girls. I asked her for the negative and had a black-and-white copy enlarged to portrait size. I loved hand tinting black and white photographs, so I wanted to do one as a gift for Lori. It was my way of loving her without inadvertently saying the painful, stupid words that sometimes get said to grieving parents, even when people's intentions are good.

Sometimes long minutes would go by where nothing would be said. Other times we'd talk about insignificant things. Every now and then God would give me words . . . but mostly I'd try to make her laugh, which is my way. I felt so incapable of putting any kind of salve on so huge a wound. As we spent time together, we became close friends. It felt as if walking with her during this time included me in their fellowship of suffering. I had no idea what God was preparing me for.

And so it made sad sense that when my own day of tragedy would come ten years later, Lori would be the first person I would call.

12

Laughter

Before you make your final decision about adoption please remember that there are children being born as you read this letter that have no hope for the future. All they will know is a crib or one small room with work that comes along with it. Not everyone in this world can help these children but not to brag, we are financially equipped & I know deep down in your heart you would love a baby but you say you're scared of the challenge. Look you have 4 people under the same roof as you that would be a help to you. I know we're gone for 7 hrs. in the day but we are home for 6 hrs. Before we have to go to bed. Please pray about adopting.

Note written by Emily Chapman, age eleven, 1997

Do not be afraid, for I am with you;
I will bring your children from the east
and gather you from the west.

Isaiah 43:5

Our daughter Emily has always been a very compassionate person.

In 1997, when Emily and her friend Carrie Coley were about eleven years old, my friend Terri Coley and I took our girls on a mother-daughter trip to Haiti with Compassion International. Emily was deeply touched by the poverty and needs of children and families who had nothing. And once she got home and did some research, she engaged on an all-out adoption campaign. This wasn't just adoption in theory, as in us helping other people adopt, which I was happy to do. This was up close and personal: Emily wanted us to adopt a little sister from another country, like the orphans she'd seen in Haiti.

After Will was born, I had had my tubes tied. As far as I was concerned, we were done. Steven would say in concert, "We have Eenie, Meenie, and Minie, and we hope to have no Mo!" I was so thankful for our three children, and I just wanted to get our life in order and keep it that way. Adoption was for other people, mentally healthy people, more flexible people.

But as far as Emily Chapman was concerned, it was God's will that her mother's orderly plans be disrupted. Again. Emily would write letters to Steven and me, laying out all the reasons we should adopt. At the bottom she would sign her own name and leave two lines for "witnesses." And there would be the scribbly scrabbly signatures of Caleb and Will Chapman, official witnesses, ages eight and nine.

When her birthday rolled around, Emily's list was short and sweet:

1. Baby
2. Four wheeler
3. Concordance

This tells you a lot about Emily's personality.

For his part, Steven didn't need much convincing. He loved the idea of us adopting. He thought it was a beautiful theological picture of how God adopts us as *His* children. He also thought that since we had been so blessed, it was a way to share our blessings. And since we were in the public eye, it might also inspire other families to open their homes to adopt orphans.

The only little detail Steven was worried about was my, uh, mental stability.

I had my hands full already, and I, too, wondered if I could psychologically handle the stress and the demands of a new baby in our busy family.

Meanwhile, Miss Persistent had bought a book on international adoption with her birthday money, and while I drove our minivan to soccer practice and errands, Emily would sit in the back and read out loud to me.

"Mom!" she'd say. "Did you know it only costs this or that to adopt a child from here or there?" She was relentless.

Then Emily went with Steven while he sang at a fundraising event for Bethany Christian Services, a Christian adoption agency. "Mom!" she said when she came home. "Did you know that Bethany is trying to build up their China program? They're discounting Chinese adoptions right now!"

Because Emily was so adamant in her adoption PR campaign, I'd done a little reading on my own.

"You know," I told Steven, "when I think about adoption, I always picture a little girl from Asia. And I always think I'd name her Hannah, since that means 'gift of God's grace.'

"But there are a couple of problems," I went on. "I read that you can't have more than two biological children at home if you adopt from China, and we already have three. And I've read about attachment issues and how hard it sometimes is for older children to really attach to their adoptive families. The children coming out of China right now are mostly older toddlers. If we were to ever adopt—given my issues—I'd be more likely to pursue an infant less than a year old."

So the next day Steven called Bethany's headquarters. We were sitting on the side of our bed, and I could hear his part of the conversation.

"I understand the law is that you can't have more than two biological children at home, so I'm afraid we wouldn't qualify," he was saying. There was a pause. "Oh really?" he responded. "That's interesting. Let me tell my wife."

Steven put his hand over the phone and turned to me. "Sweetie," he said, "get this. The Chinese government changed that law just last month! Now you can have four biological children at home."

"You're kidding!" I said.

But I had another card to play.

"Ask about the age of the kids they're placing. They probably don't have babies under the age of one."

Steven was back on the phone. I heard the nice Bethany person talking, and then Steven said, "Oh really? Hold on for a second and let me tell my wife.

"The average age of the kids available for adoption used to be older," he said to me, "but things have changed and now they're placing children who are between six and ten months old."

"Unbelievable," I said. "Okay, ask her if they have any blond-haired, blue-eyed Chinese children!"

I'm sure the nice people at Bethany didn't think much of my humor, but the surprising information did make me agree to at least pray seriously about adoption. Down deep, I really did want to be open for whatever God wanted us to do. I was just really, really scared of my abilities as an adoptive parent.

So we prayed regularly—but guaranteed, not as regularly as Emily Chapman—for God's leading about the adoption decision.

Then Steven and I decided to spend one whole day together thinking about what God wanted us to do. We had a few errands to run and then it was off to lunch before a doctor's appointment.

Everything we saw was Asian. We looked in the window of an antique store . . . everything was Chinese. An Asian clerk checked us out at Target.

"Hey," Steven said, "if we were to end up adopting a child from China, we would be so *old*! We'd be like Abraham and Sarah. We'd have to find out what the Chinese name for 'laughter' is, so we could name our child like they did when God told them they were going to have Isaac in their old age."

I laughed at him as I shut the car door to go into the restaurant. We knew absolutely no words in Chinese. I got a table and looked up when the waitress asked me what I would like to drink. Yes, she was Asian.

I had a doctor's appointment right after lunch. I needed to get a possible infection on my ankle checked out. There were all kinds of magazines in the waiting room. Suddenly Steven said, "Mary Beth! You are not going to believe this! Look!"

He was reading a tattered *Reader's Digest* and had opened it to an article about a Chinese couple who were desperate to find a cure for their little son's heart problem. The story described the little boy, and then there was this line: "*The boy they called Shao-Shao* (pronounced Sho-Sho), *meaning 'laughter' in Chinese*, had a rare and very dangerous heart disease."

Only an hour before, we had been asking what the Chinese word for "laughter" was, which is not exactly the sort of thing you wonder about every day. And now here we were in this doctor's office, looking at an eight-month-old *Reader's Digest* we otherwise would never have seen and reading the exact answer to our question.

The hairs on the back of my neck stood up. I took the magazine and chucked it across the room.

A few minutes later I wasn't particularly surprised when the doctor called me in, examined my ankle, and told me it wasn't infected. I knew what God was up to: the ankle had just been the means to get us to read that old *Reader's Digest*!

I realize this could have simply been a coincidence. But I was beginning to believe that God was nudging us down the road toward adoption, building my faith as He did so.

But I was also full of fear.

"What if I can't do this?" I wondered. "What if I feel differently toward this child than I do toward my biological ones?"

I'd seen *Cinderella* a million times. I could just see myself in the evil stepmother role. I felt like I couldn't possibly love an adopted child as much as our other kids.

But then I'd think about what it might be like to be an abandoned child in China, living in an orphanage. Let's see . . . was it better for an innocent little girl to have *no* mom, or a loving family and a halfway okay, half-crazy mom?

Meanwhile, Steven gathered Emily, Caleb, and Will together. "Okay, listen up. We're gonna head down the road to adoption"— he was interrupted by wild cheers—"but you know that on every road there are detours. We don't know if this road will end with us actually getting a little girl from China, but it's the road we're heading down."

This image helped me a lot. It captured my faith journey at that time. As you know, for many of the events in my life I'd made plans and barreled toward what I wanted. With this big life decision . . . sure, we wanted (I think) the outcome to be that we'd adopt a little girl from China. But I felt like I was making that journey one little step at a time, walking each step *God* showed me to walk, not taking matters into my own hands and churning toward where *I* wanted to go. I didn't know where I wanted to go. I was conflicted and chose to believe that being conflicted was right where I needed to be in order for my faith to be put into action.

For the first time in my life, I began to learn to live the verse from Psalm 119:105—"Thy word is a lamp unto my feet, and a light unto my path."

"God!" I prayed. "I don't know that I've ever been on a journey where I really needed faith before. I could always see the path just fine. But with this, I truly don't know where the road will lead. I can only see enough by Your light to take the next little step. And the next . . . "

"I'm willing to do this, Lord," I prayed. "But I'm *scared!*"

I was scared I'd be the evil stepmother. I was scared that I was too unbalanced to handle another child on top of the challenges of Steven's crazy tour schedule. I could see in my mind how the implications of this would play out over a lifetime.

I was scared that life the way I knew it was over, and I didn't like not knowing what was coming. Many, many nights my husband would just hold me in our bed as I sobbed and tears of fear ran down my face, dribbling into my ears.

The one good thing in my favor through all this was that I've always been a champion at paperwork, and the beginning stages of adoption are all about paperwork. I filled out all our forms and tracked down our certified birth certificates, marriage certificate, and all kinds of other certificates. We had background checks and fingerprints done.

So in May 1999 we finished our adoption dossier, including our home study and everything else in our paperwork pile, which made up one fat stack of papers. After getting every kind of notarization, state seal, and government authentication, I felt like I'd followed God's path step by step, and now all I was supposed to do was wait.

We didn't have to wait long. The following January, we received our referral from Bethany. This was the packet that gave us a picture of our child-to-be and what little information existed about her health, birth, and abandonment. There was also the acceptance letter . . . which we had to sign within forty-eight hours of receiving it to say that yes, we will adopt this child.

The agency had sent me the picture electronically, and as I downloaded it, my stomach was in a knot. Back then downloads were so slow because of dial-up speed. Finally the photo opened on our computer screen while Steven and I held our breath. Little by little, our new daughter's face appeared.

Her name was Chang Yan Yan, from Hunan Province. Chang was her surname, but in China they always put that first. Yan Yan was her first name. It meant "doubly adorable." The photo was basically a chubby little Chinese face swaddled in blankets, but I thought she was the most beautiful, incredible baby I'd ever seen. I was halfway thrilled and halfway scared, still convinced I was going to be a terrible mother for this poor little, doubly adorable Chinese orphan.

Finally the time came to saddle up our horses and head to China. Emily had just turned fourteen, and she was beside herself with joy. We waited until she'd finished her performances in the school play—she was starring as Little Red Riding Hood—then packed up ten-year-old Caleb and his nine-year-old sidekick Will, and got ready to head to China.

I took a photo as we left our home to go to the airport. It was early in the foggy morning, and there were our three towheaded Chapman children, sleepy but full of excitement.

And so was I, but as I got on the airplane and flew halfway around the world to retrieve the sixth member of our family—certainly *not* towheaded—I was still afraid. I had no idea that God was going to do a miracle in China. It wasn't just the wonder of adopting our daughter. It was a spiritual miracle inside of me, one that would begin to heal me of some of the guilt and shame I'd been carrying around since I was a teenager.

13

When Love Takes You In

I will not leave you as orphans; I will come to you.

John 14:18 ESV

God sets the lonely in families.

Psalm 68:6

Our friend and Steven's road manager, David Trask, came along to help keep us all on time, organized, and sane. The plan was for us to meet our adoption guide and acclimate to the time change for a few days in Beijing while we saw sites like the Great Wall, the Forbidden City, and Tiananmen Square. Then we were to fly south to Changsha, capital of Hunan province, where little "doubly adorable" Chang Yan Yan would be brought, like the best room service ever, to our hotel room.

We had decided to call her Shaohannah. *Shao* for laughter, of course, and *Hannah* for the gift of God's grace.

We were all weary but anxious. The kids and Steven were anxiously awaiting the arrival of the newest member of the family . . . while *my* anxiety was more the kind that made me want to run the other way.

Heavy fog in Beijing delayed our takeoff for five hours. I could barely keep my calm; I felt like the moment that everyone else was waiting for was relentlessly closing in on me.

We arrived in Changsha. Our guide called the orphanage people to tell them that we had finally arrived. She discovered that they had already traveled from the orphanage and were in the city, waiting for us because of our delay. They'd been there a few hours, and they had only brought one bottle of formula. They said they needed to get the baby to us as soon as possible . . . as a matter of fact, they were in the lobby and wanted to bring her up to our room right away.

Of course I had plenty of bottles, formula, and everything else. But things were accelerating way too quickly. I was about to come eye to eye with what had terrified me for the past year. I was getting ready to give birth, and I didn't at all feel prepared. I didn't even feel pregnant! I was scared to death. What was about to happen?

As we checked into our hotel, the staff was very professional. They were used to hosting American families, who stayed in this hotel all the time to do the very thing we were getting ready to do.

We had no more than entered our room when the phone rang and a voice informed us in broken English that the people were there with our baby and they wanted to bring her up to us right then, if that was alright. I didn't have formula unpacked, nothing was settled or nested in our room. I was frantic.

My stomach was turning cartwheels, my hands were clammy, and my heart was racing. There was no backing out now. What had I been thinking? I didn't even know this little person from China, and now she was being carried up the elevator, down the hall, straight toward my arms . . . and I didn't feel prepared in the least!

"God," I prayed, "please, I don't even know what to say, but, HELPPPPPPP!"

Steven was looking at me, worried. I could see him thinking, *She's gonna completely flip out, and when she does. . . . What do I do?*

Meanwhile, David Trask was in the hall with the video camera pointed toward the elevator, his finger ready to push the little red "record" button.

I was like a caged animal, pacing, frantic. If I could've jumped out the window and lived, I would have. Jet lag, anxiety, and the Enemy's lies were skewing my brain. It was like Satan was whispering in my ear that I *couldn't* be a good mom, I *couldn't* do this, I *couldn't* love this little girl the way she needed to be loved.

I grabbed Emily, Caleb, and Will and lined them up at the end of the bed. "Kids!" I struggled to say. "This is going to change our family forever! Whatever happens in the next twenty-four hours, just remember, *I love you!*" They stared at me, all in a row, their eyes big and their jaws wide open.

I heard in the distance the "ding" of the elevator. I heard our facilitator's voice calling from the hall in Chinese/broken English, "They here! They here!"

Terrified, I walked slowly toward the door. Everything went into slow motion. I looked back over my shoulder one last time at my three little towheaded kids sitting in a row: the way things were. It was a kind of death to the familiar life I'd known. I took a deep breath, told God that I trusted Him, and walked through the door.

I saw a Chinese woman carrying a bundled baby. She was wrapped in a million layers, but the outside one was a pink, polka-dotted flannel blanket that I had made and sent from home.

I couldn't get to her fast enough. I opened my arms, flew toward the woman, and took the baby. Tears poured down my face. I couldn't believe that this was my child. I stared down at her, crying over and over, "*This is my baby!*" I wept and clutched her tightly as the nanny handed me everything I had ever sent her: a stuffed pig, a plastic photo album of her new family.

Steven had stepped back. He could see that something miraculous was unfolding. It was like I had walked out into the hall as one person, and now I was holding this baby as a new person altogether.

In that moment, time stopped. It was like God was speaking to me directly. "Mary Beth, you thickheaded woman, do you not understand now that this is the very way I see you? You are this orphan! I adopted you and you are Mine! I bought you for a price! Do you see how you love this baby? That's just a faint reflection of how much I love you! You didn't have a name, and I gave you a name. You did nothing to deserve my love, and I love you anyway. You had no hope, no future, and now you are the daughter of the *King!*"

I saw it. The second she was placed in my arms, I would have fought to the death to protect her. I loved her with everything inside of me.

"Do you get it *now*?" God was saying to me. Under the blanket, this baby was wrapped in rags. She was poor. She didn't smell good. She was hungry. There was nothing about her that had "earned" my love. But I loved her powerfully, deeply, absolutely. Period.

I got it.

Steven saw the transformation in my spirit. David Trask saw it through the lens of the video camera. In an instant, God had bonded

I know you've heard the stories
But they all sound too good to be true
You've heard about a place called home
But there doesn't seem to be one for you
So one more night you cry yourself to sleep
And drift off to a distant dream

And somewhere while you're sleeping
Someone else is dreaming too
Counting down the days until
They hold you close and say I love you
And like the rain that falls into the sea
In a moment what has been is lost in what will be

When love takes you in everything changes
A miracle starts with the beat of a heart
And this love will never let you go
There is nothing that could ever cause this love to lose its hold

When love takes you in everything changes
A miracle starts with the beat of a heart
When love takes you home and says you belong here
The loneliness ends and a new life begins
When love takes you in it takes you in for good
When love takes you in

"When Love Takes You In"
Words and music by Steven Curtis Chapman

me forever to this little girl, and nothing would separate us. In doing so, He also showed me the forever fierceness of *His* unconditional love for me, doing a work of grace in my life that I'd never known before.

Then we heard three little voices from the hotel room. We had forgotten all about our three "natural" children. We had told them to wait because I had been afraid, and we weren't sure what was going to happen out in the Hallway of Life.

"Hey! What about us?" they called. "You forgot us!"

Steven and I looked at each other through our tears of joy and began laughing. It scared Shaohannah and she puckered up and started to cry, which made it even funnier in a weird way.

"Come on out!" Steven shouted.

14

Show Hope

I saw the face of Jesus
In a little orphan girl
She was standing in the corner
On the other side of the world
And I heard the voice of Jesus
Gently whisper to my heart
Didn't you say you wanted to find Me
Well, here I am
Here you are

So what now
What will you do now that you've found Me
What now
What will you do with this treasure you've found
I know I may not look like what you expected
But if you'll remember
This is right where I said I would be
You found Me
What now

"What Now"
Words and music by Steven Curtis Chapman

We came back from China with Shaohannah Hope Chapman in March 2000. This was, of course, back in the days before airport security had become as restrictive as it is today. There were about 250 people gathered right at the gate when we got off our airplane, jet-lagged, clutching our new little Asian princess. There were camera crews as well as friends and family cheering us across the finish line, taking pictures and waving welcome home signs.

I had already told Steven I was sure that when my brother Jim met Shaohannah, he was going to want to adopt as well. And sure enough, one of the first things he said—after we had hugged and introduced him to his new niece—was something like, "Okay, what do we need to do to start the process to go bring one of these little girls home to our family?"

Before we ever left the airport, five other families had told us that they'd love to adopt too, but they'd looked into it and couldn't afford it.

Just days before, I had walked through the orphanage where Shaoey had spent the first seven months of her life. My heart broke over and over again as I looked into the faces of so many little ones lying there in their iron cribs, their eyes looking into mine as if to ask, "Did you come for me?"

So when people were telling me that they'd just love to take one of these little ones into their home if they only had the money, what was I to do? I started writing checks. As Steven says, a line started to form around the block as I tried to help wonderful families with the resources they needed to adopt children in need.

In the summer of 2001, we went back to China with my brother Jim and his wife Yolanda, as well as our great friends Geoff and Jan Moore, to be with them as they adopted Isabelle Chapman and Anna Grace Moore, two little girls from the same province as Shaoey. Several other families followed suit, and so we needed to figure out a better way to help as many people as we could to experience this miracle of adoption.

We had worked with Bethany Christian Services for our adoption of Shaohannah, so Steven called Bethany. "Is there a fund where we can direct people who want to adopt?" he asked. "We keep being approached by people who want so badly to adopt but don't have the money to make it happen. We want to help people experience this miracle we've experienced . . . not to mention the fact that there are so many children waiting right now for families, and families wanting to give them a home!"

The people at Bethany were wonderful. They told us that they once had such a fund, but it had long since been depleted. They agreed that this was a huge need for Christian families. They were willing to help us if we decided to start something.

We continued to look around for some other organization that helped people who wanted to adopt. Steven felt that he could use his music platform to give a lift to whatever already existed. He'd gladly call attention to the need for believers to adopt, if only he could connect himself to the right organization.

But we couldn't find what we were looking for. We began to prayerfully consider starting something ourselves. It wasn't like we didn't already have enough to do. Our lives were crazy . . . but this idea stayed with us, so we connected with various people who had the same vision.

In September 2001, Steven and I were chosen by the Congressional Coalition on Adoption Institute to receive their annual National Angel in Adoption award. At the time, an amazing woman named Kerry Hasenbalg was serving as the executive director. On September 10, the night before the event, we got together with Kerry and her husband Scott, along with other friends, to talk, dream, and pray about how we might do something to help the orphans and vulnerable children in the world.

The next morning, September 11, Steven woke up early to do an interview with CNN. We even had a meeting scheduled with President Bush later in the day to talk about orphan care and adoption.

When Steven returned from his interview at CNN, we sat down at a table in our hotel restaurant to have breakfast. Suddenly there was a news report that a plane had crashed into one of the twin towers of the World Trade Center in New York. We watched the television in shock, along with the rest of the world. Then the second airplane slammed into the second tower.

We ran back to our room where Uncle Dave—Steven's road manager, David Trask—was watching Shaoey. We stared at the television . . . and then we saw smoke rising in the distance beyond our hotel window in Washington. The Pentagon had just been hit.

Needless to say, our event was cancelled that night, as was our meeting with President Bush. But we had forged important friendships during that trip, in particular with Scott Hasenbalg, who would eventually help us create an adoption and orphan care ministry and would become its executive director. We would call it Shaohannah's Hope.

We officially incorporated Shaohannah's Hope as a nonprofit 501(c)(3) organization in February 2003. God had given us a burden to inspire and educate believers about the plight of orphans and vulnerable children. If Christians could become advocates for orphans who could not help themselves, we would truly be doing the work of the body of Christ and be a witness for the reality of Jesus' love in a hurting world.

There are about 140 million orphans in the world today. As we became aware of their needs, we read our Bibles with fresh eyes. We saw all the times that the Bible talks about both orphans and adoptions. In Steven's music and in the platforms God gave us, we started talking more about them as well.

As Shaohannah's Hope grew, our mission became clear: to care for orphans by engaging the church and helping Christian families reduce the financial barriers to adoption. We provide Christian couples with financial grants so the overwhelming cost of adoption doesn't discourage them. Our average grants are about three to four thousand dollars. We believe that we shouldn't fully fund the entire adoption: we want families to raise funds on their own as well as be supported by their local community of faith.

It doesn't matter which country the child comes from; we've given grants to families who have adopted from forty-five different countries.

Beyond that, we felt called to do something about the care and needs of orphans and vulnerable children who might not be adoptable. We believe that even those children who may not survive for very long are still little treasures whom God has put in our world to reveal something unique about Himself.

We committed to help, however we could, those who could be cared for medically and eventually become adoptable, those who would need long-term medical care and not be adopted, and those who would simply need a place to be held and rocked until they peacefully entered heaven.

We also felt that God had called us to help believers in the U.S. become more aware. If there was ever an issue that followers of Jesus should be all about, it would be caring for orphans in their distress. So we've become increasingly involved in mobilizing churches and communities to care for orphans.

The only problem with the ministry was that our name was a little hard to spell properly or to Google. I knew this would be a problem from the start, but God had so clearly given us Shaohannah's name that we felt strongly we needed to name the ministry after her. Eventually we would change the name to the far simpler Show Hope. And incredibly, as I write this, we've given more than 2,500 grants! That's 2,500 children now home with loving families . . . and that number just keeps on growing.

For more current information about Show Hope, check out our website at www.showhope.org.

Even though I had become passionate about adoption, helping everyone I knew adopt kids from China, Africa, and wherever else, my husband had serious reservations about us adopting again. He felt—understandably—worried about our family's sanity. Especially mine.

In spite of how much we all loved Shaoey and how God had so clearly worked in her adoption to communicate His love to me, Steven didn't want me to take on too much. So he told God, "I'm open to adopting again, but I need a burning bush if it's Your plan for us."

Before Shaoey, I'd been the holdout and Steven and the kids had all engaged in a prayer conspiracy against me.

Now it was my turn . . . and so the rest of the Chapman family began praying for Steven to get his burning bush. If it was God's will, of course.

15

I'm Signing, You're Signing, We're All Signing

A person who lives in faith must proceed
on incomplete evidence, trusting in advance
what will only make sense in reverse.

Philip Yancey

One Sunday morning in the fall of 2002, our family was all lined up in a pew at church. Our great friends, Dan and Terri Coley, were at the front of the sanctuary dedicating their new little boy Daniel to God, as well as two of his siblings, Michael and Katie.

During my second trip to China in 2001, I had met Daniel when he was a sickly, tiny infant. Steven and I had met up with Terri Coley's daughter, Rachel, who was a college junior studying in China that year. We traveled to a Christian foster home about an hour from Beijing where a group of houses had been set up to care for the orphans who somehow found their way to this place.

You could sense the love and care for the children. They were divided by age and special needs. Some were in rooms full of toys, and they were playing with balls and blocks. Some were in high chairs, being fed by nannies. Then there were the tiny babies who had not been there long. I saw a little white crib with a mosquito net streaming from the ceiling to cover it.

Rachel and I walked to the crib and peeked in. A baby boy was lying there. He was so tiny, probably just a few weeks old. He had a cleft lip and palate. It undid me to see him. He was so small, so helpless. *He's just lying there,* I thought, *waiting. Waiting for someone to come. A rescuer.*

I picked him up and held him close.

Rachel and I decided we should call her mother back in Nashville.

"Terri," I said, "I don't know why on earth I thought of you, with all the children you've already adopted, but I felt like I just had to call and tell you about this little baby here! I think you may need him in your family!"

Terri laughed for a minute. "Mary Beth," she said in her matter-of-fact voice, "I already have seven children. Seven is the biblical number of perfection. I don't need any more children!"

It wasn't like I knew God's will for Terri's life . . . but still, this itty bitty boy touched my heart, and something inside of me knew that, in spite of Terri's certainty that seven children was enough, this tiny Chinese baby would touch her too.

After we left China, Rachel Coley began taking a bus every weekend to visit with the kids, particularly the little guy with the cleft palate. When Terri came to China to help Rachel move from one city to another after her semester was over, Rachel took her mom to the foster home.

After they left, Terri had tears in her eyes. She kept thinking about the orphans . . . what would happen to them? One of her other daughters, Carrie, was traveling with her. Seeing her mom's tears, Carrie said, "Why don't you think about adopting one of them?"

"Oh, Carrie!" Terri said. "I'm too old!"

"Well, let's think about that," said Carrie, who was sixteen at the time. "Is it better for an orphan to have an old mom . . . or *no* mom?"

When Terri got home, she and Dan felt God tugging on their hearts to adopt again. They started their paperwork . . . and within a year, on their twenty-fifth wedding anniversary, baby Daniel—the same little guy Rachel and I had met in the foster home—was placed in their arms. His cleft palate had been repaired in China, but he would still need many more surgeries in Nashville.

It was a tough road. Daniel had recurring infections, hearing loss, eventual speech therapy . . . and several of the Coleys' other seven children had tough needs and difficulties.

Now, on this Sunday morning, I felt teary as I looked at our friends. Terri and Dan were—and are—my heroes.

They were in the front of the church with Christi, Rachel, Carrie, and Johnson (their biological children), and Josh, Katie, Michael, and baby Daniel (their adopted children, who are, respectively, Caucasian, biracial, African American, and Chinese). (Later they would adopt Anna, who was named by Christi, and who also had a cleft lip and palate and many medical needs.)

We'd walked with Terri and Dan through many struggles. They had adopted Josh at age six out of the state system. He had suffered neglect and abuse, and he'd brought hard issues to the Coley family. They had been through so much . . . and now, as I looked at the Coleys up in front of the church, they looked like a picture of God's family: children from all kinds of backgrounds and all kinds of suffering, joined together by love.

Love isn't easy. It's hard. And the Coleys were *doing* hard, swimming against the current of the brokenness of their children's past, as well as against the flow of our comfortable culture, which so often encourages the wide, easy road.

I looked down our row and saw my husband, tears streaming down his face, scribbling furiously in the front of his Bible. I didn't think much about it because he often writes lyrics and other ideas when things are triggered in that creative mind of his.

He must have a song idea, I thought.

After church, as our Land Cruiser pulled out of the parking lot on our way to get some lunch, Steven announced sort of formally that he had something to say. It caught our attention, which was hard because everyone was hungry and talking all at once about where each person wanted to eat.

He cleared his throat.

"Chubby Chapman" was a damaging nickname. Years later I finally realized its effects on my life.

My grandparents and me. I thought the red culottes were fine for church camp meeting.

Farrah Fawcett hair was the style for senior pictures in the '80s. The perfect feathered look.

Anderson University homecoming football game after an all-night "discussion."

Livin' on love!
19 and 21 years old.
Fifty dollars and a green
Ford Pinto to our name!

Strollin' down memory lane
during a 2008 visit to
Anderson University campus.
Notice the mailboxes behind us?

Where's Emily? After freshly laundering what stuffed animals I could after the fire, I seized the photo op while the animals were laying out drying.

Pill-eating puppy named Peso, with the result named Emily.

Sweet Emily at age 13. "The Fingerprints of God" says it all!

Celebrating Gold. We saddled up for the Great Adventure, but I was barely hanging on to the reins.

Band name: 2 Car Garage (Caleb was missing his two front teeth). A glimpse into the future?

© Paul Wharton

One of my favorite pre-adoption family portraits. We love to laugh together, and now we love to cry together. It's a privilege.

Our Compassion trip to
Haiti in 1997 captured
Emily's heart for orphans
and vulnerable children.
The faith of a child!

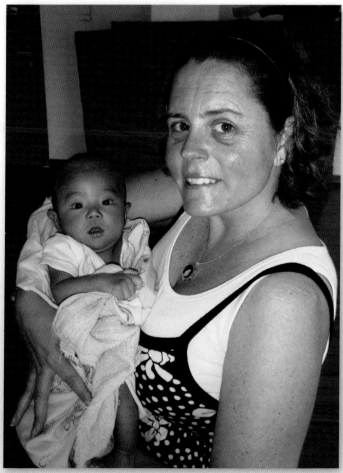

I named this Maria's Big House of Hope baby after Hudson Taylor. He giggled
at the name Maria and is with her now in heaven.

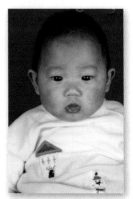

XU CHUN XI
(MARIA SUE CHUNXI CHAPMAN)

CHEN BI RU
(STEVEY JOY RU CHAPMAN)

CHANG YAN YAN
(SHAOHANNAH HOPE YAN CHAPMAN)

The first look at our precious daughters. These are the three referral pictures that came to us with all their other pertinent information.

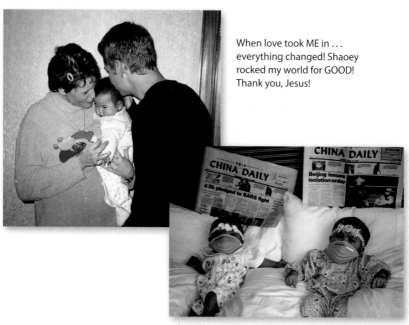

When love took ME in . . .
everything changed! Shaoey
rocked my world for GOOD!
Thank you, Jesus!

When the going gets tough, the tough find the humor.
While in China adopting Stevey Joy, I found some fun
with photos! Warped? Maybe.

Adoption day in China, and
it was as if Steven and Maria
had known each other their
whole lives.

© Tucker Photography

And Maria makes eight! Now we look complete.

We were blessed with a private tour of Cinderella's Suite at Disney World, and all *my* Cinderellas loved it!

Vacation! "I love it when my whole family is together" was one of Maria's favorite lines.

Giddyup! Isn't that what brothers and daddies are for?

Dancing at a wedding in 2006. Will and I have always been close and have so many awesome memories together.

© Tucker Photography

It's true! Chapman family tradition. Chinese or Japanese food on Christmas Eve, before Christmas Eve service.

Maria could make a "Rock Face" like none other! I cut the sleeves off the shirts to improve them.

Two peas in a pod! Maria and Stevey Joy were born seven months apart and were best buddies, inseparable.

Maria's third birthday. She loved Tinker Bell and fairies. Shaoey says Maria's finally a fairy because she has her wings!

Rub a dub dub, three girls in the tub.

In China, pools require swim caps. Why? Don't know. Will was a great sport and they all got to pick out their own cap.

© John Price

Family picture day! Will was the only sibling who had his picture taken individually with each of the three girls. He makes everything fun.

Caleb had ways of making Maria laugh and smile so hard her eyes would disappear.

Spring break 2007. One of these is not like the others! I'm grateful God used Emily to speak into my life.

Taken in China, this picture of Steven and Maria would be sent to us later, confirming that this was Daddy kissing his daughter.

After a long weekend in Maine, Tanner proposed to Emily on an airplane flight.

When I look at this picture, I can smell Maria's sweaty skin, I can hear her sweet voice, and I can feel that chubby little hand on my neck.

Maria's favorite blanket. She had to have that one. Will kept it with him in the days following the accident.

Goggle Girl. Many days, this is all she swam in. For that matter, I would occasionally catch her watching TV with them on and nothing else!

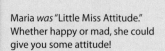

Maria *was* "Little Miss Attitude." Whether happy or mad, she could give you some attitude!

A trip to South Dakota in 2009 with our friends, the Moores, and their girls to help adjust to "the new normal."

© John Price

Caleb and Will on tour with
Casting Crowns, 2010.
Showing hope by wearing hope!

October 4, 2008. Emily and Tanner Richards were married. In honor of Maria, the family portrait was a "Rock Face" pose.

© Divine Images

May 10, 2009. Caleb and Julia Chapman were married. In honor of Maria, the family portrait was another "Rock Face" pose.

© Tec Pataja

© Austin Mann

Grand opening and dedication in honor of Maria—the complete earthly Chapman family at Maria's Big House of Hope, 2009.

"I have an announcement," he said. "This morning when we were on our way to church, if someone had asked me if we were going to adopt, my answer would have been no."

Everyone groaned.

"But as I was watching the Coleys today," Steven continued, "God spoke to me so clearly."

We were afraid to get too excited yet. Maybe Steven was just processing his thoughts, or preaching a second sermon of the day. But we had a little bit of hope. Could this be the burning bush Steven had been praying for?

He handed me his Bible, since he was driving. "I want Mom to read you what I wrote down about this."

I opened to the page where Steven had been scribbling.

Daniel, Michael Ray, and Katie Coley were baptized this morning at Christ Community Church. As I watched these great friends and faithful servants celebrating their children's entrance into the covenant and being received into the community of those who stand under the waterfall of God's grace, God's Spirit spoke to my heart and said, "Go and do likewise. Somewhere there's a child that I have plans for to know my love and grace and take his or her place under the waterfall. Will you trust me with the details that you've been worried about and walk in faith where I'm leading you and your family?"

Who knows (God does) how this act may be multiplied within our close circle of friends and family, and I will pray and ask for that, but that's not the point. The point is that there is one life somewhere (probably China) that is or soon will be in need of a family who will introduce him or her to his or her Savior. Today I commit to respond to God's revelation and give Mary Beth my full support to begin paperwork for another adoption.

Emily, Caleb, and Will started screaming. I started crying. The joyful noise startled an almost-asleep Shaoey, who promptly started crying, as if to say, "Oh *no*, my throne is going to be captured!"

I was completely excited, completely fearful of the implications, but the wheels were already turning in my madly multitasking brain. In my head, I was half done with all the adoption paperwork, and somehow I was already brewing a plan to get some of our closest friends to adopt again with us so we could all go to China together.

A week later, Steven was reading his Bible and a verse from 1 Thessalonians 2 hit him: "For what is our hope, our joy, or the crown in which we will glory in the presence of our Lord Jesus when He comes? Is it not you? Indeed, you are our glory and joy" (v. 19).

He felt that God was reminding him that when we all stand before Christ in the end, the main thing we'll have to show for this life will be the spiritual children we've been a part of bringing into His kingdom. *What a joy*, Steven thought, *to present our children to Christ as our joy and our crown in His presence!*

We had already picked the name "Stevey" for our new daughter-to-be. We knew it meant "crowned one" because "Steven" means the same thing. Who knew God would give us a tiny little girl, who out of all the Chapman children would be a princess in training, a girl who loves sparkly crowns and tiaras? God knew. And as Steven read his Bible that day, he felt like God was showing him, "Here's your hope (Shaohannah Hope) and your crown of joy (Stevey Joy)."

The next week I wasted no time in ordering various documents, scheduling the home study, and making my way through adoption agency applications and all that comes with the daunting task of assembling a dossier for a China adoption. As I worked on all the papers, I felt for some reason that I should order two of everything: two birth certificates each for Steven and me, two marriage certificates. Later this would be exactly what we needed to add to our family again, quickly. Of course, I didn't know that then. But God did.

The other crazy thing that was going on inside my "don't take no for an answer" brain was that, as the unofficial fourth member of the Trinity, I had decided it was God's will that our great friends Geoff and Jan Moore should adopt again with us. The only small problem was that God had not yet revealed this to Geoff and Jan.

So, sucking Steven into my plot, I asked him to invite them to Loveless Café, our favorite breakfast spot. We ate a dozen or so biscuits with our favorite strawberry jam, eggs, and bacon.

"We kind of need to talk to you guys about something," Steven said.

I pulled out a giant envelope full of adoption paperwork.

"This might shock you," I said, smiling, "but we've decided to adopt again!"

Of course they weren't surprised. They had seen us become intoxicated with Shaoey and adoption and orphan care, to the point of helping several friends adopt and even starting Show Hope. They grinned.

"And," I went on, "we think *you* want to adopt again too! We would love to have you on this journey with us, so let's do it together!"

Cue the crickets.

Our friends just sat there looking at us, and then slowly they looked at each other and smiled. Geoff's grin said a dozen things at once. Things like, "Oh, crap! I knew it! We were already thinking about it! Only Mary Beth could try something like this!"

"Don't worry," I said. "It just so happens that when I filled out our preliminary applications, I filled out yours too!" I dramatically pulled out a manila folder full of their preliminary agency applications, with all the correct information filled in.

Jan was teary and thrilled all at once. She and Geoff had talked about adopting again, but all this information was a little sudden for her. Geoff was looking down, shaking his head, and grinning. Steven and I were beside ourselves.

It was a beautiful day, so—since we were all getting a little too emotional for the restaurant—we decided to take our conversation outside to the grassy area in front of our cars.

We talked some more and prayed, and then, after lots of hugs and jumping up and down, I handed them the papers and we quoted one of our favorite movie lines from *That Thing You Do*: "Okay! I'm signing, you're signing, we're all signing!"

As the Chinese proverb says, the journey of a thousand miles begins with a single step. In our case it was about eight thousand miles, but the journey to bring home Ashley Rose Moore and Stevey Joy Chapman began as we laughed and cried and signed our paperwork in front of that little home-cookin' restaurant.

As our kids at home prepared for our new arrival, the reality of a new sister was setting in with Caleb and Will. Shaoey's first year with us had been filled with broken sleep and screams from night terrors. So the boys really wanted a low-maintenance, happier sister who would have no problems sleeping through the night, and they decided it would be good to pray fervently for a chilled-out Chinese baby.

Then we began to hear about a weird viral epidemic in China, something called severe acute respiratory syndrome, or SARS. The World Health Organization was picking up reports of an outbreak of deaths from a highly contagious, flu-like virus. The Chinese government wasn't revealing much, so news reports were pretty vague.

China is huge, I thought, *and it has like two billion people, and they're saying that a few hundred have died. How bad can this SARS thing be?*

I was trying to convince myself that this wouldn't affect Chinese adoptions. But deep in my heart I began to suspect that this could be a problem. I began to pray and hope that we would travel as planned, and to fret that we would not.

Our referral packet arrived from Bethany Christian Services in early March 2003. We were thrilled with Stevey Joy (aka Chen Bi Ru), but her photo looked pretty pitiful. She was tiny—1.7 kilos (3.7 pounds). She'd been found outside a police station in a cardboard box, carefully wrapped in a man's suit jacket. Her report went on to read that she had IVs for various things and that the people in the orphanage were concerned about her, even though she was officially listed as "healthy" rather than "special needs."

Though the orphanage had evidently tried some traditional Chinese medicines to fatten her up, Stevey Joy's little picture was of a pasty white, sad, tiny girl who desperately needed a mom to come get her. Caleb and Will continued to pray diligently that she'd be a chilled-out kid.

While we waited for word from Bethany about when we could leave for China, I got four visas for Steven and me and Jan and Geoff. All we needed now were our official travel letters from the U.S. government. Meanwhile, the rumblings about SARS were getting louder. The virus was lethal, fast, and extremely contagious.

One evening shortly after receiving our referrals, Steven and I were at the Moores' home, talking about life and wondering if SARS would affect our travel plans. We joked, dreamed, and reflected back on our journey together. Geoff and Jan had been the first people we told when we were pregnant with our Emily . . . and now here we were, hopefully adding to both our families again. Jan told us how she was going to paint their master bedroom the next day. She wanted to get home projects out of the way before the adoption.

All I kept thinking was that SARS just could not stop our adoption arrangements. I had a plan, and nothing was going to get in my way. But, true to the way He so often seems to deal with me, God wasn't running the world—or writing my story—according to *my* plans.

16

Rambo Goes to China

It's crazy when love gets ahold of you
And it's crazy things that love will make you do
And it's crazy but it's true
You really don't know love at all
Until it's making you do
Something crazy

"Something Crazy"
Words and music by Steven Curtis Chapman
and Matt Bronleewe

About ten hours after our cozy evening at the Moores', I got an email from the adoption facilitator who would help us while we were in China. We had worked with her before and had stayed in contact ever since.

The facilitator's email title was simple: CANCEL ALL CHINA PLANS!

The Chinese government was going to close adoptions until the SARS epidemic passed. Each province was closing at a different time, but the whole country would eventually shut down regarding adoption. We'd just have to wait it out.

My first thought was about Stevey Joy and the pitiful picture of her, so pasty white and frail. What if SARS swept through her orphanage?

"Okay," I said to my safety-conscious, follow-the-rules husband. "What if I go to China *today*?"

Steven just stared at me like, "Oh, no, here we go again with another Mary Beth idea that could get totally crazy." He knew better than to say, "You're kidding, right?" He knew I wasn't.

At this point it was about 8:00 a.m. I got Steven's then-assistant, Melissa Banek, on the phone and asked her to start checking on flights to China. I had a visa; all I needed was to somehow get my official travel letter. I convinced Steven to call the facilitator in China. He asked her if by chance we could intercept the final travel documents before they were put in the mail to us, if we could fly today, go straight to the province before it closed, and have someone meet us there with the travel papers. (If those papers had already been on their way to us from China, there would have been nothing that we could do but wait . . . and wait . . . and wait.)

The facilitator told Steven that she would check with the China Center of Adoption Affairs to see if we could pick up our documents in Hunan. She'd call us back.

We held our breath.

Melissa called back on another phone; she was on the line with a travel agent.

"There's a flight at 1:00 p.m.," she said. "Oh, wait, it just disappeared off the screen."

I freaked out. China was starting to cancel flights! I had to get there!

"Okay," Melissa said, "there's another flight at 3:00 p.m. It goes to L.A. and then on to Guangzhou. From there you can fly in-country to Changsha."

"Hold two seats!" I told her.

I called my calm, steady, wonderful friend Jan Moore. Jan had her overalls on and was in the middle of painting her master bedroom. As far as she was concerned, our trip to China was at least a couple of months away.

"Jan!" I said. "Whatcha doin'? Do you want to go to China, like *today*?"

Silence on the phone.

"They're going to close China because of SARS!" I said. "Right now Hunan Province is open, but they're going to close! I'm not sure we can pull it off, but if we go today, I think we can get there before Hunan closes. We've got to try! Let's go bring our baby girls home!"

Jan started hyperventilating and crying at the same time.

"Here, talk to Geoff," she said, handing the phone to her husband.

"Geoff," I said, "here's the deal. China's going to close, but it's still open right now. I don't know if this will really work. We may just get as far as L.A., look at the palm trees, grab an In-N-Out burger, and then turn around and come home. But you know me; we've got to at least try. Just dump all your adoption paperwork in a bag and have Jan bring it. We'll figure it out later."

While all of this was going on, I had also realized that if our husbands weren't going to be with us in China, Jan and I needed powers of attorney to sign the adoption papers without them. We could get the paperwork done in Nashville and have it state sealed, but it had to be authenticated in Washington, D.C. Once executed, it could be sent by FedEx from D.C. to China.

The whole time my husband held to a relative calm but was not sure if he should try to protect me from myself.

"This is crazy," he said. "Am I supposed to try to stop you from doing this?"

"I've got to try," I said. "If I can just get there, I know they won't say no!"

I called our friend Terri Coley and gave her the rundown. "Go to Target," I said. "Buy a suitcase and fill it with everything Jan and I might need in China: formula, clothes, medicine, bottles, pacifiers, blankets, granola bars, wipes . . . whatever. If you think I'll need it, then buy it. I'll cover it, and I'll meet you in the parking lot of Target at 12:30 p.m."

"You've lost your mind, but I'm on my way," said Terri.

Melissa called on the other phone. She had gotten the powers of attorney papers moving through lawyers that we use for estate and tax purposes, had walked them into the state capital in Nashville for their state seals, and was sending them to a friend who lived near D.C. He was going to walk the paperwork through the proper channels at the embassy.

I threw random clothes in a suitcase. Steven videotaped me doing so for a bit of humor later, if and when we could all laugh about it. We had to be at the airport by 1:30. Geoff and Jan were going to pick up all our kids from school and bring them to the airport so we could tell them that, by the way, Mommy was going to China that afternoon, and we loved them.

We zoomed to the airport, stopping at the Target parking lot first to pick up the bag of baby stuff. Jan and Geoff met us in the terminal. Usually Jan is as cute as can be . . . but today she was ever so slightly stressed out, with red, puffy eyes. She looked like she'd been crying ever since I called her that morning.

"I don't even know if I have the right paperwork," she sobbed. "It was all in a laundry basket in my office, and I just dumped it into a duffel bag. I can't believe we're doing this! I would only do this with you!"

We kissed our husbands and kids goodbye and got on the flight to L.A. We left without even knowing whether we would be able to continue on to Guangzhou.

We had a long layover at LAX. I called Steven when we landed. "The facilitator says the travel documents had not been mailed yet, and they can make it work from their end," he told me. The documents could be sent to Hunan's provincial affairs office in the city of Changsha, where our adoption—if it worked out—would eventually take place.

I began sorting through Jan's pile of papers. Miraculously, she had everything she needed, plus half of the papers from their first adoption.

I love putting things in order. I organized all of Jan's papers, put them neatly in a folder, and handed it back to her with great satisfaction.

We boarded the flight for China. Our seats were in business class, which was unusual because we always fly coach. *Oh,* I thought, *that's so nice! We're so exhausted, and the travel agent must have upgraded us because we're under all this stress about the adoptions.*

I called Steven. "No, they didn't upgrade you," he said. "The only two seats left on the flight were business class, and they were $3,500 each. So Stevey Joy just got a little more expensive . . ."

Oops!

Meanwhile, Jan was such a trooper. "Let's see," she said. "What are we doing? I left behind a half-painted room! I don't even *know* what's in my suitcase. Are we really going to China?! Are we going to catch SARS and die?"

Hours passed. I could not sleep. We flew through the skies above the dark Pacific Ocean, getting closer and closer to two little girls who needed their mommies—two mommies who were determined to rescue their daughters.

We landed in Guangzhou early in the morning, local time, and called home while waiting for our flight to Changsha, Hunan Province. It was obvious we weren't in Kansas anymore. The airport was quiet, and every single person we saw was wearing a surgical mask. Jan got her disinfectant wipes out of her purse and insisted on wiping down everything we might possibly touch. I love that girl.

Our adoption escort was waiting at the airport in Changsha. He told us his name was Smile, that our paperwork had been sent to the provincial affairs office, and that he would have what he needed to complete the adoption once our powers of attorney arrived from the U.S.

"And by the way," he said, "your babies are waiting for you at the hotel."

Jan grabbed my arm. We looked at each other after all our hours of traveling and said, "I think we did it!" We were overwhelmed . . . not home yet, but God had clearly moved mountains of paperwork and other obstacles for us.

Outside, there weren't many people on the streets. They scurried by, wearing masks, not looking at us. We got to the hotel. On other trips it had been full of American couples and Chinese babies. Now it was deserted. No other Americans anywhere. For that matter, once you left the first floor there were no other guests in the entire hotel.

We got to our room with no time to waste. Our babies would be here any minute, and we didn't even know what kind of bottles or formula we had for them. Jan started getting the video camera ready to capture our historic moment. I opened the suitcase that Terri had bought at Target. I had no idea what she'd bought; all I knew was that whatever was in there had cost almost nine hundred dollars.

I unzipped the bag, and the first thing we saw were tons of Clorox wipes. Nothing could have made Jan happier. "We'll need to ration them," she said. We had been told we might have to be in the country for three weeks or a month, and she wanted to be sure we had enough. "Are there scissors in that Target bag?" Jan continued. "I'm going to cut all these wipes in half and put them in Ziploc bags—"

I was laughing, and then the phone rang. Our babies were being brought up to the room.

We weren't ready. Freaked out. We ran around trying to set up the video camera so it would automatically film this amazing event on tape, as both of us would be busy meeting our new children. We splashed cold water on our faces so we wouldn't look like we had been up for five hundred hours. Then there was the knock on the door. I almost peed in my pants.

The orphanage director, Smile the escort, and two nannies holding two babies were standing there. One nanny handed Ashley Rose to Jan. She was a plump, healthy baby, about seven months old. Jan was crying with joy, the Chinese people were all talking at once in Mandarin, and then it was my turn to receive my baby.

There she was—I think. She was wearing a huge, red, puffy traditional Chinese outfit, and somewhere in all that puff, I found a very tiny, very pale, very sickly . . . Stevey Joy! She weighed almost nothing. She wouldn't have had half a chance against SARS.

As quickly as the adoption group came, they left. Jan and I were on our own. The two had become four, and all was quiet, except for Stevey Joy Ru Chapman. As Jan doted on Ashley by stripping her down and bathing her in the lavender baby wash we'd brought (thanks to Terri and Target), I was trying to console a very unhappy, loud, tiny, sick new daughter. I was so glad I'd felt the need to act quickly to get this precious little one out of China, but now I had this sick feeling in the pit of my stomach. Caleb and Will had prayed for a mellow new sister, and she was screaming at the top of her tiny lungs. And on top of it all, she looked like someone, I just couldn't think who. Then it came to me. She looked like Phil Collins, the singer. I told Jan.

"Will you stop it?" Jan said. "She does not look like Phil Collins. She's cute as she can be!"

The next day, Smile gave us a little update about the situation. "We don't really know what will happen or how this will all play out," he said, "but you could be here for about three weeks." This was because of SARS and our uncertainties about how long it would take for the powers of attorney to arrive.

I watched as Ashley would sit for hours playing with toys. She was a bit passive; you could tell she'd needed the love of a mom, and Jan was beginning to take care of that.

But Stevey Joy wouldn't even look at a toy. She was sick and sad. I had her on antibiotics now and was doing my best, but it was hard. And to top it off, we discovered that our wonderful adoption video had malfunctioned. All we had was lots of footage of some Chinese adoption worker's butt, and then the camera had turned itself off.

Jan was beginning to fall apart, and I wasn't feeling much better. We were looking at three weeks, minimum, in this SARS-infested ghost town with chilled-out Ashley and tiny, sickly Stevey Joy, who pretty much did nothing but squirm and wriggle and yell and scream.

I finally got up the nerve to call home. Caleb and Will got on the phone. "Mom, we've been praying so hard," Caleb said. "Is Stevey Joy all calm and chilled out?"

"Well," I said, "uh . . . *Ashley* is."

Caleb could hear Stevey Joy screaming bloody murder in the background. "Is that her I hear?" he asked.

"Well, she's so sick—" I started.

"Oh, no!" Caleb moaned. "But Mom, we *prayed*!"

Jan was still convinced we were all going to get SARS and die. At one point—though I didn't know it at the time—she locked herself in the bathroom and videotaped a pitiful last will and testament message for her family in the event that we never made it home.

Meanwhile, our friend in D.C. had gotten the powers of attorney documents authenticated in Washington. Steven had checked on FedEx. Because of the SARS crisis, the overnight company could take three weeks to deliver a package. Our friend flew to Nashville, got off his plane and handed the papers to Steven in the terminal, and then turned around and flew back to D.C.

By God's providence, Steven had the following week off, which was pretty unusual. Because he had his visa, he decided to bring the powers of attorney to China himself. So he booked a flight to China and took on a new job as an international adoption courier.

"You wait," I said to Jan. "I'll bet you anything that when Steven sees Stevey Joy for the first time and I ask him what pop star she looks like, he'll say she looks like Phil Collins."

"There is no way Steven will say Stevey Joy looks like Phil Collins," Jan responded.

Steven arrived at the hotel late in the evening. I couldn't believe he was actually there. Stevey Joy was asleep. I took him over to her little crib. He just stood there, staring in wonder at his newest baby daughter.

"What pop star does she look like?" I whispered.

He rolled his eyes at me and then gazed at Stevey Joy carefully for about ten seconds.

"Phil Collins," he said.

Smile, the adoption consultant, came to meet with us the next day. He was still saying that we'd be in China for three weeks at least.

"At home we can get express passports if we pay extra money," I told him. "Do you have anything like that here?"

"I don't know what you talk about," said Smile in broken English.

"Well," I said, "usually there are lots of Americans here in Changsha, and that makes a big demand on the passport office and in all the government offices. So of course it makes sense that adoption groups usually need to stay in the province for five days to process everything.

"But because of SARS, there's no one here. So it seems like there would be less of a wait for us to get the adoption papers signed and the passports processed quickly. Can you see about us getting our passports soon? I mean, we like you and all, but I'd love to go home sooner rather than later."

Smile stood up. "You ask me to be Tom Cruise!" he said dramatically. "This is *Mission Impossible*!"

We all looked at each other, trying to figure out if this was Chinese humor or what . . . but we soon found that we had no problems finalizing the adoption papers at the provincial affairs office. They had not shut down yet because of SARS, and that part of the process went smoothly.

After that, Smile left us at the hotel and said, "You wait here, I see what Mission Impossible Man can do about passports!"

Within four hours he was back, holding two Chinese passports for the babies. "Ha!" he said. "I *am* Tom Cruise!"

We had been in China for only one week. This kind of paperwork turnaround was unheard of. Even an adoption under normal circumstances usually takes ten to twelve days. It was as if SARS had been the very thing that sped up our process!

While Jan and I packed up our things and got the girls ready to travel, Steven and Smile worked on getting us the heck out of Dodge. They booked us on the first plane home.

Steven upgraded his ticket using frequent flyer miles, so we were all in business class together. As we settled into our nice, wide seats, we looked at each other and smiled like little kids who had just pulled off the ultimate practical joke.

Steven reclined in his seat, and Stevey Joy snuggled on his chest, covered by a warm blanket. They both went to sleep.

I stared at them. I couldn't believe that after just one week, we were on a plane bound for home. In spite of the curveball SARS had thrown us, it was one of the few times in my life where God had actually allowed my plans to work out.

"God," I prayed, "I don't know what just happened, but I do know You were with us every step of the way! Thank You for continuing to walk with a Rambo woman like me who has issues with taking no for an answer. I know it can get me into trouble . . . but thank You for the gift of this crazy trip!"

I finally felt a huge wave of emotion come over me. I was exhausted. I pulled the flight blanket up to my chin and went to sleep.

Next stop, Nashville, Tennessee!

17

Fingerprints of God

I can see the tears filling your eyes
And I know where they're coming from
They're coming from a heart that's broken in two
By what you don't see
The person in the mirror
Doesn't look like the magazine
Oh, but when I look at you it's clear to me that . . .

I can see the fingerprints of God
When I look at you
I can see the fingerprints of God
And I know it's true
You're a masterpiece
That all creation quietly applauds
And you're covered with the fingerprints of God

"Fingerprints of God"
Words and music by Steven Curtis Chapman

For the LORD sees not as man sees: man looks on the
outward appearance, but the LORD looks on the heart.

1 Samuel 16:7 ESV

Even as we traveled home from China with a new little daughter, my mind was on my firstborn. Emily had been the catalyst for us entering the wild world of adoption, and it was amazing to think that the passionate prayers of a young girl could bring such life-altering changes. Now Emily was in high school. She'd traveled a long way since those middle school years.

It's safe to say that no amount of money could convince Emily—or me, for that matter—to travel back in time and repeat the dark ages of middle school. Since she was our oldest, I wasn't quite prepared for the change in her environment when we turned the corner and left the safe, happy world of elementary school. I should have remembered from my own experience. Ah, junior high—that jungle where the strong devour the weak, where hormones, cliques, and gossip rule.

In the midst of jocks, popular kids, musicians, nerds, and whatnot, Emily struggled to find her place. While many of her classmates spent their Friday evenings at the movies or the mall, our Emily was at home passionately campaigning for the expansion of our family through the miracle of adoption. Emily was mature beyond her years. It's just how God made her. At an early age she tuned in to that which carried *eternal* weight and significance . . . something that just hadn't quite come into focus for most of her peers.

As she struggled to discover a group of friends who would accept her for who she was, Emily eventually began spending most of her time with the "smart kids." Before, academics had not been her strong point. But now she spent tons of time studying. She made high grades and her teachers recommended her for honors classes.

While these achievements were understandably exciting, Steven and I began to notice that Emily was putting a lot of her identity and worth in her academic work. Since she was like me—a performance-driven perfectionist—she wanted to do everything just right. There were times we'd have to tell her to go to bed and quit studying. We didn't have a whole lot of friends who were telling their kids not to work so hard on homework.

Middle school was also the season in Emily's life when her body started changing. She was not one of those skinny-mini girls with an overactive metabolism. Like many of us, she got wider before she got taller. It was so hard to find clothes that fit her like they did on "other" girls. I anguished for Emily as I remembered the sting of being called "Chubby Chapman" in my own early years.

We avoided shopping. It usually led to tears, frustration, and self-hatred. One afternoon, I went out on my own and returned with a bunch of clothes for Emily. She started making her way through the pile, taking each outfit, trying it on in the bathroom, and coming out to show me.

But her frustration grew with every outfit she put on. Her eyes filled with tears. She didn't look like the size zero girls in the clothing ads or the girls at school who could throw on tiny jeans and have them fit just right. By the time Steven came home, Emily and I were both crying on the floor, surrounded by shopping bags and heaps of rejected clothes.

It was after this fashion show gone wrong that Steven wrote the lyrics of his song "Fingerprints of God." Mature as she was for her age, Emily didn't recognize the beauty we saw in her. And she certainly didn't understand how unique she was in the eyes of God. But as Steven's song became a hit and connected with so very many people, Emily realized that she wasn't alone in her inadequate feelings . . . and gradually she learned to place her worth in *God's* view of her rather than the fashion magazines' perspective. It wasn't like she had it all figured out perfectly. But Emily began the lifelong journey of learning to rest in who God had created her to be. She found that her worth was not in what she could do but in what had been done for her through Christ.

Even during those tough teenage years, though, Emily adored her little sisters from China. Shaoey joined the family during Emily's final year of middle school, and Stevey Joy came home while Emily was in high school.

Emily spent countless hours in the dress-up closet playing princess with the little girls. She took care of them and saved my sanity when Steven was traveling and Caleb and Will had places to be, and I was just one parent running back and forth between five children.

Then, during Emily's final year of high school, Steven became convinced we should adopt again. Emily, our outspoken adoption advocate who had relentlessly campaigned for us to bring home her first two sisters, was surprisingly resistant to the idea of gaining another sibling. She says that part of her reservation was selfish: she wanted focused attention from all of us since it was her last year living at home. But she also knew how much stress would fall on my shoulders with her heading to college in the fall, Steven launching his "All Things New" tour, and neither Caleb nor Will being old enough to drive.

But in her thoughtful and deliberate way, Emily came to Steven and me and said something like this: "Mom and Dad, I'm a bit weary about the idea of adding another child to the Chapman clan. But if God confirms in your hearts that we're to welcome home another little girl from China, I'll support you and watch expectantly for what God will accomplish!"

God did bring Maria into our family, and it didn't take long for Emily to have a change of heart about her adoption. Of course, none of us knew quite what to expect once Maria came into the picture . . . or all the things God was going to do through her little life.

18

I Just Met a Girl Named Maria

I found you in the most unlikely way
But really it was You who found me . . .

I wish You could stay
But I'll, I'll wait for the day

And I watch as the cold winter melts into spring
And I'll be remembering You
Oh and I'll smell the flowers and hear the birds sing
And I'll be remembering You, I'll be remembering You

From the first moment when I heard Your name
Something in my heart came alive
You showed me love and no words could explain . . .

And though You've gone away
You'll come back and . . .

And I'll watch as the sun fills a sky that was dark
And I'll be remembering You
And I'll think of the way that You fill up my heart
And I'll be remembering You

"Remembering You"
Words and music by Steven Curtis Chapman and Caleb Chapman

I n April or May of 2003 . . . no one really knows the exact day . . .
a baby girl was born outside a city in China called Tian Jian . . .
no one really knows exactly where.

There are two billion people in China, with eleven or twelve million in Tian Jian alone. Somehow this tiny infant was found on a riverbank, cold and blue, when she was about forty-eight hours old. She was taken to a state orphanage. From there she ended up in a Christian foster home for special needs orphans.

She was placed in the care of an Australian family who lived outside of Beijing. The orphanage had a Chinese name for her, but this new family called her Rowena. She captured the hearts of these people for four months until the family was unexpectedly transferred back to Australia. They would have pursued her adoption, but at the time there was no adoption agreement between Australia and China.

Little Rowena was taken back to the Christian foster home and then placed in the home of missionaries named Tim and Amy Hedden. Tim and Amy, along with all of their children, quickly fell in love with this little girl. They named her Maria.

Why Maria? It just seemed to fit her.

Meanwhile, our home in Franklin, Tennessee, had become nonstop busy. We were definitely done with adopting. For ourselves, I mean. We loved helping family and friends adopt, and as a result of an amazing staff and God's blessing, Show Hope's ministry was going great. We were helping families adopt orphans from all over the world and becoming more and more involved with orphan care and advocacy.

But as far as we were concerned, the Chapman family's quiver was full. We were looking forward to Emily's senior year in high school, celebrating her graduation, and pushing her gently from the nest into whatever college God had for her.

Then Steven was invited to China to do the music for a Luis Palau outreach there. One Sunday morning in April, Luis preached for Beijing International Christian Fellowship. Steven sang and led worship for this community of mostly Western expatriates. After the service, an American family serving at a special needs foster home came up to Steven. They were Tim and Amy Hedden, their four biological children, and two Chinese foster babies.

Steven was missing his two little Chinese girls back home in Tennessee, so he was drawn to the girls. "This is Natalie," Amy told him. Natalie had the biggest Chinese eyes that Steven had ever seen.

Her special need was a cleft lip, but her smile and charm warmed his heart. The Heddens told Steven that they were in the process of adopting Natalie.

Then the attention shifted to the next little one. "And this is Maria," Amy continued. "She doesn't have a home yet."

Maria was a tiny drooling machine, with the smallest Chinese eyes Steven had ever seen. They made her look very mischievous . . . which, we would find out, fit her to a T. Steven held out his arms, and Amy smiled and handed her over. He hugged Maria and tickled her and told her how beautiful she was, intending just to love on her for a minute.

But then something unexpected happened.

When he handed Maria back to Amy, Steven felt like he was giving his own daughter back. The rush of feelings caught him completely off guard. He'd held dozens of babies and toddlers on this trip as well as all the other trips . . . but this was different.

As he left, Steven strained his neck to watch the Heddens as they turned to walk to their van, doing his best to watch little Maria for as long as he could. When he could no longer see her, he dialed my number. As I picked up my phone, I wondered what was wrong. My husband was all choked up.

"I'm okay!" he told me. "But the strangest thing just happened. I just met a girl named Maria . . ."

I don't know how I knew what he meant, but I did.

"Don't even think about it!" I told my softy of a husband. "If we are even going to consider another adoption, she better know how to play guitar, because she is going on the road with you!"

We laughed a few seconds, but somehow I knew this was going to come back up.

The rest of the week in China, wherever Steven went with Luis Palau, he was thinking about Maria. At first he tried to plan how he could help the Heddens adopt her. China had a law that said you couldn't adopt two children at once, but Steven kept trying to think of a way to help them give Maria a forever home along with Natalie.

He was perplexed. We weren't adopting again. But down deep, all he could think about was how much he wanted us to adopt Maria.

He didn't know why. It made no sense. It was like an instant, permanent connection in his heart.

The following Saturday was the day before Easter, and Steven was able to go to Maria's foster home. He played music for the kids and carried Maria around all day long while the kids had a big Easter egg hunt.

The next day, Steven arrived at the same church where he had met Maria a week earlier. The Heddens met him in the hallway, carrying Maria in a beautiful pink Easter dress. After the service they said their goodbyes and took a few pictures in the parking lot before Steven left for the airport to come home. One of those pictures would become of monumental importance in the coming days.

"Can you believe this?" he asked me on the phone. "I've fallen in love with this little girl!"

I had sent him to China with strict orders not to fall in love with any more little Chinese girls in need of a family. But as I thought and prayed about my husband's new little love, God took hold of my heart and changed it. By the time Steven traveled the twenty-some hours home from China, I was in full adoption mode. As far as I was concerned, we were going to China to get Maria as soon as we could. I'd completed all the adoption paperwork, and it was sitting on the kitchen counter waiting for his signature.

But by now Steven had shifted gears and tried to tone down his excitement about Maria. He had argued with himself about it all the way home on the flight from China. He had come to the conclusion that we didn't have any business adopting again.

When he told me this, I just shrugged. As far as I was concerned, it was a done deal.

A few days later, I got a call from Steven while he was at the recording studio. He had checked his emails, and Amy Hedden had emailed a picture taken in the church parking lot in China as he was kissing Maria goodbye. When Steven saw that picture, it hit him: this wasn't a photo of a man kissing the forehead of a little orphan. It was a picture of a daddy kissing *his* daughter.

"I know what we're supposed to do about Maria," he excitedly told me on the phone. "Let's go get her!"

It was like God had planned it from the beginning.

Maria was a special needs orphan. The doctors in China had said that she was born with a hole in her heart, and she was diagnosed with ASD, atrial septal defect. This is a common congenital heart defect. Over time it can lead to irregular heartbeats, hypertension, stroke, or enlargement of the right side of the heart.

Oddly enough—God knew what was coming even though we didn't—when I had prepared for Stevey Joy's adoption, I had gotten two of every official paper that I needed. It was one of those random, "just in case" kind of things. So I already had all of the documents that it normally takes quite a while to get hold of.

Maria hadn't yet been listed on a special needs adoption list. Special needs children are put on different lists for different agencies. At the time, if you met an orphan you would love to adopt, you would search around on various agencies' lists, and if no one else had yet been matched with him or her, you could ask to be matched.

I'm sure the process is different now, but anyway, we waited . . . and eventually Maria was placed on a special needs list and we were able to be matched with her through a Kentucky adoption agency. After climbing the now-familiar mountain of paperwork, it appeared as though all was well for us to make our trip to China to get Maria.

When we got to China, there was good news and bad news.

The good news was that Maria was there and her papers had been collected to be able to complete her adoption. However, the medical papers with her initial heart diagnosis had been lost.

She was just tiny when she had the tests to determine the ASD. Now, when she was examined again so her adoption papers would be complete, her heart was healthy. We had no way of knowing if her original condition was a misdiagnosis or if her heart had been healed. Sometimes these types of holes close up on their own as the child grows. At any rate, there was no evidence that she still had the condition.

So while that was good, the bad news from an adoption standpoint was that now officials wanted to reclassify Maria as "healthy" instead of "special needs." This meant that she would have to reenter the system and go through a completely different process, which in essence would make our being able to adopt her next to impossible.

We started praying immediately.

We were told to come back in a few months, and that they would have it figured out. I was devastated. I tried my best to hold it together, but the tears came in spite of my best attempts. The officials asked us to go to a nearby building to wait.

We paced, cried, and prayed. Our case was being considered by everybody from the official in the big office with the leather chair to the clerk in the finance office with the steel stool and the rubber stamp . . . and it seemed like everyone in that hierarchy had an equal vote.

Over the next few days, we'd get word that it looked like we were going to be approved to adopt Maria. We'd prepare to leave the hotel to go pick up our little one. Then we'd get a message that it looked like it was not going to work out. So we'd stay at the hotel for a few more days.

We were on a roller coaster of excitement and despair, and by the time it was all over I was sure that, due to stress, *we* would have developed the heart problems that Maria no longer had. But in the end, after many tears and a lot of sweating, God allowed us to adopt Maria. Her paperwork was approved and completed, and with much excitement and laughter, we went to the Heddens' home to pick her up.

This was really, really difficult. It was like Maria had a family, one that wanted her, but because of the Chinese law they couldn't adopt her. I was grieving as I saw how hard it was for the Heddens, but at the same time I wanted to shout and scream with joy that we would become a forever family. We prayed and all cried together.

Then it was time to take Maria with us. There was a long, sad moment, and then Amy looked at me and calmly said, "You need to go now." She had packed a little bag for Maria. "Pick up her bag and take her things," Amy continued. "It's time." She was being the mom who needed to pick up the pieces and comfort her family once we had gone.

We gave Maria the middle name "Sue" in honor of Amy Hedden's middle name. We will never forget the wonderful family who loved and guarded our little girl until it was God's timing for us to come and make her our own.

But then our new life with Maria Sue Chapman began . . . and it was wild and crazy, right from the start.

19

I'm Divin' In!

The long awaited rains
Have fallen hard upon the thirsty ground
And carved their way to where
The wild and rushing river can be found
And like the rains
I have been carried here to where the river flows, yeah
My heart is racing and my knees are weak
As I walk to the edge
I know there is no turning back
Once my feet have left the ledge
And in the rush I hear a voice
That's telling me it's time to take the leap of faith
So here I go

"Dive"
Words and music by Steven Curtis Chapman

If you want a nice, tidy, organized life, you don't marry Steven Curtis Chapman. And you don't adopt orphans. And you don't start an adoption/orphan care ministry. But I did all that . . .

As time went on and I felt God pulling me toward the needs of orphans around the world and the former orphans in my home, I knew I had to bid goodbye to my former hopes that I could neatly arrange every detail of my life into a nice, orderly existence. My story was not being written the way that I had planned. My grasp on orderly and predictable was slowly being pried from my fingers.

A trip we took to Uganda in the summer of 2005 illustrates my farewell to my old friends Orderly and Predictable. If I felt my life was already like riding wild, foaming rapids in a flimsy boat, all I had to do was go rafting on the Nile River—and over the famous Bujagali Falls—to experience that metaphor in wet, living color.

The trip started as a ministry opportunity. Steven and I, along with some of our children and close friends, headed to Uganda to meet up with missionaries from Far Reaching Ministries. I had been eager to get Show Hope involved if there was orphan care we could do in Uganda.

At the time, a terrorist group known as the Lord's Resistance Army (LRA) had been abducting children at night from villages in northern Uganda, killing their parents in front of them, and brainwashing them to serve as child soldiers in the conflict between the LRA and the government of Uganda. Because of this danger in the countryside, whole communities of children would leave their huts before sunset and walk miles to the safety of lighted areas in larger cities. These children were known as "night commuters." They would sleep in big groups in parking lots, often protected by government troops, and then return home to their villages in the light of day.

Churches had been working in the city of Kitgum, trying to help these children with food, shelter, and the gospel. Steven and Caleb took their guitars and Will took his djembe, an African drum . . . and they did a concert for the night commuter children in a protected parking lot outside of a church in Kitgum.

When we first arrived, it was still daylight and there were no children to be seen. The people at the church had put up a small stage for our guys. While Steven and the boys set up their gear, the rest of us waited and wondered when the night commuters might show up. We had all kinds of candy and hundreds of glow-in-the-dark plastic bracelets for them.

As the sun set, the children began to arrive: one by one, then group by group, and then there were hundreds of them, ranging in age from about three years old to teenagers. Some were tiny, carrying thin rolled mats to sleep on. Most were barefoot. They had walked miles and miles, just to get to a place where they could spend the night in relative safety.

As soon as the kids found out that we had candy and glow-in-the-dark stuff, they flocked around us. As Steven, Caleb, and Will started the music, the children sang along as best they could. They laughed, clapped, and raised their hands in worship to God, and we all felt His presence with us.

Later on this trip, God did give a way for Show Hope to help: we were able to commit funds to build a home for children who had been orphaned by AIDS in Kitgum.

After our visit with the commuter children, we took a side trip to the Nile River. Friends had told us that rafting there was an adventure we had to have. But I had somehow missed the rafting memo and didn't even have on a bathing suit. I was wearing athletic shorts and a T-shirt, but that was fine with me since I had no intention of getting wet.

Our friends had told us that there are long stretches where you could just lie back and float, taking in the African scenery.

That sounded good.

What nobody bothered to share was that this idyllic float also included a bunch of class 5 rapids at Bujagali Falls.

At the nice, calm place where the rafting company was located, we got our life jackets—I wondered what those were for—and divided into groups of about ten people per raft, including guides. Our family and friends were part of a larger flotilla of eight rafts, each with experienced guides manning the main oars. There were a number of other random tourists in the other rafts, mostly visitors from England, Australia, and the U.S.

As we got ready to start, our guide walked us into the shallows and told all of us to get in the water.

"Why?" I asked. "I'm not planning on getting wet."

"We need to teach you how to flip the boat over in case it capsizes," the guide said. "And you need to know how to get back into the raft when you fall into the river."

They showed us how to flip the big boats. This should have been my first clue that things might get crazy later. We were told that if our rafts flipped, we were to swim to any boat in our group—whichever was easiest to get to—and grab the ropes with both hands, crossed over each other. Then, as the guides would grab us by the wrists and pull, the idea was that we would rotate because of our wrists being crossed and fall neatly into the boat on our backs.

Once we'd practiced our little safety precautions, off we went. One of the other rafts drifted by. It was full of excited Americans who looked like they had been on a missions trip. As they went by we could hear them all singing at the top of their lungs:

> The river's deep, the river's wide,
> The river's water is alive
> So sink or swim, I'm divin' in!

They were thrilled that they could actually sing the lyrics of Steven's hit song "Dive" right to its author out there on, of all places, the Nile River.

Our SS *Chapman* headed out into the river. It was calm, quiet, beautiful. I lay back, perfectly at peace.

We continued this way for a mile or so . . . and then, in the distance, something intruded on my bliss. It was growing louder and louder, like the sound of a thousand freight trains. As I strained to see what in the world that sound was, I finally saw it in the distance: Niagara Falls on steroids. And our little fabric boat was being sucked straight toward it.

I didn't even have time to scream. Our guide was shouting as loud as he could and we could still barely hear his instructions: "If I yell 'paddle,' then *paddle* with all you've got. And if we flip over, try and grab hold of the side of the boat!"

The last thing I saw was the front of the boat rising up in front of me, vertically. Then the bottom dropped out of my life—and my stomach—as I heard that daggum guide yelling, "Paddle!" And then I was underneath tons and tons of churning, rushing water taking me down and around and around and around, like a washing machine. I struggled, somehow popped above the surface of the mad water for a second, took a breath, and then down I went again, swirling into the abyss.

I popped out again, hyperventilating. *I'm gonna die!* I thought. *Steven has killed not just me, but half our family!*

Miraculously, when I popped up again, my eyes caught Steven's as the boat was almost on top of us. If looks could kill, he would have been dead. I was panicking, worrying about Emily, who was not the strongest swimmer. But eventually the whole Chapman group was found alive and gathered back into that death trap of a raft.

"Wasn't that *awesome*?" our guide yelled.

I looked at him like he was out of his mind.

"Are there any more like that?" I asked.

"Oh yeah, there are five total," the guide bragged. "They get worse the further we go. Remember, if our boat flips, just swim to the closest raft."

"Didn't I hear something about a *safety* boat, you know, a different boat for people who panic?" I asked. I was envisioning something like an aircraft carrier, but larger.

"Oh yeah," said our guide, who I was beginning to dislike more and more with every passing second. "Yeah, well, sometimes the safety boat flips too."

"Then why do they call it the *safety* boat?" I yelled.

No more time for chatting. I could hear the roar of billions of tons of water. It was Niagara the Second.

It was the same drill as before. Our raft went vertical, and I was driven down into the vortex of washing machine hell. Again.

"Oh, well," I moaned in my oxygen-starved brain. "At least I'm gonna die on a missions trip in Africa!"

I popped up to grab a gasp of air. I saw Caleb floating by, clawed desperately for him, couldn't quite reach, and then down I went again.

I somehow surfaced. The water was calmer; I'd made it through the rapids. No idea where my raft was. But there was another raft a few yards away. I might make it . . . but I had a problem.

Due to the incredible underwater force, my elastic-banded athletic shorts *and* my underwear had been pulled down and were swirling, dangling around my ankles, terrifyingly close to flying off and being lost forever in the Nile River.

Swimming with one arm, I bent down with my other and grabbed hold of my underwear and shorts. I thrashed with my one arm and arrived at the nearby raft, the raft that would pull me to safety and get me the heck out of the Nile.

A guide was at the edge, ready to rescue me.

"Both hands on the rope!" he yelled. "Both hands on the rope!"

I grabbed the rope on the side of the boat with one hand, since my other hand was busy holding onto my underwear to prevent it from swirling down the river, never to be recovered.

The guide yelled down at me. "*Both* hands on the rope!" he bellowed.

"I can't!" I yelled back to him.

Clearly the guide was mad that I wasn't following his stern instructions. Or maybe he thought he couldn't pull me in if I just held the rope with one hand.

"*Both* hands on the rope!" he yelled. "*Now!*"

In a split second I had to decide which was worse, having the guide continue to yell at me in front of everyone, or being pulled into the boat with my underwear and shorts around my ankles.

Then, wincing, I spread my legs apart so my shorts and underwear wouldn't wash down the Nile, and put *both* hands on the rope on the side of the raft, though I forgot to properly cross them like we had been taught earlier.

The guide, completely put out with me, grabbed my wrists and pulled me in the raft in one fell swoop. I flopped up and over the edge of the raft, landing completely face-planted on the bottom of the raft, my bare bottom up in the air, draped over the rounded, inflatable side of the boat.

What I didn't know was that Caleb had already been pulled into this particular raft. I also had no idea just whose boat I had floundered into.

I just lay there for a minute. Silence from all the people on the raft.

"Please, God," I prayed, "don't let this be that boat full of the nice American missions team that was singing 'Dive' and waving to Steven!"

God heard my prayer . . . though the first face I saw when I finished flipping and flopping around like a landed fish was Caleb. He was just sitting there . . . staring . . . jaw dropped . . . looking at me . . . but trying not to.

I wriggled around, trying to pull up my soggy underwear and shorts to cover up, well, the bottom half of my body. Then I looked around. It was the raft full of tourists from England.

"Well," I heard a chipper British accent proclaim, "I suppose if you've seen one bum, you've seen 'em all!"

20

Cinderellas Everywhere

She spins and she sways
To whatever song plays
Without a care in the world
And I'm sitting here wearing
The weight of the world on my shoulders

It's been a long day
And there's still work to do
She's pulling at me saying, "Dad, I need you
There's a ball at the castle and I've been invited
And I need to practice my dancing
Oh please, Daddy, please"

So I will dance with Cinderella
While she is here in my arms
'Cause I know something the prince never knew
Oh I will dance with Cinderella
I don't want to miss even one song
'Cause all too soon the clock will strike midnight
but I know the truth is the dance will go on.

"Cinderella"
Words and music by Steven Curtis Chapman

Our life at home in Franklin, Tennessee, was as wild as rafting on the Nile, though in different ways. I felt like I had blinked and all of the sudden I had six children. Emily was twenty-one years old, Will and Caleb were in high school, Shaoey was in first grade, and our two littlest ones—only seven months apart—were both three.

Steven was doing concert stretches for three or four days, then he'd be home for a while. It was nonstop commotion—wild, fun, and at the same time exhausting. I had a front-row seat—even though I had no time to sit down—to watch my dream of an organized life morph into a life of craziness that I never wanted . . . or so I had thought.

How had this happened? Does God really have this weird, calculated sense of humor?

One typical night in the Chapman home in March 2006, Steven was in full "writing mode" for his upcoming CD, *This Moment*. However, he was also on bath and bed duty for Stevey Joy and Maria this particular evening, so he put the songwriting on pause to take care of the girls. He explained to them that they needed to do a fast bath and bedtime tonight because Daddy had to get back to work.

They did not exactly share his priority.

He got them in the bathtub and was working quickly, but as he turned around to get the shampoo and a washcloth, the girls escaped, leaving two little sets of wet footprints leading to their bedroom. A few moments later, two little giggling princesses appeared around the corner, Cinderella and Snow White, wearing their Disney costumes complete with matching shoes, tiaras, and wands.

"We're going to the ball, Daddy!" they told him.

"No," he said, "you are not going to the ball. You're going back in the tub!"

Two or three escape attempts later, Steven finally got them clean, shampooed, and to bed.

"Daddy, can you read us a story?" they asked.

"No, no stories tonight," Steven said. "It's too late. We're going to pray and go to bed! Pray a short prayer, immediate family only tonight! Pray fast!

"Okay," Steven continued. "Heads on your pillows! No more drinks of water! No more questions! I love you! Kisses! Lights out! Now go to sleep! I mean it, good night!"

Finally! Steven thought as he headed back to his studio. *Why do they get so wound up on the nights when I just need them to settle down?*

Then a thought hit him. It was as if God had whispered a name in his ear: *Emily.*

It was just yesterday that Emily was splashing in her bath, spinning and swaying her way through childhood without a care in the world. Steven used to call her "Queen Tuck" as he would tuck her in and tell her silly stories about Looney Larry the Coconut Hunter . . . and now she was an adult, twenty-one years old, away at college.

The years go by in a heartbeat, and then your children twirl right out of your life and into their own.

All that flashed through Steven's mind in a second. It was as if God was saying, "Steven, are you really going to rush through moments like this? You already know how fast they go by! Remember Emily? She's grown now, no more tuck-ins, baths, or make-believe balls."

As he sat with a weight on his chest and tears in his eyes, he began to put his thoughts into a song. Within an hour, he had written a complete song called "Cinderella." He played it for me the next morning as a work in progress.

I cried. "Don't touch it!" I told him. "Record what you just sang for me and it's going to affect a lot of people!"

So Steven put "Cinderella" on his *This Moment* CD. It became a hit song on the radio . . . and an all-time favorite song for our two little princesses, Maria Sue and Stevey Joy.

When the Fourth of July came later that year, we celebrated in classic Chapman style. We began the day with a pool party in our backyard with a big crowd of family and friends. Steven cooked up some of his famous burgers (they're really not that famous, but since it's pretty much the only thing he cooks, we let him believe they are). Chips, baked beans, and Nutty Buddies rounded out the nutritious feast, and the adults sat talking while the little ones played in the pool. Then, as the sun went down, it was time to light up the nighttime sky.

In Tennessee, fireworks are legal outside the city limits, and if it could be blown up, be lit on fire, or create massive amounts of smoke, it had been purchased by the Chapman men. The rest of the evening, the testosterone-filled "boys" lit things on fire for the women and girls to ooh and ahh over. We gave approval by clapping loudly and cheering at the top of our lungs, scoring each one. If a rocket didn't meet our high standards, we would yell "Boo!" and "Dud!" at our explosives experts.

After all of the fireworks were blown up and the smoke settled down, we gathered food plates, trash, water bottles, and blankets while Steven and the guys collected all the scraps and pieces of burnt-out fireworks and put them in a big cardboard box. He made sure they were extinguished and put the box on top of our big plastic trash cans at the back of the house.

A little after four o'clock in the morning, Steven and I woke up in a panic to the shrieking of our smoke detector/alarm system. Steven ran around the room trying to remember where the keypad was to turn off what we assumed was a false alarm.

When he was finally fully awake and realized that the keypad was downstairs, he noticed a glowing orange hue outside the French doors in our bedroom. He yelled at me that the house was on fire. The ashes looked liked snow, but they were floating upward into the sky.

"Call 911, and get the girls out of the house!" Steven yelled.

He rushed down the stairs to see just where the fire was. I tore up the stairs to Shaoey's room, pulled her out of bed, and woke her up enough to follow me to Maria and Stevey Joy's room. Somehow I managed to get both little girls scooped up into my arms. I ran down the stairs and out the back door in record time, holding a little one under each arm, with Shaoey right behind me.

I put all three girls in our Jeep. I told them that the fire department was on the way, that they were not to get out of the car, and that they could watch how Mom and Dad put out a fire . . . kind of like a field trip . . . and then they could watch the firemen once the professionals arrived.

By then, Steven had taken a rake from the garage and pulled the wooden trash bin away from the side of the house. The side of the house had caught on fire from some tiny live ember in the fireworks trash. The windows were already breaking out of my office that held the family computer, files, and legal stuff. I flew into the house to try to save at least the girls' adoption files, but when I felt my office door, it was too hot to even think about going in.

I grabbed two fire extinguishers from the kitchen and came out of the garage spraying white foam on the fire for all I was worth. Once the extinguishers were empty I ran for the garden hose.

Meanwhile, Steven was breaking up the fire, stomping and stamping on embers . . . in his sleepwear, which consisted of a little pair of tightie whiteys. I dragged the hose to my firefighting superhero and turned it on full blast.

Then, in the distance, we could hear the wail of fire engines approaching. And there was Steven Curtis Chapman out in the driveway, hose in hand, wearing nothing but a pair of undies. All he needed was a "junior firefighter" hat.

At the sound of the sirens, Steven looked down, realized he was in his underwear, and was prompted to take action.

"Here," he said to me. "Can you take the hose? I've got to run inside and get some clothes on before that fire truck drives up the driveway!"

"Of course, go!" I said.

I took the green hose and started spraying down the side of the house. My nightgown was all wet from the hose, but since it was July I wasn't cold. As the fire engines came roaring around the back of the house, I looked over at the girls to make sure they weren't scared of the sirens. They were just staring at me. Not moving a muscle. Then the engine stopped and Franklin, Tennessee's finest firemen and paramedics hopped out.

I was so glad to see somebody who could take over. I was quite certain they would be impressed with the firefighting that Steven and I had done.

About that time, Steven came out of the house with more than underwear on. He looked at me with an odd face that made me realize I needed to look down. As I did, I realized that thanks to the hose, my thin cotton nightgown was absolutely sopping wet . . . and I didn't have anything on underneath it. I looked like a disheveled participant in a wet T-shirt contest.

"Uh, hi!" I called weakly to the firemen. Then I handed the hose off to Steven and backed myself into the garage, arms crossed in front of me, trying to disappear into the diminishing smoke.

21

February 20th

It was like any other weekday morning in the Chapman house. The alarm went off at 6:00 a.m., the snooze button got pushed until 6:20, and then we were all running late.

When Steven is in town, he usually drives the girls to school. That day, as usual, Shaoey needed to be taken first for her 8:00 start, then he'd come back and get Stevey Joy and Maria for preschool at 9:00.

After prayers and kisses with Shaoey, I sent her on her way with Steven. Now it was time for round two.

I came into Maria and Stevey Joy's room, and there was Maria, sitting on the floor, pajamas wadded in a pile beside her. If I didn't get to her before she attempted to get dressed, it was almost a guarantee that she would have on her favorite bright pink, fuzzy snowman outfit, and so that was today's attire. She was grunting and groaning, trying to pull on her socks. Whenever Maria concentrated really hard, she drooled. So here she was on the floor, drips on her chin and drool running down her neck.

"Maria," I laughed, "would you like for me to help you?"

Out of the blue, she said, "Mom, is it true that God has a big, big house?"

"Yes," I said. "It's true! God does have a big, big house."

"Does it have lots and lots of rooms?" Maria asked.

"Yep, it has lots and lots of rooms," I responded.

"Is there lots and lots of food?" she asked. Just the thought of food made Maria smile. She loved any part of meal time, snack time, ice cream time, anything food-related time!

Trying not to laugh, and knowing where this conversation was going since she was reciting lyrics from a familiar Audio Adrenaline song, I said, "Yes, tons and tons of food! The best food ever! And you'll never run out!

"And you know what else?" I added. "God also has a big, big yard where you can play football!"

Maria gasped, and said with complete amazement, "Mom! How did you know?"

I said, "Maria, are you learning a song at school about God's big, big house?"

She started belly laughing, her eyes completely disappearing, her mouth a big Cheshire cat grin. "Yes, we are! How did you know?"

I laughed with her.

"Mom," she said, "I wanna know more about God's big, big house! I wanna go to God's big, big house! How do you get there? Can I go there?"

Oh, my goodness! I thought. *Here she is, four years old, and she's asking how you get to go to heaven!*

When it comes to the spiritual stuff in our family, I'm always afraid that I'll mess something up or leave out some important part. Not wanting to screw up this key prayer with little Maria, I did what the rest of the world would do: I went to find Steven Curtis Chapman!

"Come on," I said. "Let's go find Dad so we can both help you understand how you get to live in that big, big house forever!"

I scooped her up, giggling with her, and took her down to the kitchen where I set her on the counter. Steven, just back from taking Shaoey to school, came in and did his best to explain the gospel in four-year-old terms. He told her how wonderful it was that she wanted to go live with God forever because that's what all of us are created for . . . to know God and to be with Him. He talked about

On the floor with her mom
Putting her shoes on
Getting ready for another day
February 20th
She says, "Mom, is it true?"
"Does God really have a big, big house?"
"Does it really have a lot of rooms?"
And she said,
"I really, really want to go there."
And I said,
"So why don't we just talk to Him?"
That's what we did
On February 20th

February 20th
I did my best to explain
How it is that we all will be with God
How it was the Savior came
February 20th
If it's true what He said
Then God Himself sang along
With the beautiful song of rejoicing in Heaven
As she prayed, "Jesus, please come and live in my heart."
"And someday can I come live with You?"
And we could never have imagined
She'd be going there so soon

"February 20th"
Words and music by Steven Curtis Chapman

how Jesus made it possible for us to go to that place when we leave this earth, and how if we ask Him to, He will come and live in our hearts. He tried to explain sin and the cross and resurrection and forgiveness.

Then he asked, "Maria, would you like to talk to God about this?"

"Yes," she said. Then she prayed in her own words, asking Jesus to come live in her heart and to take her to God's big, big house when it was time.

It was so simple, so sweet, so real—one of the best memories that I will carry for the rest of my life.

Steven and I were both crying as we raised our heads, and then Stevey Joy, who'd been watching from the sofa, jumped up and yelled, "Well, if she's going to God's big, big house, I wanna go there too!"

So we put Stevey Joy up on the counter and she prayed a similar, sincere prayer. These two small sisters, sitting side by side on the kitchen counter, were now *new* sisters in Christ!

We celebrated with maple syrup kisses and hugs as coats were zipped and Dad took them out the back door on that morning of February 20, 2008. Maria could hardly wait to get to school, find her teacher Miss Megan, throw her arms around her, and tell her she was going to God's big, big house.

Later, of course, what transpired in the kitchen that day would give us specific, sweet comfort because of Maria's big decision. But at the time it was just a normal Wednesday, a crazy Chapman morning, running late and getting ready for school.

Soon, though, a day was coming when I wouldn't have any more "normal."

22

May 21, 2008

DEAR MOM AND DAD
I love you. I will always be with you. Bye. Kiss.
LOVE MARIA

Note Maria dictated to her preschool teacher in spring 2008

It was a beautiful, warm spring day. The evening before, I'd gone shopping with Emily for her wedding dress. I couldn't believe it: my firstborn girl was getting married! We had prayed since she was little that God would bring her the right man at the right time. Since Emily had struggled with self-esteem issues, the fact that she was marrying a wonderful godly gentleman like Tanner had overwhelmed us all with a sense of God's goodness and faithfulness.

Tanner's mom, Janie; his sister, Tabby; Caleb's then-girlfriend (now wife), Julia; Anna-Ruth, Emily's best friend since first grade; and Karen, Julia's mom and one of my best friends, all crowded into The Bride Room, a boutique outside of Nashville.

I held my breath as the consultant collected several dresses in styles Emily had described. I had spent many shopping outings with Emily while she cried her eyes out in disappointment because the latest, greatest styles just didn't fit her body shape. Today I prayed that my daughter would put on a gown, look in the mirror, and not only know that this was the dress in which she would marry Tanner, but that she would see herself as the beautiful woman God created her to be—a daughter of the King!

Emily tried three dresses on for us, and everyone was polite, but you could sense the self-image "liar" beginning to make his way into Emily's head and heart. She went back into the dressing room, shoulders drooping in disappointment, and my heart ached for her.

Then Anna-Ruth, who had been in the dressing room with Emily, pulled back the curtain, and Emily walked out in a simple but elegant dress with an empire waist, beadwork at the top, and lace and netting at the bottom.

Emily walked to the platform in front of a long line of mirrors. Keeping her eyes down, she stepped up and waited while the wedding consultant straightened the dress and fluffed the train.

Emily slowly looked up into the mirrors . . . and tears started streaming down her face. The rest of us followed suit. It was one big blubber-fest. Even the consultant started crying. The gown fit Emily perfectly, as if it had been custom-made for her. It was a Cinderella moment.

She could not wait to call her daddy. She was so excited, but she wanted his approval. She would not take the dress off, and she continued to cry off and on for 45 minutes until Steven could get there to see it on her.

My prayer changed from spiritual to practical. Emily was so thrilled with that dress . . . and I hadn't even seen the price tag yet.

The look on Emily's face was priceless; I just hoped the dress wasn't!

All of us had just about finished sniffling when Steven arrived. We made him sit on the couch with his eyes closed as Emily waited in the dressing room. Then Emily stepped up on the platform, the gown was fluffed and arranged, and Steven opened his eyes on the count of three.

For just a split second, I saw a familiar look in his eyes. Kind of like the day he saw me in my wedding dress. Then there were more tears, a big group hug, and the dress was a "yes"!

I made my way over to the consultant. To my surprise and delight the dress was reasonably priced for a wedding gown. As Emily came out of the dressing room, the consultant said that since the dress was in pretty good shape and fit her so well, we could buy the floor sample if we wanted to. This would mean a reasonable discount. Other than a little dirt around the hem, the dress looked like new.

But I wanted to buy her a new one.

"Mom," my practical Emily said. "I'm getting married outside at home, in the grass! It doesn't matter. Let's just get this one and save some money!"

So we did. I was happy about the discount, and Emily left the dress shop floating on a cloud, grateful that the big moment of choosing her gown had gone so well and that her closest girlfriends and family had experienced it with her.

Steven and I grabbed an early dinner with some friends and then headed home. I took the bagged dress out of the trunk of the car and headed upstairs to hang it in my closet. Shaoey, Stevey Joy, and Maria came running in. They couldn't believe that we actually had Emily's wedding dress. I unzipped the bag and pulled out the lacy, flowing gown.

Maria, being the youngest and most unrestrained, laughed and wrapped the lace around herself. She was excited that Emily had asked her to be a flower girl, and you could see her little mind churning, pretending it was her own wedding day.

Now, the next morning it was warm and sunny, a flawless spring day. Steven headed off, coffee in hand, to take Shaoey to school. Stevey and Maria had graduated from preschool six days earlier, and they were excited about getting to stay home and play.

My friend—Steven's assistant, "Amazing" Grace—came over. She was helping me choose colors for a bedroom I wanted to paint. As Grace and I walked up the stairs, Maria was just ahead of us, giggling as I pinched her tiny butt all the way up the steps. When we got to the landing, she was already there, sitting on a bench next to an almost life-size Chinese doll, frozen in place, pretending to *be* a Chinese doll.

"Where'd Maria go?" I asked Grace. "I don't see Maria, just this doll sitting here."

Maria jumped up and flew into my arms. "I'm right here, Mama!"

A little bit later our babysitter Melissa arrived. Since Maria and Stevey Joy were both bouncing around the house while Steven and I were trying to work on wedding lists and final plans for Caleb's graduation party that weekend, Melissa and another friend, Wendy, had asked if they could take the girls to a playground that had just opened, the Monkey Tree House.

Melissa and the girls were gone for a few hours. When they came back, they'd had a wild time at the Monkey Tree House and lunch at McDonalds. Around three o'clock, I told Melissa that it was such a beautiful day and she'd been working so many hours, why didn't she just head home? So she kissed the girls and went on her way.

By now Shaoey was home from school, and the girls were running in and out of the house, having a big time. They loved to hang out on the playground pretending that they were the Chapman Sisters, and that they were going to an after-show party with the Jonas Brothers.

At one point, Maria came and asked me to help her get her Cinderella Barbie's little white gloves on. She stood for as long as that busy little body could wait while I worked and wiggled to try to get those tiny white gloves onto Barbie. Then she tore off to do something else.

I never knew until later that she had changed into a maroon and pink ballet tutu . . . this was her dress for the Jonas Brothers aftershow party.

Finally I managed to pull the tiny gloves onto the doll. "Maria," I called, "I got Cinderella Barbie's gloves on her!"

No answer. She and her sisters were outside in the sunshine, playing on their playground in the backyard, which was a good thirty yards into the grass away from the driveway. Maria wanted to hang from the monkey bars, but she couldn't get up to the bar by herself. Shaoey tried to lift her up, but she wasn't quite strong enough.

Steven and I were still at the dining room table, talking about wedding plans. His cell phone rang; it was Jim Houser, his manager. Steven left the table and went outside to our wraparound front porch where he'd get better reception.

While he was talking to Jim on the phone, he saw Will turning into our driveway. He didn't think much of it, though later he would remember that he noticed Will was driving slowly and wasn't talking on his cell phone.

"Yes!" Shaoey said to Maria as she heard Will's old Land Cruiser on the gravel part of the driveway near our front gate. "Here comes Will! He'll help you get up on the monkey bars!"

Will rounded the corner, heading toward the garage.

"Will!" Maria yelled, running toward the car.

"Maria!" Shaoey screamed. "Stop!"

Maria was a hard-headed little girl. If she got something on her mind, she was going to do it. And by golly, she was going to get her brother Will to help her get up on those monkey bars!

"Will!" Maria called again, waving her arms and running, though she was so little that Will couldn't see her.

In the dining room, I was writing a list, thinking about all the wedding details. Suddenly I heard confusing noises. Not the normal commotion of the girls at play. Screaming. But not the kind of screaming where you wait to hear if it's a false alarm. This was different.

I jumped up and tore through the kitchen, heading toward the hall to the back door, just as Shaoey ran in from the back driveway.

"Mom!" she screamed. "Will hit Maria with the car!"

I ran down the few steps to the garage and rounded the corner toward the driveway. Will was holding Maria, crying and pleading for her to wake up. Both of them were covered in blood.

"Mom!" Will screamed. "I hit her with the car!"

"Call 911!" I yelled. "Get your dad!"

I took Maria from Will. She was limp, like she was asleep. I ran across the driveway and laid her down in the grass. There was a puddle of blood about four feet in diameter on the driveway. Blood was streaming from her ears, her nose, her mouth. I tried to clear as much of it from her mouth as possible and started rescue breathing. I was afraid to compress her chest; because of the blood, I didn't know what bones might be broken. I just tried to breathe for her. But she wasn't responding.

Will was in shock. He couldn't dial 911. Later we would find his cell phone broken into a million pieces where he'd thrown it.

I stopped rescue breathing for a second. I was screaming and pounding my fist into the ground, yelling for help, yelling for God to save her, yelling for time to rewind.

Steven came around the back corner of the house, still talking on his cell phone to Jim Houser. He saw me covered in blood. Jim heard him say, "Oh my God!" and then heard the cell phone being dropped in the grass and the sound of screaming.

Steven ran to me and Maria.

"Will hit her with the car!" I cried. Steven picked Maria up and carried her to a rug on the floor right outside our back door in the garage. He took over the rescue breathing while I ran into the kitchen and called 911 on the home phone.

"911," a woman's voice said. "What is your emergency?"

"The first thing you need to do is dispatch LifeFlight!" I screamed. "My little girl has been hit by a car and it's really bad . . . my husband's working on her."

The dispatcher told me to slow down.

"Look," I said, "this is a trauma situation and we *will* need LifeFlight! Please, believe me, get LifeFlight here! Help me, oh my God, please help me!"

The 911 operator dispatched all the various rescue vehicles, even as she was telling me what to tell Steven.

Steven did everything I told him to do. He rescue-breathed and did chest compressions. I kept hearing him beg Stevey Joy to breathe.

"Steven!" I yelled. "It's not Stevey Joy! It's *Maria*!"

It was awful. Because of the blood, his panic, and the fact she was wearing a tutu, Steven had assumed it was Stevey Joy, since she was the one who was always dressing up.

"Is there any response yet?" the dispatcher asked.

"She's gurgling," I cried.

A paramedic who lives close to us heard the dispatch on the scanner. He was the first responder to pull into our driveway.

"Is the ambulance there?" the dispatcher asked me.

"No! Not yet!" I sobbed. "Is LifeFlight coming? Are they coming?"

I saw the paramedic getting out of his truck in the driveway. I ran toward him and grabbed his arm. "You've gotta save my little girl!" I screamed over and over.

"You've gotta calm down and show me where she is!" he yelled. I pulled him around the corner and into the garage. He took over working on Maria.

Will was running down the driveway and across the yard. Shaoey was chasing him, crying and yelling for him to stop. Caleb came tearing out of the house. He ran after Will and tackled him on the grass by the pond in front of our house.

"I can't stay here!" Will was screaming. "Why was she taking a nap on the driveway?"

He was in shock. Caleb held his brother on the ground, using all his strength to hold him down. Will was struggling, fighting back. He just wanted to get away.

"Where would you go?" Caleb yelled. "We love you! It's gonna be okay!"

I somehow called my friend Lori, whose daughter had been killed in a car crash nine years earlier.

Jim Houser, who had been talking with Steven until he dropped his phone in the grass, had called David Trask, Steven's road manager. David lived close enough to be able to get to our house within a few minutes.

Caleb grabbed at Will's shirt, which was covered in blood. "We've got to get this off of you," he cried.

"No!" Will sobbed. "Everyone needs to know that I'm the one that did this!" He wrestled against his brother. "*I* did this!"

Caleb grabbed Will's white V-neck undershirt, tore it off of him, wadded it up, and threw it into the pond.

Steven's brother Herbie, who'd been up at our barn, came running. After he realized what was happening, he got hold of Shaoey and went to look for Stevey Joy, who'd gone missing in all the chaos. He eventually found her curled up in a ball, as small as she could get, under her desk in the room she shared with Maria.

David arrived. Herbie, weeping, told him what had happened. David ran to Will, who collapsed in his arms. David held him. He, of all people, knew what Will was going through. When David was seventeen, he was driving down a crowded street and a little boy darted into traffic. David had hit him . . . fatally.

Will sobbed as he lay in David's lap. David stroked his hair. "Maria is in God's hands, Will. She's in God's hands."

Sirens. The ambulance arrived, pulling up the driveway and around to the back. They loaded Maria onto a stretcher while continuing to work on her. The LifeFlight helicopter landed in a neighbor's field down the street; our property didn't have a clear enough landing area.

Rick, a friend who'd been taking a walk, came running up our driveway. "Let me drive you to the hospital," he said. We loaded into our minivan, Lori and me in the back, Steven up front.

A policeman appeared as we were getting into the van. He wanted to see Steven's driver's license. "Were you driving the car that hit your daughter?" he asked.

"No," Steven said. "My son was, but you are not talking with him right now."

As we followed the ambulance down the driveway, we saw David holding Will in the front yard. Steven lowered his window.

"Will Franklin!" Steven yelled at the top of his voice, though he wouldn't even remember this later. "Just remember, your father loves you!"

We pulled out of the driveway. We drove past the place where the paramedics were loading Maria into the helicopter. It felt so weird, driving past our daughter . . . but we couldn't go on the helicopter with her. The best thing we could do was get to the hospital as soon as possible.

Our friend drove as fast as he could from our home in Franklin toward Vanderbilt Hospital in Nashville, but it was rush hour and traffic was crawling. In the front seat, Steven beat his fist on the window over and over as hard as he could, praying out loud for God to please, please breathe life into Maria, breathe life into Maria.

I was in the backseat next to my friend Lori, crying, screaming, praying, and calling people on my cell phone. David Trask was driving Caleb and Will to the hospital. Caleb had called Emily; she had just gotten off work. She picked up Tanner, and they were heading to the hospital. They knew nothing other than Maria had been hit by a car.

Finally, finally, in the crawl of rush hour traffic, we arrived at Vanderbilt.

As we came into the emergency room, we were walking in slow motion. I saw someone curled up on the floor of the waiting room, crying. I saw my brother Jim and his wife Yolanda, the Lipscomb family, Reggie and Karen Anderson, Chris and Miriam Chesbro, and several other friends. Everyone was just standing there looking at us . . . a moment frozen in time. Then I saw one of our pastors, our friend Mike Smith, walking toward Steven and me.

At about the same time a hospital staff person came up to us as well. "You need to come this way, with me," she said.

I started backing up.

"No! No!" I screamed. "No, I don't want to go that way, please, no!"

I think I knew in my heart that Maria was gone, but I was hoping that the LifeFlight team had been able to either resuscitate her or keep her breathing. I couldn't comprehend what was happening. I kept trying to wake myself up.

They took us to a small room beyond the ER. The doctors who had worked on Maria were there, along with several nurses. They told us that while they had done everything they could, Maria had, in fact, passed away.

"No!" I screamed. I fought the nurses and doctors to get out of that room.

"*No!*"

They eventually walked us to the trauma room where they had worked on Maria. They had already disconnected most of the equipment that had been used to try to save her life. She was just lying there, like she was asleep. The only mark on her was a small abrasion on the side of her forehead.

"Oh, God!" Steven cried. "Breathe life into Maria! You can bring her back to life! Please bring her back to life!" He knew God could do that if He chose to.

I knew that too. But something inside me also knew that God had healed Maria in a way we didn't want. I went up behind my husband and gently put my hand on his back.

"We've got to let her go, Sweetie," I whispered. "It's okay to let her go. It's time to let her go."

Somehow in that unthinkable moment it became clear to Steven and me that we were standing at the very door of heaven, placing our little girl carefully in the arms of Jesus, desperately trusting that she would be safe there until we could come and join her.

Somewhere in the distance I heard Steven's voice explaining to those in the room that this was an eternal moment, and how everything in this life really comes down to this moment for each of us.

Heaven is the face of a little girl
With dark brown eyes
That disappear when she smiles
Heaven is the place
Where she calls my name
Says, "Daddy, please come play with me for a while"

God, I know, it's all of this and so much more
But God, You know, that this is what I'm aching for
God, You know, I just can't SEE beyond the door

So right now
Heaven is the sound of her breathing deep
Lying on my chest, falling fast asleep while I sing
And Heaven is the weight of her in my arms
Being there to keep her safe from harm while she
    dreams
And God, I know, it's all of this and so much more
But God, You know, that this is what I'm longing for
And God, You know, I just can't SEE beyond the door

Heaven is a sweet, maple syrup kiss
And a thousand other little things I miss with her
    gone
Heaven is the place where she takes my hand
And leads me to You
And we both run into Your arms

Oh God, I know, it's so much more than I can dream
It's far beyond anything I can conceive
So God, You know, I'm trusting You until I SEE

Heaven in the face of my little girl

"Heaven Is The Face"
Words and music by Steven Curtis Chapman

"As crazy as this seems right now," he said, "the only thing I can say to honor the life of my little girl and our terrible loss at this moment is to ask you, please don't miss this . . . we will all stand here one day and face eternity. If you don't know the One who can give you eternal life, His name is Jesus . . . you need to meet Him and you really need to meet my little girl in heaven . . . she's amazing."

Steven and I bent over and kissed Maria's forehead. My hand shook uncontrollably as I stroked her face and tucked her hair back behind her ear one last time. Then we walked out to meet our friends and begin our long journey of grieving and waiting until we would pass through heaven's door ourselves.

23

Not As It Should Be

We're not necessarily doubting that God will do the best for us;
we are wondering how painful the best will turn out to be.

C. S. Lewis

Time stopped.

We could barely breathe. I walked slowly out to the hall, where the rest of the family was waiting. Our pastors were there too.

Some other part of my brain took over. "I need Caleb, Emily, Julia, Ruthy, Tanner, Danny, and Melissa," I said.

Steven was holding on to Will as the rest of our family filtered into the little room. I told our children that their sister was no longer with us. Tears. Disbelief. Pain.

There was screaming. Crying. Rocking back and forth in anguish. Desperate hugs as we held each other up. Steven, Caleb, and our pastors holding on to Will. Collapse.

"I'm going to go tell everyone else," I said. Emily and Tanner came with me to the emergency room waiting area where friends had gathered. People were on the floor praying, waiting, hoping. My brother came next to me. He held me up.

"Maria didn't make it," I said.

People have told me I was calm, that I quoted Scripture, and that I gave them all a real sense of hope. I don't remember. Emily and Tanner actually started leading everyone in singing a praise song.

I went back to the other room and the rest of my family. I passed members of Steven's management team huddled together, tears rolling down their faces as they made decisions for us about how to handle the media.

Maria's body—her shell—was taken to a private room and covered with a soft blanket. I sat quietly with her as our closest friends and family streamed in to say goodbye. After everyone had gone, Steven and I prayed and kissed her goodbye.

I asked for a few minutes alone with her. I wanted to hold her, but I didn't know that I was allowed to.

This is not how it should be
This is not how it could be
But this is how it is
And our God is in control

This is not how it will be
When we finally will SEE
We'll SEE with our own eyes
He was always in control

This is not where we planned
   to be
When we started this journey
But this is where we are
And our God is in control

Though this first taste is bitter
There will be sweetness forever
When we finally taste and SEE
That our God is in control

"Our God Is In Control"
Words and music by
Steven Curtis Chapman
and Mary Beth Chapman

I consciously gave her back to the One who had allowed us to have her in the first place. But then I felt stabs of guilt. Had I let Maria down? Was this my fault because I was "busy"? I tried to talk with God louder and louder as I felt the voice of the Accuser become louder and louder inside of me.

Finally, in all my tears and anguish, it was time to leave without my baby girl. One last kiss.

Will asked if he could be alone with her for a little while. I stood outside the door, watching through a small rectangular window as Maria's hero and big brother wept over her. I never asked him what he said.

Then Geoff and Jan Moore took Steven and me by the hands and walked us out of the hospital. They drove us back to Franklin, to our church. Everyone who had been at the hospital had gathered there, as well as hundreds of other people. I saw dozens of high school kids all sitting close together in a hallway, completely quiet. They were there for Will and Caleb.

My best friends were there for me too. Karen, Jan, Terri, and Lori took me into the ladies' room.

"Sweetie, you need to take off your clothes," Karen said gently but firmly.

I was in a daze. I didn't even really know where I was. I didn't realize that my clothes were completely stained with Maria's blood and that it would upset people—especially Shaoey and Stevey Joy—to see me this way.

"What?"

Karen told me they had asked Grace and Wendy to go to our house and get clean clothes for me.

"I don't want to wait," I said. "I need to see all these people who have come here for us! Can you guys give me your clothes?"

They would have given me anything. I stripped off my shirt as Jan took off her blouse to give to me. But my bra was saturated with blood.

"Take your bra off," someone said.

"No one will see it," I said.

"Take it off now," my friends said. "We are going to throw it away."

Terri stripped off her own bra and handed it to me. Someone else gave me their pants. It was almost funny.

"Okay," I said to my friends. "You wait here for Grace and Wendy to bring clothes so you can come out of the bathroom!"

Once I was dressed, I walked outside as Steven's brother Herbie and his wife Sherri pulled up outside with Shaoey and Stevey Joy. Stevey Joy had changed her clothes; she was wearing a lime green T-shirt I'd never seen before. It read, "Heaven is better."

Steven and I held our girls tightly and carried them to a grassy area under a tree, which offered a bit of separation from all the people arriving at the church.

We knelt with them on the grass.

"Where is Maria? How bad was she hurt?" Shaoey asked.

"Did they have to put a Band-Aid on her?" Stevey Joy added.

"You know what?" I whispered, my throat raw with pain. "She was hurt really bad. She was hurt so bad that Jesus came and took her to heaven where she will never hurt again."

"It's like Maria has gone on a really long trip," Steven added. "It's going to be a long time before we see her again, but we will see her again!"

We held the girls for a while as they sobbed against our chests, Steven and I crying along with them. Finally, we prayed together and walked toward the church. I was carrying Stevey Joy, and Shaoey was holding tightly to my leg.

24

SEE

Right now all I can taste are bitter tears
And right now all I can SEE are clouds of sorrow
From the other side of all this pain
Is that you I hear?
Laughing loud and calling out to me?

Saying SEE, it's everything you said that it would be
And even better than you would believe
And I'm counting down the days until you're here with me
And finally you'll SEE

"SEE"
Words and music by Steven Curtis Chapman

Now we see but a poor reflection as in a mirror; then
we shall see face to face. Now I know in part; then
I shall know fully, even as I am fully known.

1 Corinthians 13:12

There were many, many people whispering and milling around
in the narthex . . . and many more who had found their way into
the sanctuary to pray.

I felt like a ghost, watching a moment that I didn't belong in, and yet somehow I was one of the main characters. I floated from person to person.

"I'm so sorry!" some would say. Others would just give me a giant hug. Still others knelt on the floor weeping and praying. I felt deep gratitude that so many people had come to offer their support and love, to be sad and broken with us. I didn't know if Steven and I were supposed to be taking care of them or if we should just sit and let them come to us.

At some point adrenaline kicked in. I went into the sanctuary and was able to thank people for coming. I vaguely remember seeing friends staring at me, stunned, as if they couldn't conceive what we were going through. It scared me. I realized that we were at the very beginning of what was going to be a long, long journey.

Finally, I stood up in the front of the sanctuary and said, "It's all true! It's *all* true! The gospel is true. If we believe anything about our faith, we have to believe that we know where Maria is right now and that God didn't make a mistake. He didn't turn His head, He was in complete control. Maria's days here were numbered. We don't like it, but He will give us the strength and the hope to walk this journey."

Did I really believe that in this moment? Or was I on autopilot and the right "Christianese" terms just popped out of my mouth?

Meanwhile, Steven was dealing with the authorities and their questions for Will. Since the police didn't get their statement earlier at our house, they wanted to talk with him outside at the church, where it was a bit more quiet.

The good news is that the officer was not the same person who had tried to stop Steven in our driveway. This police officer was kind with Will, understood his anguish, asked him if they could pray together, and then gently asked him to tell what had happened and draw it out on graph paper.

My friend Karen became the mother hen for all of us. She could see our energy fading as we tried to encourage everyone who had come out to encourage us. She and her husband Reggie pulled us out of the crowd and drove us to their home.

Caleb, Julia, Emily, Tanner, Will, Ruthy, Melissa, Danny, Geoff and Jan, Karen's son Dave, who is a great friend of Will's, and Brandon, another friend, all headed out to the Andersons' as well. We just huddled together in the living room, some on chairs and sofas, some on the floor, no one really saying anything. Eventually I may have dozed a little from time to time, and when I did I would have these thoughts, or mini-dreams, that the whole thing was just a bad, bad nightmare

But it wasn't.

The next morning I couldn't eat. I couldn't even take a shower. We just sort of got ourselves together and went to the funeral home and cemetery where little Erin Mullican was buried . . . it seemed like a good spot for Maria's shell.

We had a million details to handle, and our friends were there to help us think. It was unbelievable, in the space of one day, to go from planning a wedding and a graduation to planning a funeral for our five-year-old.

The funeral director was a gentle man. He led us through the maze of decisions we needed to make. Somehow, together, we created an obituary and made plans for the private family ceremony that would be held at the funeral home.

"We don't have as many children's deaths," the funeral director explained, "so we only have two caskets here to choose from. Or of course we have catalogs if you would like to order something. It can be here by tomorrow."

Steven and I didn't feel the need to look at casket catalogs. We walked down a hallway that seemed about five thousand feet long. The man opened a door and there were two little caskets, one white, the other gray.

I started backing up, just as I did in the hospital when they told me Maria was gone. I fell to my knees. "I don't care!" I wept. "The white is fine. Whichever is more girly!"

I needed to breathe. I needed to get out of that room. Caskets that small should not exist.

It was like a bad movie with no end.

We decided to bury her in the dress she would have worn as a flower girl in Emily's wedding. It was traditional Chinese silk covered in embroidered butterflies . . . beautiful, perfect.

"She needs lots of roses," I told the director when he asked about flower arrangements. "I can't stand carnations; they smell like the flower of death. I don't like baby's breath, and please, no yellow!"

Even in my grief, I was pretty particular.

Then we went to the cemetery, where the kind funeral director took us around in a golf cart so we could look at burial plots. Surreal.

We got out of the cart at a plot with a little tree beside it. My friend Terri Coley bent down in the grass. "Look!" she said. "There's a lady bug!" She carefully picked up the little spotted creature.

Maria loved lady bugs. "This is fine," I said. The funeral director asked if we wanted to think about plots for ourselves.

"Why not?" I said. "We'll take three plots, and Steven and I will be buried here beside her."

I turned and walked away. Done.

Later our friends took us—except Shaoey and Stevey Joy—back to our house for the first time since the accident. It was more difficult than I can describe to pull into the driveway. None of us wanted to go in the back door, which was our normal routine. The memories of the accident were too fresh in our minds.

We parked in the front spots that visitors use and went in our little-used front door. Quietly. Pausing every few steps.

I needed God to show up, because I thought I could never live in that house again. I went upstairs, my legs feeling like thousand-pound weights were attached to them. I walked into Stevey Joy's room—which up till yesterday she had shared with Maria. I fell down on the floor and started sobbing. I grabbed some clothes for Stevey Joy. Then I thought carefully and selected the things of Maria's that we would display at her memorial service.

I climbed up into her bunk bed, laid my head on her pillow, and took in deep breaths of my little snuggle bunny who had loved her bed. I lay there and sobbed and sobbed, never wanting to leave.

But I somehow made myself get up. I went to Shaoey's room to get clothes for her.

Then I rifled through my own closet, pulled out random clothes, and threw them all in a bag.

We walked into the family room and made a big circle. The house was so still. We prayed. We asked that God would honor our pain and surprise us with joy that could only come from Him.

Steven and Caleb had been praying like crazy since the night before, something like, "God, we know you're in this, but we're so confused and hurt. You've got to show us something tangible so we can know Maria's with You! Please, we need to see you in this, please let us see!"

Steven was slowly making the rounds of the house, retracing some of Maria's steps from the day of the accident. He walked into our dining room. Next to the bay window Stevey Joy and Maria had two little art tables where they had spent tons of happy hours creating things. They loved coloring and gluing and taping and glittering just about anything they could get their sticky little fingers on.

Steven looked down at Maria's table. There was a piece of notebook paper there. Maria had drawn a six-petaled flower with a green stem and two leaves. Only one of the petals was colored in. Blue. Maria's favorite color. The center of the flower was orange.

Steven saw something bleeding through from the other side of the paper. He turned it over. Maria had colored an orange butterfly, and written a word she'd never, ever put down on paper before.

Maria could write her name and little things such as "I love you," but she hadn't started writing other words yet. Since Stevey Joy was a little older and a year ahead of Maria in preschool, she had a list of words to learn. Steven's best guess is that Maria must have copied one of the words off the list.

And the word she wrote was SEE.

SEE.

Staring at Maria's artwork, Steven had tears spilling down his face. It was like Maria was speaking to him from heaven, from the very realm of eternity, saying "SEE? Can you *SEE?* Everything is going to be all right. I am here with Jesus. I am fine. Heaven is real, the gospel is true, you just have to SEE!"

Several days later, when we were getting ready to leave Karen's house, I drew Maria's artwork on a white board there. As I drew the flower, I realized it had six petals. Like I had six children. And only one of the petals was colored in. Like only one of my children was safe at home in heaven with Jesus. And the petal that was safe was blue—Maria's favorite color.

Some people might see little things like this as coincidences, no big deal. But to us, these small signs were like a little trail of bread crumbs on a shadowed path, showing us the way to walk.

I could only see a few feet in front of me. If I could see any farther than that, the journey ahead would be too scary. But He was showing me all that I needed, just a few steps at a time . . . giving me little glimmers of grace . . . if I would choose to SEE them.

25

Jesus Will Meet You There

Every act of evil extracts a tear from God, every
plunge into anguish extracts a sob from God.

Nicholas Wolterstorff, Lament for a Son

We were physically and emotionally exhausted. The sad had
settled into every part of us as we headed back across town to
the Andersons'. We all had worries and concerns about Will.
I had lost one child, and I just kept crying out to God, "Please
don't let me lose Will too!"

Will had such a special connection with all three of his little
sisters, and he had been Maria's constant playmate. He called
her "little dude" and would always take time out to play. He'd
let her climb all over him. He'd swing her high in the air and
tickle her until drool flowed freely from her mouth because she
was laughing so hard.

Now that his little chubby buddy was gone, Will was in a
deep, dark place. Wearing Maria's favorite pink blanket around

his neck, he'd walk down to the Andersons' dock and sit there for hours, or he'd stay in the basement and not come up.

Someone was with him at all times. We felt like we were all fighting in a spiritual battle for Will . . . like the Enemy had come calling for him and we were praying him back from the edge of despair, in a conflict for his very soul.

On Thursday night, Steven and I went downstairs to check on the younger crew. We found Tanner and Emily, Caleb and Julia, Ruthy, David, and Brandon all circled around Will. Will was weeping, clutching Maria's blanket. The others were praying fervently over him, interceding on Will's behalf and begging God to help Will, to heal him, to prevent the Accuser from whispering lies of guilt into Will's heart.

Then Emily and Tanner slipped away, and when they came back they had gotten a basin of water and some soft towels. While the rest of us surrounded Will, they knelt and washed his feet, praying that the Enemy would not get a foothold in his soul, praying that God would give Will peace and rest.

When you think you've hit the
  bottom
And the bottom gives way
And you fall into a darkness
No words can explain
You don't know how you'll
  make it out alive
Jesus will meet you there

He knows the way to wherever
  you are
He knows the way to the depths
  of your heart
He knows the way 'cause He's
  already been where you're
  going
Jesus will meet you there

When you realize the dreams
  you've had
For your child won't come true
Jesus will meet you there . . .

"Jesus Will Meet You There"
Words and music by
Steven Curtis Chapman

Steven and I looked at each other with tears flowing down our cheeks: we could not believe the profound sadness and the deep beauty of that moment.

Darkness fell on our second night without Maria, and just as the night before, the young people stayed close together in the basement family room on couches, blow-up mattresses, or the floor. Karen, concerned about my lack of sleep, made Steven and me go get in their daughter Ashley's bed. She thought we might have a better chance of getting an uninterrupted night's sleep in a real bed.

This real bed was the same one in which Maria would sometimes spend the night with Karen. On her last visit, she had absolutely loved a big stuffed yellow flower that Karen had for her to play with. It had a bright butterfly on it, and Karen had wrapped it around the bedside lamp so it would be the first thing Maria would see when she woke up in the morning.

Eventually, exhausted by grief, Steven fell asleep. But I was fitful and could not rest. I stared at the yellow flower that Maria had loved . . . and every time I closed my eyes I would see the accident, with all its trauma, in my mind. Or I would see sweet Maria's face . . . I couldn't believe she was gone, so quickly. I was in such pain and anguish . . . and I was scared beyond belief. I don't know exactly what the fear was, but I felt very alone, and I was so worried about my children.

Whenever I thought of Stevey Joy, she was the continual reminder that her almost-twin, her best friend and constant companion, was gone. They did everything together; they had even dressed alike. And in a split second, Stevey Joy was alone, her whole sense of security ripped away. She was so young, she couldn't understand what was going on in her world and how much everything had changed. I was so old . . . and I couldn't even understand it.

Then there was Shaoey . . . so responsible for her age and carrying the terrible pictures in her head of having seen the whole accident, a burden no child should ever have to bear. She was so smart, so logical by nature . . . and she could not make any sense of this. She wanted to be with me all the time, and she was becoming more and more angry.

And Will . . . so caring, so tenacious, so strong, so broken. Clinging, just barely, to what he knew to be true, that God was with him even in this. Such a hard concept for anyone to grasp, let alone a seventeen-year-old boy and Maria's best buddy.

I thought of Emily, trying to be the helpful firstborn child and clinging to Tanner with all her might . . . of Caleb, the prayer warrior, who kept a constant watch on Will. He was trying to be a strong man, and he leaned on Julia for encouragement.

I felt completely numb and non-functioning, yet at the same time I was going through the motions and making the decisions that had to be made. But even in my pain I could see that my children's pain was worse. More than anything, as a mom I wanted to fix all this for my kids. To make it all go away. To turn back the hands of time.

And of course I couldn't.

Hours went by. I finally crept out of bed and tiptoed downstairs to Karen's room.

"Karen!" I whispered. She was dozing and so was Reggie. She woke up right away.

"I can't sleep!" I said. "Can you come and sleep with me?"

My wonderful friend understood my loneliness and panic. She got out of bed, and we headed up the stairs to our bedroom. I crawled into the bed, squishing Steven over against the wall on his side. I was in the middle and then Karen got in next to me, clinging to the outer edge of the mattress.

"Okay, Karen," I said, "now you can tell everyone you slept with Steven Curtis Chapman!"

We actually had a few seconds of giggles.

Steven woke up. "What are you doing?" he asked groggily.

"I can't sleep, and you're asleep," I whispered. "So I need Karen here so she can recite Scripture to me and I can go to sleep!"

My sleepy husband smiled, rolled over toward me, and fell back to sleep, totally understanding.

26

Sown in Tears

I don't even want to breathe right now
All I want to do is close my eyes
And I don't want to open them again
Till I'm standing on the other side

I don't even want to be right now
I don't want to think another thought
And I don't want to feel this pain I feel
But right now pain is all I've got

"I Will Trust You"
Words and music by
Steven Curtis Chapman

Those who sow in tears
will reap with songs of joy.

Psalm 126:5

We had a public visitation at our church on Friday afternoon. Thousands of people came. The support from our community, and the expressions of love and sadness that came from across the country and around the world, were unbelievable to us.

As Steven and I greeted the people who were able to come to the church, a lot of them didn't know what to say. The thing that helped us most was when people would just hug us and say, "There are no words."

Some people did their best to hold it together, but as soon as they made it through the long line and to us, they fell apart.

Others would innocently try to connect our sorrow with some event in their own lives. They were simply trying to relate the best they could. But when people would say that they knew how we felt because they'd lost their dad or their mom or their grandmother, I felt numb. I know that grief is grief, and pain is pain . . . still, in the natural order of this life we do tend to lose our parents and grandparents first. Burying a five-year-old isn't in the usual order of things.

I remembered when I was a young teenager and my middle-aged aunt died. It was so sad to see my grandmother so upset. When I had walked into her house, she put her hands on my thirteen-year-old shoulders. "It's not right for any mother to have to bury her child," she had sobbed to me. It *wasn't* right . . . and my grandmother's child was forty-three years old.

Now here I stood, greeting people while trying to reconcile the fact that my five-year-old daughter was lying in a casket not three feet from me. *God, where were You? Where are You?* my brain whirled. *I don't get it.*

A couple of people actually told me they could sympathize with our grief because their dog or cat had been hit by a car.

Really?

There were also expressions of great encouragement. One card that helped Steven and me a lot came from Greg Laurie, our friend who is a pastor and evangelist in Southern California.

Greg wasn't able to come to the visitation, but he wrote to encourage us that Maria was a far bigger part of our future than our past. We'd known her for a few years down here . . . but we would be spending *eternity* with her soon. The sad irony is that Greg would lose his own son in a terrible car accident just two months after Maria died.

At the visitation, I was in a daze, seeing people and scenes like it was a movie. I saw Amy Grant come in at the same time we did. I don't remember words, just a big platter of cookies (for the children's room) and her endearing Amy smile, full of compassion for our family. I was told later that she sat quietly in the back for a long time, alone, praying.

I saw our Show Hope partners from China, Robin and Joyce Hill. They had flown in from Beijing. I saw Jon Rivers, the "Countdown Magazine" radio host, and his wife Sherry. They'd adopted from China as a result of our story and had come up from Texas to be with us. I saw the staff of Show Hope. Teachers from Maria's preschool. Friends from church, from our neighborhood, from everywhere.

We were overwhelmed by the outpouring of support. The line of friends went on and on . . . and finally, seeing how exhausted Steven and I were, Jim Houser and Dan Raines made the difficult decision to end the line. They invited everyone left in line into the sanctuary, and Steven spoke to them all at once, thanking them for their love and support, asking everyone to continue to pray for us as our names came to mind.

Meanwhile, Will was in a separate room where his buddies from school could come see him but he wouldn't have to stand up in front and hear the comments, no matter how kind people thought they were being. It was an unusual, special time for these soon-to-be senior boys, and Will was actually able to encourage some of them. God was already using our son—and his brokenness—to minister to his friends.

It was very late when we left the church on Friday night. I was one of the last to leave. I deliberately walked from flower arrangement to flower arrangement by myself, reading the cards and thinking about the friends who had sent them.

One of Caleb's and Will's good buddies, Trevor, was right there as well, quietly loading arrangements to take to the house or the burial site or wherever.

Even in my sad daze, his humble help touched my heart.

On Saturday morning we went to the funeral home, where our extended family and close friends would gather for a private time with the casket open. We'd say goodbye to Maria, then have the memorial service in the afternoon, followed by a private burial.

I felt like I was on the outside looking in, more of an observer than a participant.

It seemed so random, walking toward a tiny white casket that held our beautiful flower girl. Friends had spent hours enlarging pictures of Maria and framing them; they had been placed all around her casket. There was

Stevey Joy's letter to Maria

I'm sad you had to leave & sad you left earth to go to heaven. Melissa misses you. Our Mommy & Daddy love you so much.

I want Jesus to take good care of my sister. Me & Maria played together a lot. Me and Maria talk about when we die & go to heaven & how our shells will have to be buried. I love you.

Have fun with Jesus, Maria!

Love, Sissy

Maria as a ballerina, as a giggling baby, as a princess . . . so many beautiful, funny, happy times. I wept over a little life that would no longer make memories for her mama! The ache was almost more than I could bear.

Family and friends walked in slowly, so full of sorrow and yet full of support. They came up to the casket and wept with us.

None of us wanted to leave. Shaoey and Stevey Joy both had written letters to their sister, and now they put them in her "box," as they called it. The others followed suit. (The letters were actually copies, as I wanted to keep the originals.)

We also tucked in some Tinker Bell wings, one of Maria's favorite Tinker Bell dolls, and the tutu and ballet slippers that she would have worn in her upcoming recital. (Stevey Joy would, in fact, dance without her sister just six days later, in an auditorium right across the street from the emergency room where Maria was taken. Her teacher would award her with a flower at the end of the recital, for being the smallest—and the bravest—dancer there.)

My brother Jim is an art teacher. Whenever the kids were together, they would all line up for Sharpie marker tattoos from Uncle Jim. Steven always hated the girls getting them, because they took so long to wear off.

Shaoey's letter to Maria

Dear Jesus and Maria
I want you to know that Maria's stuffed animals are going to be packed away and put in the attic. But we found your last flower picture and on the front you wrote "SEE" and a butterfly. Dad cryed because you are special to him and all of us. Enjoy Heaven. I will see you soon but not too soon. I will come to you. I hear the roads are made of gold and the throne of God waits for everyone who believes. When you see that I am coming wait for me at the gate and pray for Will he has been sobbing so has Mom and Dad. I hope I see you soon but not too soon.

Love,
Shaoey

But today, when Jim pulled out his markers and asked to draw one last tattoo for Maria, Steven agreed. Maria loved it when Uncle Jim would give everyone Sharpie tattoos, especially her.

Jim took his markers and drew three ladybugs to represent Sha-oey, Stevey Joy, and Maria. We all cried as he took his time, doing one last masterpiece on his niece.

Later, after the memorial service, all the little ones waited patiently in line for Jim to draw the same tattoo on their arms. (And even later than that, my six-foot-four-inch brother would get the same ladybug tattoo on his arm, but his was the real deal.)

Our pastor Scotty had a counselor lingering in the back of the viewing room, just in case Will Franklin needed someone. There was also a slide show being shown in the back so that the cousins could watch some of Maria's funnier moments.

Then slowly, one by one, family and friends left. Then Steven and I were left alone to say a final goodbye to our little girl, whose face we would never see again until eternity. I gripped the side of the casket and fell to my knees as Steven held on to me. We cried and prayed, kissed her goodbye, and walked out of the room.

Will's letter to Maria

I Love you so much! I'm so sorry, and if I could go back in time I would change it so fast and I know I would have seen you. I'm sorry! How's it going up there in Heaven? I bet it's pretty unbelievable, and I just wish I could see the incredible smile on your face. I'm having a pretty stinkin hard time down here and it's going to be so hard and miserable, but I know ur looking down on me with God and you guys are just smiling at me. I just wish I could see you one more time or just see you running around and flying around. You're a big bundle of joy Maria, and I'm so sorry for not seeing you. Oh, Man, I'm gonna need your prayers in the many many years to come b/c its not going to be easy!, and I'm gonna need you Maria. I can't do it without you. I can't, I can't, I CAN'T!!!

Will

We had no sense of time. We continued to stay at the Andersons' home, and they took such good care of us. But it was as if the chronological passage of minutes ceased to exist in our world; random, disjointed events were happening, but everything seemed out of order. In the midst of our grief and struggles, we were also living with an experience of special grace . . . a sense of God's presence, as if the veil between the temporal and the eternal had been lifted.

I believe this is because of the prayers of hundreds of thousands of people around the world who had heard about the accident and were lifting us up before God. We felt a supernatural sense of God holding us. We had a heightened awareness of what really mattered, a clearer vision of eternal things that we normally could not see. We were desperate for God. The Bible was like oxygen for us as we searched for comfort within its pages.

At one point, Caleb had been talking with a friend down at the Andersons' dock, and he came running up to Steven, a fire blazing in his eyes.

"I see it, I get it," he shouted. "God is real and Maria is with Him and we're going to be there. . . . Satan doesn't want us to be able to see it this clearly, because if we did we'd be so dangerous for God!"

As we planned Maria's memorial service, I asked Steven if Matt Redman could be there and sing some of our favorite worship songs, "Blessed Be the Name of the Lord" and "Never Let Go." Steven called Matt on the off chance he was in the U.S., since he lived in England at the time.

When Steven's call came, Matt was standing in line at the Atlanta airport, getting ready to board a flight back to the U.K. He walked away from his flight and drove to Franklin. He not only sang the worship songs, but also a song that he and Steven had written together just four months earlier to mourn the stillborn death of a friend's baby. Now . . . sad, sweet irony . . . he would sing those words for our sweet Maria. When I heard that Matt was coming to be part of the service, I was overwhelmed by gratitude and grace. His was a true gift that I will never be able to repay.

At the same time we were experiencing God's grace through our friends and the sweetness of the Holy Spirit's presence, we were also just plain getting beat up by grief, sometimes when we least expected it.

At the Andersons', someone brought us a bunch of yeast rolls from our favorite home cookin' place, Barbara's. As soon as Steven saw them, he flashed back to a night or two before the accident, when he had taken the little girls to eat at Barbara's.

As I've said, Maria loved food, and she *loved* Barbara's yeast rolls and homemade butter. She'd spread a thick layer of butter on a roll and then lick it off . . . then she'd spread more butter on the roll and lick that off . . . then she'd stick her finger in the pats of butter and lick *that* off. We'd always tell her to stop eating all that butter. It wasn't good for her.

But now, as he looked at the rolls, Steven started to sob. "Why didn't I just let her have all the butter she wanted?" he cried.

We both knew the answer to that. He was simply trying to parent her well. But the pain was so strange, so huge, set off by a thousand ordinary memories every time we turned around.

And we had only just begun our long, painful journey of grief.

27

Beauty Will Rise

Out of these ashes
Beauty will rise
And we will dance among the ruins
We will see it with our own eyes
Out of these ashes
Beauty will rise
For we know joy is coming in the morning
In the morning
Beauty will rise

"Beauty Will Rise"
Words and music by
Steven Curtis Chapman

The LORD gave, and the LORD has taken away;
blessed be the name of the LORD.

Job:1:21 ESV

Selections from the Memorial Service Transcript

Steven Curtis Chapman

Thank you all for being here. . . . We know God has told us
He is revealing Himself here in a profound way. [Inviting family

members up to the podium.] You guys just share your heart. I'm going to let you tell how you knew Maria.

Melissa Northup

I had the privilege of taking care of the Chapmans' beautiful daughters.

Maria had an amazing spirit. She was love itself. She was laughter, silliness, passion, beauty, sweetness, and a determined little soul, a super funny soul and a little Curious George, so full of questions. She was so full of wonder, happiness, desire, detail, creativity. She was a giving, caring, cuddle bug who would snuggle for hours if you would let her. Sometimes at our little slumber parties, I would wake up with her as close as possible to me with her little hand somehow in mine, not knowing how it got there.

I know it is true there is a time for sadness, but Maria would want us to be happy again, living with fullness of life like she did. Maria loved things that little girls do. She loved dressing up for princess balls, being a ballerina, being a bride in a pretend wedding, dancing and singing with Shaoey and Stevey in their Chapman sister band, and just playing pretend. She would always say, "Let's pretend such and such . . . 'K?"

Maria always asked me what was pretend and what was real. When talking about Jesus with her, it always made sense to her that Jesus was real. The greatest peace I have today, what helps me take one step at a time, is knowing where Maria is. This place called heaven is real, and Maria is there with her real King Jesus!

Maria loved God's creation. She loved smelling His flowers and picking bundles of them. She always loved God's flying creatures. She loved ladybugs, and she loved God's little birds. Sometimes when swinging—she loved to swing—she would pretend she was a birdie and ask if I could make her fly higher and higher.

She noticed every butterfly that flew by, every dandelion that needed to be picked and blown so she could watch the fuzzy white pieces fly away.

And if you knew Maria, it would be no surprise to see her running around with a pair of fairy wings on. And her funny Buzz Lightyear costume with his big ol' wings.

Now I have come to realize that Maria was created with a pair of wings on her heart. God had a plan to have her fly home to Him. Just like the plans He has for us to fly home one day too.

Maria would want us to remember the verse Jesus spoke, "Let the little children come." And she would want us to carry on her childlike faith, living this life as if we all had wings, longing to fly to Jesus.

We are not home yet, and if we trust in Jesus like Maria did, we will find deep within our hearts a pair of wings He has waiting for us too.

> Maria once told me that her favorite songs that Daddy sang were "Dive," "The Great Adventure," "Children of God," and "Cinderella." I can honestly say that Maria dove into life, learned what it's like to be a child of God, felt like a Cinderella, and has lived the great adventure!
>
> Megan Thompson

It makes me smile to think that Maria is getting to see those mighty angels' wings . . . and I can hear her now asking if she can touch them.

Emily Chapman (now Richards)

May 13th, just a few weeks ago, Maria turned five. Two days later, on May 15th, she graduated from preschool. And then two more days later, on May 17th—a week ago today—Tanner and I got engaged. We got engaged on an airplane; I couldn't wait to call my family when I got off. I talked to the girls one by one, Shaoey, then Stevey, then precious Maria. And Maria asked me a question that the other two girls didn't ask.

She said, "Ooooh, yay, you're getting married!" And then she asked, "What did you say?"

And I told her, "I said 'yes,' you silly girl!"

When we got home, Maria was the first to run up to me and she handed me this little happy engagement card that was done backwards, of course, with way too much glue, and she gave me a really big hug, and she said again, "What did you say when Tanner asked you to marry him?" I didn't understand why she kept asking me that. I told her, "I said 'yes!' and I'm going to need you to be a flower girl on October 4, okay? We've got to start practicing!"

In case you guys haven't heard, Maria is being buried today in her flower girl dress. So she is a flower girl.

In the midst of all the confusion and pain and grief that I don't ever wish on any of you, God has brought comfort through little Ria's words. Maria cared deeply about how I responded to the proposal. You see, Maria too had said yes to a glorious proposal in February this year, when she accepted Jesus.

I woke up this morning asking the Lord for a Scripture to bring to you guys, and he brought me to Revelation 22:17. It says, "The Spirit and the bride say, 'Come!' And let the one who hears say, 'Come!' And let the one who is thirsty come; let the one who desires take the water of life without price."

A proposal has been made through the death of Jesus Christ . . . and so in honor of Maria, I would like to ask each and every one of you: What did *you* say?

Caleb Chapman

"When the righteous cry for help, the LORD hears, and the LORD delivers them out of their troubles. The LORD is near to the brokenhearted and saves the crushed in spirit" (Ps. 34:17–18).

All of our spirits here are really crushed, and I know a lot of y'alls' are too. . . . Any of you that have walked through something like this know that it's a new emotion and there's nothing that can describe it. The only word I've been able to come up with is confusion. . . . We feel so many different things. We have joy and we have sadness, we feel loved and we feel lonely . . . but I have never been this confident in Jesus Christ. And I've never been this confident of heaven.

> And the pain falls like a curtain
> On the things I once called certain
> And I have to say the words I fear the most
> I just don't know
>
> God is God and I am not
> I can only see a part of the picture He's painting
> God is God and I am man
> So I'll never understand it all
> For only God is God
>
> "God Is God"
> Words and music by
> Steven Curtis Chapman

The only analogy I can come up with is this: it's like God is an abstract artist . . . and when you're real close to a painting like this, it's hard to focus, it's blurred, and you can't see what's going on. You have to walk really far back, and then the whole painting comes into focus and you can see what the artist was doing.

That's what this experience is like for us. We're just really, really close to this mess . . . but I think the farther we get away from it in time, the more we're going to see this picture come into focus. Man, it's a really big one too, so we'll have to walk pretty far away.

You know, I feel like as Dad held Maria, I held my brother. I held Will that day. We prayed for healing for Maria, but God healed her in a way that we didn't like. But God is going to heal my brother in a way that I think we're all going to like a lot.

[At this point, people all over the sanctuary jumped to their feet, and soon seven hundred people were applauding in a standing ovation of praise to God and support for Will Franklin Chapman.]

I just challenge you guys, nothing matters in this life except for relationships, especially with Jesus Christ. I know we're coming from a bunch of different backgrounds, but I can tell you, because I'm in the midst of this, that Jesus is real, and man, He shines through some really, really dark places. So thank you everyone for supporting us. We love you guys.

Mary Beth Chapman

This is something I wish I wasn't doing. And I really don't have a whole lot to say, because so many beautiful people standing with us and behind us have already said everything. But I just wanted to tell you a couple of things about Maria so you will remember her the way we do.

Probably no less than ten times a day Maria would say, "I love it when my whole family is together!" And obviously, it's hard schedule-wise for us all to be together. So on those occasions when we were, she would just love it when we would do the group hug and "kiss the monkey," and Maria was always the monkey. And she loved, loved, loved to be naked.

I don't know if this is appropriate, but I'm going to say it anyway because I'll regret it if I don't. Besides my husband, Maria loved my boobs. Any way she could get her hand down my shirt, she would. I don't know why, maybe it was just the physical closeness and touch.

Anyway, I have lots of last memories, but one sticks out in my mind, and this is going to be another one that will make Steven blush. Then I'm going to sit down and let him say all the spiritual stuff. I always let him kind of sweep up my mess.

Some of you know that with young children, it's hard to find time to be alone in an intimate way. One morning it was early and Steven and I were together, and Maria came walking into our room.

She was always the first one up, and I'm sorry that I ever complained about it now, but she woke up talking a hundred miles a minute and she went to bed talking a hundred miles a minute.

And so she came busting into our bedroom early one morning while Steven and I were connecting—I'm sorry y'all, it's okay, Maria would want us to laugh even though maybe this is grief and I'm really going to regret this tomorrow when it all comes crashing down. Anyway, she comes crashing into our room while we were together, and luckily there were covers over us . . . but she just stopped and looked at us with her little eyes as big as they could get and said, "What are ya'll all like (putting her little hands all crinkled together) smushed together for?"

She was so full of a million questions, and that's one of the last questions I ever heard her ask me!

Every time I got to ask her a question I'd say, "Maria, do you know how much Mommy loves you?" She'd always answer, "To infinity . . . and beyond!"

And she was right.

Steven Curtis Chapman

Well, obviously I'm married to a very amazing, incredible, and uh, unpredictable wife! And I've just been blown away at watching God reveal Himself through her.

You guys, help us live differently because of this! We don't know what "normal" is or will ever be, but we don't want to go back to it, because time is short. We've looked into eternity . . . we're doing it today. This is the kind of thing we need to spend our time doing, just seeing and celebrating the glory of God where it shows up, in the pain and the joy He gives us in this life.

You know, I think Maria would say to us today, "Taste and SEE that the Lord is good." Maria loved tasty things. She loved to eat. And she would say, "See, just SEE the glory of God today!"

If you've never seen it, if you've been afraid to see it or too proud to see it or whatever, just see the goodness of God in the midst of this. We can't see it all right now. Like Caleb said, it's a huge painting, it's too big to perceive all at once and we have to keep backing up to see it. But allow Him to remove the fear of death from your heart, reveal and show His love to you so you can know, really know Him!

Thank you all for coming.

20

Goodbye . . .

Why have I waited for so long
To be singing you this song
I thought that time was all I had
I have so much left to say
But time has faded now

Caleb Chapman

Then the Lord said to him, "Take off the sandals from your
feet, for the place where you are standing is holy ground."

Acts 7:33

After the service, we got into a long, white limousine that was
waiting to take us to the cemetery. Another limo followed, full
of extended family and close friends. Then there were hundreds
of cars behind that.

The silence is the noise I still hear inside my head. Not a word
was spoken. Shock. It was so hard to believe that we were actually riding in a funeral procession following a hearse that carried
the shell of our sweet Maria. Shouldn't she be riding in the car

with us? Shouldn't she be hanging from the ceiling, making us all laugh and worry about her safety at the same time?

We were facing what we knew was going to be one of the most difficult moments of this whole nightmare. Surely we would wake up before we had to do it, before we had to put Maria's body into the ground.

As we got closer to the cemetery, my heart was beating faster and faster. I wanted to jump out of the car and run as far away as I could.

Then, even though I was anxious, it seemed as though everything stopped and went into super slow motion. I looked around the car that carried the people most important to me. Will, with the pink blanket around his neck, clinging to his girlfriend Ruthy. Emily holding tightly to Tanner's hand. Caleb and Julia holding on to each other for dear life. And right in the middle of it all were Shaoey and Stevey Joy. Too young to completely understand, they kept our minds from going completely crazy.

I held Steven's hand. And after taking a long look at my surviving children, I blankly stared out the window the rest of the way to the beautiful but awful place where Maria's shell would be planted to wait for the new body that Jesus would bring her one day.

We drove past many of our friends gathering to celebrate the graduation of their high school seniors from Franklin Classical School. In fact, some of our closest friends, Geoff and Jan Moore, who were at the memorial service for Maria, were now watching their son graduate instead of being able to come to the burial service.

It seemed so strange . . . one family celebrating the ending of a chapter of life called high school and the beginning of a new chapter of hopes and dreams called adulthood . . . and at the very same moment our family was grieving the reality that our earthly hopes and dreams for one of our children had suddenly and tragically come to an end and that the future of our family had been forever changed.

We arrived at Williamson Memorial Gardens and walked to the spot we had selected just two days earlier as the place where Maria—and eventually Steven and I, the sooner the better as far as I was concerned—would be buried.

I smelled fresh dirt and grass as we took our green, velvet-covered family seats. There were beautiful flowers, plants, and fresh-cut roses for people to hold so that they could throw them on the casket when it was time to say goodbye.

Many of our friends gathered around and our pastor, Scotty Smith, began to speak. He talked about this day being a day of planting . . . planting a seed that was the body of Maria. He read from 1 Corinthians 15:

> What is sown is perishable; what is raised is imperishable. It is sown in dishonor; it is raised in glory. It is sown in weakness; it is raised in power. It is sown a natural body; it is raised a spiritual body.
>
> *1 Corinthians 15:42–44*

Scotty talked about what it meant to plant a seed and wait . . . that until a seed falls to the ground and dies, it can't come to life. But because of Jesus' resurrection from the dead and His promise of our coming resurrection, and because the gospel is true, this seed of Maria's body that we were planting was going to be raised imperishable.

He talked about the promised spring that is coming when all things will be made new. He reminded us of those hopeful words of Revelation 21 and the coming day when God will wipe every tear from our eyes.

Somehow we were able to grasp that. Not fully . . . not even close to fully. But just enough that we were able to throw beautiful roses on the casket, believing that the story of Maria's life was far from over . . . that there was in fact a spring when we really will see her again . . . more alive than ever.

These are the truths that got us through that unbearable day and have kept us breathing in the days since, even when we don't want to anymore. We *know*—even when we can't feel it—that that ultimate spring really is coming.

After everyone else had left the graveside, I told Steven to go on to the limousine with the others and that Will and I were going to sit for a while.

I put my arm around Will's shoulders and hugged him hard. "There are no words for this," I said. "It's as hard as hard gets. But I promise you one thing right here by your sister's grave: it's going to be a long, long journey that won't end until we get to heaven, but it's going to be okay."

He leaned his head against mine, the pink baby blanket around his neck, and sobbed. I told him that I loved him, that I didn't blame him, that this was a horrible accident, and that we were not only going to get through it, but that God was going to give each of us a different kind of story to steward well.

I hugged him like when he was a little boy, and I got a pretty sweet hug back. I knew the Holy Spirit had given us those sweet, private minutes together. We agreed to not let this tear us apart. We held hands and walked back to the white limousine.

The next day, in the very same sanctuary where we had held Maria's memorial service, Caleb's class had their graduation ceremony. It was beautiful and surreal all at once.

Caleb had gone to Christ Presbyterian Academy from kindergarten through eleventh grade. I had homeschooled him his senior year so he could play guitar on the road with his dad. His classmates really wanted him to be a part of the ceremony. They always have a musical guest, so the class voted that Caleb would perform for their ceremony. That way he'd get to be part of it.

Our whole family had come barefoot to Maria's service. It was our way of honoring her and proclaiming that we were on holy ground. God was surely in the place where we honored Maria Sue Chunxi Chapman. We didn't know until they walked in, but Caleb's entire senior class came barefoot to honor our family, to honor Maria, and to pay deep respect to their beloved classmate, Caleb.

Before the accident, Caleb had been working on two songs that he would sing at his commencement. One was "You've Got a Friend in Me" from *Toy Story*; the other was a song that he was writing called "So Long."

Caleb's song was only half done when Maria's tragedy struck us . . . and yet somehow, in the busy and grief-filled days between Wednesday night and Sunday morning, he finished writing his song. I couldn't believe he still wanted to sing for his classmates.

But Caleb felt strongly about fulfilling his commitment, and somehow God gave him the grace and presence of mind to sing at his graduation. I watched my son and was filled with such a mixture of pride and wonder and grace. God was giving him what he needed, even in these early days after the tragedy, to be a faithful steward of Maria's story.

Steven and I sat and listened to our son sing, tears running down our faces.

Why have I waited for so long
To be singing you this song
I thought that time was all I had
I have so much left to say
But time has faded now

So take care, so long, goodbye

And if our paths don't cross in this Life
In heaven it will be
Where there's no pain, no death, just Life
Oh the day that that will be

So take care, so long, goodbye

"So Long"
Words and music
by Caleb Chapman

29

The New Normal

I am waiting for the rescue
That I know is sure to come
'Cause You are faithful, yes, You are faithful
And I've dropped anchor in Your promises and I am holding on
'Cause You are faithful, God, You are faithful

You are faithful, You are faithful
When You give and when You take away
Even then still Your name is faithful
You are faithful
And with everything inside of me
I am choosing to believe
You are faithful

"Faithful"
Words and music by Steven Curtis Chapman

Hope waits but does not sit. It strains with eager anticipation to see what may be coming on the horizon. Hope does not pacify; it does not make us docile and mediocre. Instead, it draws us to greater risk and perseverance.

Dan Allender

Karen and Reggie had been planning to visit their daughter in Ireland but had delayed their travel plans because of the accident.

After Maria's memorial service, though, Steven and I insisted that our friends go ahead on their long-planned trip.

We stayed at the Andersons' a few days after that, but then the day came . . . we knew we had to return home and face one of our scariest scenarios.

When we had been home the day after the accident to pick up some clothes and Steven found Maria's artwork, we felt like God had given us a huge gift. We had chosen to see it as a message; it was time to put one foot in front of the other and return to the place that held seventeen years of memories, good and bad.

In short, it was time to begin our "new normal"—whatever that was.

But it was still awful. Part of me wanted to have friends clean out the whole house, then hire movers to pack it all up and have the Chapmans start over somewhere else. It seemed inconceivable to go back and live in the place where Maria had died. How could I walk on the driveway every day where my daughter had taken her last breath?

As we approached our house, the morning was gray. We turned into our neighborhood. Then, as our tires hit gravel on the unpaved surface of our cul-de-sac, the skies opened up and started pouring rain . . . as if Jesus was weeping with us while we came back to this place.

We went first to our barn, which is up a hill not far past the house. Friends and family were there, and they had brought tons of food. The little girls played with friends. The rest of us watched the children, none of us saying what we were thinking: someone was missing. We made small talk, and then it was time to go to our house.

We drove down from the barn and up our driveway. There was a baby magnolia tree near the girls' playground. We never paid much attention to it, and it had never bloomed before. But as we rounded the corner, we saw that little tree, so near to the place where Maria's earthly life had ended, and there was a huge, fragrant, blooming flower on it. Just one.

We could almost hear her laughing from heaven, "SEE?"

Counselors had told us that there were some things, in terms of our grief, that we would just have to push through. Our back door was one of them.

We had lots of bags and had to make many trips from the car to the house and back again. It was amazing . . . somehow, God gave us the grace to go in and out of the back door, over and over. We put our bags down inside and tried to do normal things, even though the quiet was so loud without Maria giggling and running and bouncing around everywhere. We got some laundry started and put our stuff away. We were mostly focused on Shaoey and Stevey Joy, trying to make things as normal for them as we could . . . as if that were possible.

As we survived, breath by breath, moment by little moment, we began to have other feelings besides the terrible flashbacks of Maria's loss. Of course those awful memories were part of this place. But if we left our home and started fresh somewhere else, we would also leave behind so many wonderful memories.

Our house was not just the place where Maria had died. It was also the place where Maria had giggled and washed dishes and swam naked in the pool, nothing on but a smile and some swim goggles! It was the place where our boys had learned to ride their bikes without training wheels, eventually advancing to four-wheelers. This was where the boys had that painting party in the basement—with oil-based paints—with Grandma and Grandpa in charge. This was where Steven, while warming little Emily up for a softball game, batted the ball that whacked her right in the nose.

This was the house where Emily got her first puppy at Christmas . . . where the kids had caught Old Gus, the granddaddy catfish, in the pond . . . where Tanner asked permission for Emily's hand in marriage while kneeling on one knee in front of Steven.

This physical place, with its flowers and pond and monkey bars and bedrooms and blankets and warm kitchen and family room fireplace, had been a taste of heaven for the Chapman family. It was the site of squeals of laughter, rich music, sweet prayer, great fellowship with friends and family, Super Bowl and March Madness parties.

"I love it when my whole family is together!" Maria often proclaimed with great gusto. Maria was now in heaven, and though we felt her absence so acutely we sometimes couldn't breathe, we still knew the reality that we would see her again.

In these long, strange days of our new normal, though, I had to *choose* to believe that. It didn't come naturally.

One day I went to my favorite retail therapy store, T.J. Maxx. I bought a rounded white pitcher with a simple handle and accents of white flowers. We put it into a big Ziploc bag and sealed it shut. We then gathered as a family out on the driveway, right where Maria had run into the arms of Jesus.

Our plan was to take that pitcher, hurl it into the concrete, and then take the broken pieces and glue them back together. The jug would be an Ebenezer—a physical reminder—of God's spiritual work in our lives. Our idea was that the mended pitcher would leak water, our reminder that in our brokenness and eventual healing we would leak out the comfort to others that we ourselves had been given. The idea had come from 2 Corinthians 1:3–4:

Praise be to the God and Father of our Lord Jesus Christ, the Father of compassion and the God of all comfort, who comforts us in all our troubles, so that we can comfort those in any trouble with the comfort we ourselves have received from God.

We all gathered in the driveway. We prayed. Then I threw the pitcher onto the pavement . . . where it broke into not hundreds of pieces, but about a million. Actually, some of the pieces smashed into a fine, white powder. There would be no physical way to glue our brokenness back together again.

In theory it was a great idea. But like so many other things in my life, it didn't quite work out according to my plan.

Sometimes Steven would go up to his home studio, which is soundproof, and scream as loud as he could, "Blessed be the name of the LORD! He gives and takes away! Blessed be the name of the LORD!"

And like the rest of us, sometimes he'd just collapse at the foot of the back stairs, praying and crying out to God.

One day the rest of us were gone somewhere, and Steven was alone in the house. He took an extension cord and a pair of electric hair clippers out to the driveway, and buzzed his hair at the accident spot. In that time of deep grieving, the thought of just continuing on like normal, fixing his hair each morning, seemed like a travesty. He felt like Job; he wanted to do something as a visual representation of his mourning, like tearing his clothes and shearing his head.

When we came home, the hair was already cleaned up from the driveway. So it wasn't until we walked into the house that we came eye to eye with the buzz-headed Steven Curtis Chapman.

He decided to stop shaving as well, and grew a beard, though much, much later he shaved it off.

"Daddy," said Stevey Joy. "I liked your beard. Can you please put your beard back on?"

So he did.

30

"We Can Do Hard"

I've walked the valley of death's shadow
So deep and dark that I could barely breathe
I've had to let go of more than I could bear
And questioned everything that I believe
But still even here in this great darkness
A comfort and hope come breaking through
As I can say in life or death, God we belong to you.

"Yours," verse added after Maria's death
Words and music by
Steven Curtis Chapman and Jonas Myrin

Endurance is not just the ability to bear a
hard thing, but to turn it into glory.

William Barclay

On the night of the accident our pastor, Scotty Smith, had gotten in touch with a trusted counselor who could walk with Will through the tragedy and the hard months to come. Another doctor prescribed medication to help Will sleep, as well as an antidepressant. Meanwhile, my doctor had advised me to switch from my usual antidepressant to a more powerful one. He also prescribed additional medication to help me through the days immediately following Maria's death.

We got in touch with a trauma therapist who works with children. I'll call her Dr. Lois.

Dr. Lois specialized in working with children who had experienced trauma of various kinds. Right from the start, she was incredibly insightful and tender toward us. She asked us about our plans for Shaoey and Stevey Joy during the memorial service. Sometimes adults want to keep children away from funerals, she told us, but little people need to be able to say goodbye too. It's really important for closure.

She also gave us some great insights into how children grieve. Even though children's grief can seem almost schizophrenic, it's actually healthier than the way most adults deal with their feelings of loss and sadness.

She was right: I would see Stevey Joy, for example, go into a really deep place of sadness, crying in her room and holding a picture of Maria. I would sit and hold her. Then about ten minutes later, she'd be outside skipping and playing. She would fully enter into her sorrow and then move fully into her play.

Dr. Lois began seeing the little girls regularly. I learned a lot through her work. With Shaoey, she used a therapy called EMDR. In simple—believe me, very simple—terms, I would describe it like this: when you see a tragic loss, your brain can't handle it. This is just how the brain is designed.

So for a child who witnesses her sister's death in the driveway, or a soldier who sees a friend step on a bomb in Afghanistan, the brain takes in the catastrophic event and then the experience explodes into thousands of pieces, like shrapnel, in the mind. It's an instinctive survival response.

The problem is, of course, that these pieces of traumatic memories are all over the place in one's mind, almost like land mines. You can be doing fine, and then a chance association will detonate one of those memories, triggering a panic attack, a flashback, or worse.

The idea of the EMDR—in my layman's terms—is to bring all the pieces of traumatic shrapnel together in one place. Then you can put them in a mental file cabinet and access them when you want to . . . rather than the flashbacks coming when you least expect them.

Because of the way the brain is designed, repetitive motor movements crossing the midline of the brain, combined with mental imaging, can pull together one's mental shrapnel. Dr. Lois would have Shaoey sit with her, tapping her open hands first on Shaoey's right leg, then the left, back and forth, in a pattern.

While she would tap—left, right, left, right, tap, tap, tap—Dr. Lois would ask Shaoey to remember Maria as she saw her right after the accident. Then she would redirect by saying something like, "Okay, Shaoey, now instead of seeing Maria all bloody and lying on the ground, I want you to see her in your mind all clean and laughing in Jesus' arms."

Shaoey would replace the awful memory with a beautiful picture in her mind, which also had the distinct advantage of being *true*. This wasn't just wishful thinking; it was replacing what was visible to human eyes with the reality of what was actually occurring in spiritual reality. For Shaoey, and for the rest of us, it meant choosing to SEE how Maria really was.

This kind of therapy was—and is—immensely helpful, particularly because Dr. Lois is a believer and uses it in a Christ-centered way. These techniques don't erase what happened. But hopefully they can give the girls—and the rest of us—psychological and spiritual tools we can use for the rest of our lives in this broken world.

Another, deeper issue we have all had to deal with in varying degrees is guilt. Will feels it: he was driving the car. I feel it: I should have been outside with my children. Steven feels it: ditto. The rest of our family—and even friends who weren't connected at all with the events of May 21—feel guilt in one way or another.

I didn't realize how deeply it was affecting Shaoey, though, until we visited the cemetery a few months after Maria's death. She was mad and just didn't want to be there. She didn't want to pray with us and wasn't acting like herself.

Finally I asked Shaoey what she was feeling inside.

"I don't want to be here," said my broken, insightful Shaoey, at that time eight going on about thirty-five, "because this is where guilt finds me."

Shaoey felt like she was responsible for the accident . . . because she had told Maria to go get Will, that Will would lift her up on the monkey bars.

I said to her, "Shaoey, is it a true statement that Maria was too heavy for you to lift to the monkey bars?"

"Yes," she said.

"Is it a true statement," I continued, "that you told her, 'Here comes Will, he'll help you get on the monkey bars'?"

"Yes," she said. "Will would always play with us."

"Is it a true statement that you yelled for Maria to stop running toward Will's car?"

"Yes," she said.

"And is it a true statement that Maria was little Miss Stubborn and she just kept running toward the car anyway?"

"Yes, ma'am," she said.

But guilt is not easily defeated by mere logic.

Dr. Lois brought Shaoey into her office and asked her to pick a figure that represented her guilt from one of the shelves. Dr. Lois's shelves have everything from fairy princesses to lions, tigers, bears, crowns, swords, monsters, good guys, bad guys, you name it.

Shaoey reluctantly began to look at all the figures, not sure of what she was about to do. Finally she chose a gnarly old grim reaper skeleton guy. "This is my guilt," she said. "This is what it would look like."

"Okay," said Dr. Lois. "This is the devil. I want to tell you something, Shaoey. In these rooms with me you're allowed to say things that you shouldn't say at home or school or church. You can tell him to shut up, or whatever you want."

Shaoey was surprised and decided this might just be a fun thing after all.

But as she dealt with the gnarly devil guy, she began to get upset. "You shut up!" she yelled. "You get away from me and leave me alone! Stop saying things to me! *Shut up!*"

Together, Shaoey and Dr. Lois beat up the devil guy some more, and then they put him in a coffin in a box. They buried the box in the sand.

"When did your guilt begin?" Dr. Lois asked.

"May 21, 2008," said Shaoey. They wrote that date on a note they put in the box.

"And when does your guilt end?" Dr. Lois asked.

"Today!" Shaoey yelled. They put the date on a note and placed that in the box. Then they closed the lid and wrote Romans 8:1 on the top: "There is therefore now no guilt for those who are in Christ Jesus."

"Okay, Shaoey," Dr. Lois said. "Now find something on the shelves that represents Jesus."

Shaoey looked around for a while and then chose a crown that had diamonds on it. Together, they put the crown on top of the box, and Dr. Lois stored it high on a shelf. That way, just in case the devil guy of guilt started bugging Shaoey again, they could get him out, yell at him, and then re-bury him, reclaiming Jesus' absolute victory over him.

Jesus' victory *is* absolute, but many of our days are still difficult. One day both Shaoey and Stevey Joy were very sad, both of them crying for Maria.

"Mom, why is it just so hard living without Maria?" Stevey Joy asked.

I sat down with them.

"Yes," I said. "This is so hard! It stinks! It's the worst! It's so hard to live without Maria's giggles, snorts, slobber, and all the funny stuff she used to say!"

Tears rolled down my cheeks as my little girls continued to cry.

"It's not fair, I know!" I said. "There are lots of things that don't seem to be fair, and they're so *hard*. But girls, God has asked us to do hard. It really stinks and I wish we didn't have to, but this is what our family has been called to. If we all stick together, we can do hard."

31

The Unhappiest Place on Earth

Christianity doesn't deny the reality of suffering and evil.
. . . Our hope . . . is not based on the idea that we are
going to be free of pain and suffering. Rather, it is based
on the conviction that we will triumph over suffering.

Brennan Manning

What if we all got brave?
Enough to take away
All we're hiding behind even just for a day
And let the scars show even a little
But I know the honesty will show us all to be

Broken, we're all broken
And we all need a Savior
Broken, we're all broken
And we all need a Savior
We all have a Savior
We all need Jesus

"Broken"
Words and music by Steven Curtis Chapman

As the sad, numb summer of 2008 unrolled, our various counselors told us it would be a good idea to make some new memories

as a family. I could hardly get myself up in the morning, and the thought of a trip without Maria didn't help my deep grief.

But again, I was willing to do hard, as I've said, and it seemed like it would be good for our girls to make some new memories with us that would be helpful in their healing.

We decided to go to Disney World. The happiest place on earth, right?

Wrong.

Our make-new-memories group was Karen, Reggie, their daughter Julia (our daughter-in-law-to-be), their son David (Will's best buddy), Steven, Shaoey, Stevey Joy, and me. The rest of the family had other commitments, and we would all be back at Christmastime when Steven would sing, as he does each year, at Disney's annual candlelight processional at Epcot Center.

I won't go into all the disastrous details, but the trip was doomed from start to finish. We decided to stay at a Disney resort we hadn't been to before. We thought that might help, but it didn't. It was still Disney without our Tinker Bell, who had actually been with us to Disney World eight times over the course of her little life. We kept getting smacked with memories of Maria, the ultimate Goofy, everywhere we went. That set the stage for tension throughout our trip.

At one point Steven and I had gone in separate directions, agreeing to meet at the huge Wall-E statue at a certain time. He had Shaoey with him, I had Stevey Joy, and as we waited . . . and waited . . . and waited at the appointed spot, I got madder . . . and madder . . . and madder.

So I did what any mom would do—went into the gift store right beside the giant Wall-E. I felt myself spinning out of control as Stevey Joy was picking out a souvenir. She chose a "High School

Musical" outfit. I was so in the habit of buying two of such things . . . one for Maria, one for Stevey Joy. Holding only one outfit to buy brought Maria's death to the forefront of my mind. My friend Karen found me crying on the floor in the corner.

I tried to pull it together. I bought Stevey's outfit and left the store sniffling. When I got back to the giant Wall-E—where earlier I had already waited for my consistently late husband—Steven *still* had not shown up!

For his part, Steven had made a wrong turn and innocently missed the sign, but I wasn't having any of it. When he finally appeared, I was yelling at him from the time I could see him coming: "How does anyone miss a *forty-foot Wall-E?*"

We eventually settled down (sort of) and even took a few pictures with fake happy smiles. Then we headed to a crab restaurant (appropriate) for dinner.

As you can imagine, the short walk to the restaurant was a complete fuss fest. I was mad at Steven for missing the biggest Wall-E in the world. Steven was mad at me because I was mad. Karen was telling Steven what had happened to me in the gift shop, which started me crying again.

It was as tense and miserable as it could be. We were all close friends, and family, and we were stuck in a grief that seemed like it would never change. Nothing would *ever* be the same, and we were all realizing it by how the evening was playing out.

When we finally got seated at the table and ordered our food, Steven decided to take a little break.

He excused himself and went for a walk, crying and praying, feeling hopeless. The restaurant was built like a big paddleboat next to a large lake, with various levels sticking out over the water.

Steven was standing on the second level from the top, staring at the water, praying, "Lord, when are You coming back? If it's not in the next half hour, I'm not gonna make it. This is so hard, and we're all at odds with each other because we're hurting so bad."

Just then a little girl came skipping up to Steven. She was by herself—no parents anywhere nearby. She looked like she'd been to the Bibbidy Bobbidy Boutique, a place where little girls go and get glammed up with glittery hairdos and sashes. She grinned at Steven and said, "You know, the best view's from the top!"

Then she skipped away.

It was like God was saying, "SEE!" to my hurting, angry husband. The best view on everything we were going through *was* from the top. A heavenly view. The eternal perspective we had to cling to with all we had in us.

Steven came back to the table. He apologized to everyone for his attitude, and we all apologized to him and to each other for our own stinky attitudes. Then, since the food still hadn't arrived—the restaurant was busy that night—Steven took Shaoey and Stevey Joy up to the top of the boat so they could look across the water.

The three of them were looking at the lake when they felt someone approach from behind. It was the same little girl, still with no parents in sight. "I *told* you the best view was from the top!" she said. And then she skipped away . . . and they never saw her again.

32

October 4, 2008

Emily's Smile

Our soul waits for the LORD; he is our help and our shield.
For our heart is glad in him,
because we trust in his holy name.
Let your steadfast love, O LORD, be upon us,
even as we hope in you.

Psalm 33:20–22 ESV
(Scripture on the front of Emily's wedding program)

It was a beautiful, warm fall day. I couldn't believe it: my firstborn girl was getting married! We had prayed from the time she was little that God would bring her the right man at the right time. And He had.

But then what we never could have imagined happened, and Maria died in the spring of the year we had thought would be so happy.

From the time Maria left us, Steven and I had said privately that we thought it would be healing for Tanner and Emily to proceed with plans to marry on October 4. But it wasn't our decision to make.

On May 21, even as he wept and prayed and anguished, Will had told Emily and Tanner, "You have to promise me that you will still get married on October 4!" Will did not want Emily's wedding to change . . . despite the tragedy of losing Maria.

As time went by, Emily and Tanner felt that our home was indeed the place to begin their union, and October 4 was the day to do it. They wanted to establish their new life together on that same holy ground where Maria had been taken to her eternal home.

Yes, our home was the site where Maria was accidentally hit by a car and left this earth . . . but even though that all-consuming, terrible thing had happened here, our home was also a place of powerful, happy memories. This was the place where God had met us time and time again; He had not been looking the other way on May 21.

So, less than five months after Maria suddenly went to heaven right from our driveway, our home was to be the site of Emily Elizabeth Chapman's wedding celebration.

We missed Maria, and our hearts were sad . . . but we also laughed with the most powerful sense of joy, the kind of joy that thrusts its way right up through sorrow. We knew that something powerful was happening at our home on this day.

I know that Satan took a massive swing at our entire family on May 21 and thought he was going to destroy us for good. So October 4 was not just a good day, it was a victorious day! God overwhelmed us with a joy that eased our sorrow and allowed us to see that, out of this horrible story, there were redemptive pieces already being written by the Healer of all wounds.

Yes, we were devastated by our loss, but I know that the day we stood in faith and gave our daughter to be married, we defeated the Evil One. If by chance Satan does have a forked tail, I envisioned it tucked very uncomfortably between his gnarly legs.

On the afternoon of May 21, just before Maria passed away, Steven had been writing some beautiful instrumental music on a keyboard in our dining room. He'd planned a piece called "Sisters," which would be played as the bridesmaids and flower girls walked down the aisle. He wrote another piece called "Emily's Smile," which would be played as Emily approached her groom.

That was the plan.

Now, so many dark days after the tragedy we did not plan, the "Sisters" music started to play. The wedding party walked out of our house, down the porch steps, and through the grass near our pond. After a pause, the "Emily's Smile" music started and Steven walked his daughter through the green grass and toward her groom.

Tanner was beaming. Emily was beaming, feeling as beautiful as she had ever felt in her life. Steven, holding our daughter's hand, felt overwhelmed by a sense of rightness. We had prayed since Emily was small for her husband . . . and here was Tanner, the godly man that God had brought.

> "Emily's Smile" is the melody I heard in my head as I tried to picture my sweet little girl slowly walking down the aisle, dressed in white, with that beautiful smile on her beautiful face, to become a bride to the man of her dreams. Her mom and I know that this is a day that she has dreamed of since she was a little girl. We also know how incredibly happy she is this day because of the goodness and faithfulness of her Heavenly Father. So there's no doubt that while there will certainly be a few tears, this day will be lit up brightly by Emily's smile.
>
> Steven Curtis Chapman,
> note on wedding program

Our friends and family were all smiling and crying as the music played and Steven walked Emily closer to her groom.

This day, with its beauty and sweetness, was all we could have hoped and dreamed . . . even as we were aware, in sharp relief, of the day that our dreams had died when Maria left us. It was like a peek inside the curtain of eternity, and we all saw a little further than usual: Blessed be the name of the Lord, the One who gives and takes away!

Preceding Emily down the grassy aisle, Stevey Joy had served as the sole flower girl. She carried a Chinese lantern; within it was a beautiful monarch butterfly, in honor of Maria. As Stevey Joy arrived at Tanner's side at the front, he bent and gently helped her open the lantern. The butterfly paused for a moment and then took flight off into the golden October evening.

After the service, everyone walked the short path to our glorified barn. We'd hired a great band, had awesome food, and we all cut loose.

At one point in the evening, Steven looked across the dance floor and saw his Uncle Barry, a staid Baptist, dancing with his daughter, who had actually been the flower girl at *our* wedding. There was his ninety-four-year-old grandmother, not exactly boogying, but smiling and tapping her toes from her wheelchair. There was Steven's sister-in-law Sherry dancing with their adopted Chinese daughter, Leah Rose. My big, bald brother was doing spin moves on the floor, and then he'd pop up and dance with his wife and their two little ones from China.

There were so many beautiful adopted children there . . . so many children like Shaoey and Stevey Joy, dancing with everyone . . . once orphans, now laughing at the wedding feast. It was like every inhibition had been let go . . . not by alcohol or something external, but by the Holy Spirit, setting people free so they could dance.

For Steven, it was a realization of why Jesus loved weddings in His earthly life. And it was like a foretaste of heaven's wedding banquet, when there will be no weeping or tears, when all will dance freely in the Father's joy.

I danced and danced and had the time of my life. At one point, I sat down to take it all in. It was so right. I watched old friends talk and laugh, and new introductions take place among the young cousins and friends. I knew Maria would have wanted us to celebrate in this way; Emily's wedding was a pure gift from God, giving us fresh wind under our tired wings.

From this sublime experience at the reception, we came to the less-than-sublime time when the bride and groom would leave for their honeymoon. Emily and Tanner had wanted to be surprised by what was thrown at them as they left the reception. We were happy to keep it a mystery but wanted to figure out something creative. We didn't want to toss rice or birdseed or flower petals at our bride and groom. We didn't want to blow bubbles or release balloons.

Finally, we'd come up with the ideal choice. I ordered hundreds of small stuffed bunnies from a toy manufacturer. We thought it was perfect: bunnies were a sign of fertility, and it would be so cute to gently pelt our bride and groom with neon-colored rabbits.

Even before the wedding, a few dozen of these rabbits had hopped over to the bridal-night hotel, waiting in the room for the bride and groom to arrive. Others had been stuffed in honeymoon luggage and dozens more inside every nook and cranny of the getaway car. The bunnies were multiplying.

I should have remembered that the bride's brothers were seventeen and eighteen at the time, and the groom's friends were not much more mature than that. So in the hands of these groomsmen and other wedding guests, the cute little bunnies became, you guessed it, airborne weapons.

Emily and Tanner were ready to go. They stood at the beautiful arbor that my father had made for them. The crowd was ready to say farewell, bunnies in hand.

Then I saw Caleb—who happened to catch the bride's garter, which was a bright Irish green—wearing said garter around his head like a ninja, with a bright pink bunny tucked into it on his forehead. Other guys had their hands full of bunnies. This couldn't be good.

And as the happy bride and groom ran for the getaway car, it began. Bunny wars. Tanner tried to shield a perturbed Emily as they were painfully pelted with hundreds of cute little rabbits . . . which was not quite the fairytale end to what had, thus far, been a perfect Cinderella day.

33

Journaling, Blogging, and Sobbing

The quickest way for anyone to reach the sun and the light of day
is not to run west, chasing after the setting sun, but to head east,
plunging into the darkness until one comes to the sunrise.

Jerry Sittser

I'd been a faithful blogger before Maria's homegoing, sharing
photos, fun, and Chapman news for our friends online. After
the accident, blogging was either impossible or terrifying. I had
nothing to say.

But bit by bit, I started expressing myself again . . . in blogs
or journal entries or even text messages.

But I started short and sweet. Here's my first blog after we
lost Maria:

September 19, 2008

He is God!

I couldn't do much more than that. But I did need to write what was happening. In October I sent this text message to Steven after a trip to Florida with my best friend, Karen, during which we prayed, read the Bible, walked the beach, looked at photos, cried about the past, and prayed about the future:

October 18, 2008

I love you. Ready to see you tomorrow, but unfortunately this trip was not a magic pill to "fix" me.

I knew it wouldn't be.

It has been great and I've remembered a ton.

But in the end, Maria is still gone and her life was lived so full—but also just full enough for this mama to want her back with everything inside of me . . . thus leaving me with the same questions I came with . . . and a bunch of head knowledge as to how to live with this catastrophic loss.

I'm not sure when my broken heart will ever let the knowledge of my head in, or if it can.

I'm afraid to trust God (obviously a past issue) because in my humanness we've trusted and lost over and over.

So where do I go from here?

Once again . . . wanting Maria back and feeling as though God forgot our cumulative prayers of protection on May 21. Which sucks cuz I've read some awesome stuff this week, but it is hard to let it sink in. I love you.

The same day, I wrote Steven a card, which was as much for me as for him:

October 18, 2008

Take my hand . . . that's really it! All we can do is to grab hands, hold tight, and start taking steps!

It feels like we are walking into hurricane-force winds, but maybe, just maybe if we hold tight to each other, and then tie ourselves to the Creator of the hurricane in the first place, we will survive the storm that we are surely in!

I'm only prepared to say survive . . . not yet able to see the calm sunshine and beauty that comes after such devastation, but I'm willing to hold on, which in the end is the true meaning of faith and trust.

Thanks for helping me and not expecting me to be OK too soon. I'm scared, very scared. I'm holding tight. It's all I know to do.

All my love,

Me xxox

Most of my grief those first months went into my journals:

October 2008

Maria,

I'm sad. Brokenhearted and wounded. You are momentarily gone from me, taken without notice, way too soon for my liking.

I'm sitting on the beach with Miss Karen. She loved you so very much and with the pain of your departure she is caring for me very well during my adjustment to the "new normal." We are in Amelia Beach and it is almost sunset. You would've loved the beach because there are lots of waves, shells, flowers, and butterflies. The sand castles you would've built would have been enormous!

Mom and Miss Karen came here to talk about you and remember you! We have watched a lot of DVDs and looked at pictures. We have also read Scripture and books. We have so many questions about why you had to leave us so soon.

Mommy has been *so* sad. I know you wouldn't want me to be, but I long for the way things were and wonder why they have to be the way they are.

I'm sorry, Maria, so sorry if I should've kept a closer eye on you that day. I was too busy, as usual, and excited for the plans of Emily's wedding. I've lived the last five months wondering all of the "what ifs." Please forgive me.

Willy is sad too. He loved you with all of his heart and would never have done anything to hurt you. He didn't see you! I know and you know that now, but I wanted to tell you.

Shaoey has been brokenhearted too. She feels like in some way it is her fault for sending you to get Will. She loves you *so* much! So does Stevey Joy, who misses you terribly! It is like half of her is missing!

Thanksgiving 2008

Maria, this grief I can't express is deeply personal and isolating. It makes Mommy very sad. Sometimes I can't breathe it hurts so bad. Everybody has loved on me, but the tears still come. Shaoey and Stevey miss you so much.

By Christmas, I found I did have things I wanted to share with others, so I sat down to write my first Christmas letter without Maria.

December 12, 2008

I have been impressed for quite some time now to write a letter to all of you who have been so present with us in prayer during these last several months as we have grieved and come to terms with the reality that Maria is gone from us, but present with Christ.

We honestly don't like that very much.

As we enter this Christmas season and all of the festivities that it brings, it also makes the point even louder that one of us is missing. A stocking that won't be filled, and less presents under the tree.

Maria had a contagious giggle that would fill the room over the wonderment of finding the elf that moves to a different spot every day during the month of December. The reality that the precious laughter of Maria won't be heard for a while has been a quiet loudness that screams for Jesus to come quickly . . . not as a baby in a humble manger, but as the King of all kings who will wipe all of the confusion and tears from this sad mother's eyes! I am eagerly anticipating His arrival . . .

As I anticipate Christmas 2008, I have many thoughts flying through my heart and head. The last several days, my mind has not been able to stop thinking about Mary, the mother of Jesus. Pregnant and scared, knowing that the baby she was carrying eventually would pay the ultimate price of His life.

How would I have lived differently if I knew that my time with Maria was going to be this short?

Regretfully, I would have lived much differently. I would have purposely hugged and kissed more. I would have tried to memorize and lock away in my heart certain smells and smiles. I would have colored more and worked less. I would have laughed more and fussed less.

Bedtime wouldn't have become a chore to check off the list of things to get done. Instead it would have been more of an opportunity to listen about the day and offer whatever words were needed. The swimming pool wouldn't have been too cold to swim in. The flowers in the garden would have all been picked, and definitely more ice cream would have been consumed!

I wonder what it was like for Mary after her son's death. I know she saw Him resurrected and was certain of the fact that she would see Him again, but she was still His mom. Mary found favor with God; therefore, she was chosen to be Jesus' mom. But because God favored Mary, she was also chosen to suffer. Not just at the crucifixion, but her whole life. She was chosen to carry a baby in her womb, be persecuted, and give birth in a dirty stable.

Most of the time at Christmas we end the story there . . . in the stable with Mary, Joseph, and Jesus receiving their company. Wise men, shepherds, and angels—you get the picture in your head, right? The star, the animals, the nativity!

What about the rest of it? Mary, mothering the Son of God! She was human, she had a baby, and she raised that baby with the heaviness that she was to see Him suffer and thus she too would suffer. I think when Mary was hiding things in her heart, it was a lot more than the reality of who she carried in her womb. I am certain that she was hiding away the memories of first smiles and steps, as well as the first tears and tumbles.

Knowing what was to come, did Mary have the opportunity to live differently as a mom to her little boy? I believe she did. I am sure that she watched Him differently, taught Him differently, and prayed differently. I can only imagine the discussions that she and Joseph would have when their son wasn't listening, how they probably begged God to let the cup pass from them, but in the end yielding up the prayer we all hesitate to pray when it comes to our children . . . Your will be done.

UGGHH!!!! I don't want to. I didn't want to on May 21st, and I still don't want to now. Yet somehow we did, and somehow we will continue to. I am reminded more than ever this Christmas that it doesn't end at the nativity in Bethlehem in a cozy manger . . . it is a journey all the way to the cross on the hill on Good Friday.

Christmas for the Chapmans this year represents suffering. From here on it represents the ultimate suffering that came on Good Friday.

Isn't it amazing that it is called GOOD Friday? Why is it good if it is full of suffering? Because Easter came on Sunday and what Satan intended for evil, God intended for GOOD! Christmas ultimately ends at Easter and the reality that we will see Maria again!

If we are to live as Christ, then we will suffer like Christ. I am thankful this Christmas more than ever for Easter. When all the questions I have will be answered and all the tears I have will be wiped away. Until then, Merry Christmas with the reality that Easter came and all of this suffering will someday be gone in a moment, and all things will become new and right and awesome!

Thanks for your prayers during this journey. It isn't an easy one and your love and support is continually needed. May you be richly blessed for gracing us with your love. Longing to be washing dishes in heaven with Maria,

—Mary Beth, for all the Chapman family

Somehow, as I moved into my first full year without Maria, I found a way to share on the blog about life again, even the hard parts.

February 2009

Let me just tell you how proud I am of my Will Franklin Chapman and all his buddies on his team. Not that they clinched the District Title, but that they all spoke afterward at Senior Night, and it was inspiring, to say the least. A little background: Will has played basketball with a couple of these guys since fourth grade. They are a close bunch of friends. David Anderson is one of those guys. He just so happens to be the brother of Julia Anderson, soon to be Julia Chapman! You are getting the picture . . . close buddies.

At any rate, they all had a chance to speak tonight and they *all* did great and gave God, family, friends, and coaches the credit. When Will spoke, he talked about homeschooling last year and how hard it was on me to see him not play. Then he told the crowd he is playing this year for *me*, his biggest fan!

To stand before the crowd and acknowledge what he has been through, and thank his family and his best friend, David Anderson, for standing with him, was simply amazing.

When David spoke, he told Will it was a privilege to walk with him this past year and how it has inspired him to live his life for Christ, like him. What an awesome thing to stand there as parents and see this all unfold in the high school gym. Big boys with quiver lips and tons of love for each other in their voices is something I will never forget. Will Franklin, your mom loves you whether you play basketball or not . . . but I sure am glad you did!!

February 20, 2009

One year ago today, Maria and I had this conversation:
Maria: "Does God really have a *big, big* house?"

Mom: "Yes, Maria."

Maria: "Does it have lots and lots of rooms?"

Mom: "Yes, Maria."

Maria: "Does God's big, big house have a big, big table?"

Mom: "Yes, Maria, with lots and lots of food . . . and Maria, it also has a yard where you can play football!"

When I look back to that February morning, Maria was on a mission. I remember even questioning to myself whether she was too young to fully understand what was going on. She was only four years old at the time.

But when God took Maria to heaven just three months after that, February 20th, 2008, would become one of the most special days for our family to hold onto.

Don't ever underestimate the faith of a child. I believe with all of my heart that Maria asking and being so determined was a gift of God . . . a preparation for three months later when my whole world would crumble and life would cease to exist in the way I knew it.

I can't even begin to explain the suffering and hard places that this journey has found me in. But hear me say, with all the certainty in me, that Maria felt compelled that day to ask Jesus into her heart. Did she understand fully? As much as Christ asks us to understand.

We don't have all the answers, but with childlike faith we can trust the one who says all through Scripture that *He* is the only One to trust with your life.

Thank you, little nutty Maria, for teaching Mommy that all you need is the faith of a mustard seed and it will grow into an eternity of sitting on the lap of the One who has the biggest table of food you can imagine . . .

Be blessed today as you put whatever amount of faith you can muster into the hands of the One who holds it *all* . . . including my little girl, Maria Sue Chunxi Chapman . . . the silliest goober I know (I miss you my little sweet pea).

February 21, 2009

I *really* love the support that I've received from you all as I have begun to wander back into the blog world. Please continue to keep our family in your prayers. I really try to be honest and open, and as it relates to Maria it continues to be a very cautious place. We hurt . . . deeply . . . we *are* being held by the One who holds Maria, we believe that. At the same time I cry out to our Father . . . help my unbelief.

Will continues to allow God to work, and the twinkle has been spotted back in his eyes some. Thank you, *thank you,* THANK YOU from the bottom of this mama's heart for holding him in your prayers. He is an amazing young man, and he is simply a hero in my book. The pain of a broken heart is at times unbearable to watch, but then God smiles on us and allows us a glimpse of what He is up to.

It is a *long* and at times *dark* road . . . but the lamp of our faith is lit and we are journeying through it. God bless you all for being on the journey with us. Please don't stop praying.

February 24, 2009

Today is Emily's birthday. Yep, twenty-three years ago today, little Emily Elizabeth came into our life, forever changing it for good, but we had no idea how this little wrinkled bundle of jaundice would impact the lives of so many children and families . . . ours at the top of the list! Happy Birthday, Emily!!!! We love you so very much.

On a day when Mom is having a hard time holding it all together, I am thrilled that your life is being celebrated today. I am so proud of the woman you have become . . . and I *love* the husband that God sent to you.

March 11, 2009

I feel the need to explain my week last week so that my friends here will know how better to pray for me. About a week and a half ago, I completely came to the end of myself. I was teary . . . OK, I was just plain a puddle . . . lots of tears that kept coming. A lot of anger was just crawling all through me. I just couldn't figure it out . . . where was it coming from?

Granted, there is a part of me that feels entitled to be teary and angry. I've been through a lot. Not only last week, but this last year! However, then I quickly prayed to God, *please* . . . I don't want to feel entitled, or act like I deserve to be in this place of self-pity. It is an ongoing war in my heart and my head! I tend to stay quite conflicted these days since Maria left and went to be with Jesus.

But let me tell you about the last several days! Two weeks ago tomorrow, our good friend, business associate, father to Caleb's other band mates, awesome husband, mentor to my sons, left this world to go see his Savior and Maria . . . the result of a fourteen-month battle with pancreatic cancer.

David Lipscomb was an awesome friend and encourager . . . one of the first faces I remember seeing in the emergency room at Vanderbilt the night of Maria's accident. I miss him. I am sad.

And I'm angry. Angry at David, angry at Maria, angry at Steven, angry at whoever would allow me to be and not be angry back!

I was at that place of not understanding God taking away those I love and leaving all of us here to wander around and heal the best we know how! That's at least how I felt . . . partly because I had gone back to the doctor to ask about some medication that I had been on for awhile.

The funeral was 11:00 on Tuesday. The doctor's appointment was Tuesday afternoon. We went straight from the doctor telling me I needed to add another antidepressant medication to the basketball regional semifinals for Will Franklin. Shaoey, meanwhile, had to read a big book on Laura Ingalls Wilder and then she was supposed to put together a pioneer outfit to wear to school on Pioneer Day, then a diorama with a scene from the book, and a book report. Thursday found me at the ob-gyn having my six-week checkup after a hysterectomy (yes, there was that too!). Friday was Pioneer Day!

It was a *big, long* week. I didn't have time for anything I long to do . . . being at home, quiet, spending time reading, praying . . . you all know what I'm saying.

At any rate, I hope at this point you are all figuring out that I am really normal—or not—and on the verge of out-of-controlness! Friday night found us at Shaoey's BB tournament in which she played one game Friday night, two games Saturday night, and two games on Sunday night! (They won!!!)

All the while I am the mother of the groom, with wedding plans coming down the pike fast. I just married off my daughter last October, my little girl went to be with Jesus, and Will Franklin is graduating as well.

I think I am realizing something through all of the craziness. Yes, God wants my quiet, and yes, God wants me to rest and hear Him and learn from Him. But all along, in the crazy last two weeks where I hardly had time to think, I realized that if I always think that I am going to finally get to that place where I am constantly trying to get—like in a quiet, picked-up house— then I'm wrong.

I need to choose to SEE Christ in every birthday party I drive to, every piano lesson that gets taught, every ballet tutu that gets twirled. God is with me. He isn't waiting until I die for me to be with Him. He isn't waiting until BB season is over or until I get completely healthy. He SEES me now. He is with me now. I know this is a simple realization, but it was big good news to me.

I don't want to forget . . . I want to remember . . . God was with Maria on May 21 and God is with Mary Beth on March 10. I would ask your prayers as I try and navigate all the things that pull after me. I love looking after my family, and I really try to put that circle around them that they come first. After that . . . it gets fuzzy.

34

Spring Breaks

Though hope is clouded
It has not left us
Though pain runs deep now
You're deeper still

And You are holding
All things together
Hold us together now

"Close To Your Heart"
Words and music by Steven Curtis
Chapman and Matt Redman

But you, O LORD, are a shield about me;
my glory, and the lifter of my head.

Psalm 3:3 ESV

March 16, 2009

We are in our friend's condo about five miles down from Disney
. . . where we spent four spring breaks, all of them with Maria.

I took a long (probably not long enough) walk on the beach and I cried out to God—Why? What now? How? What?

Here is some of what I heard:

Why? "Because I am God and I know all and am in control and know what is best. Even though it looks like a mess . . . it is My mess."

What now? "I am God . . . keep walking and keep trusting . . . love well the ones still in your charge and care . . . realize that time is short, life is hard, but I've given you so much, do not squander it!"

How? "By remembering that I am God and your trust has to rely completely on Me . . . no striving of your own will to fix, heal, cure, help, calm any of what you see as mess. I allow what I allow for reasons you can't even comprehend . . . rest. You won't figure this out, but He who holds Maria holds you."

What? "Realizing I am God, do the next thing. Tell people of My amazing faithfulness, love your family and friends well . . . rest! It is okay to take the time you need for you. Make changes if you need to. Life on earth is short. I am coming to get you—soon!"

When I was on the beach crying and in a very scattered way asking God these questions above, I cried out loud with tears streaming down my face, "God, can I just hear you audibly? About all of this?"

As I was praying, tears streaming, eyes closed, waves and birds in a rhythm in the far-off background, all of a sudden—SMACK!—the loudest wave I'd heard all day, to the point where I jumped and it startled me. At once I heard God . . .

"Hello, look at this ocean that I breathed and the waves that roll, but not too far, for it is My hand that keeps them off the shore.

"Hello, do I not know how many grains of sand there are, and the number of hairs on sweet Maria's head? I put this bright sun and this cloudless morning in place and will bring the storms in as well. I do not need to speak, for I already have and you have not only heard Me, you have seen me and my power at work. If I control all of this, then I was here May 21, 2008.

"It hurts, but I am all you need. I am sufficient and I am God! Trust Me."

Looking back at my journals from this time, I can see that God helped me know truth, even when I didn't feel it. And I kept writing to Maria . . .

March 18, 2009

> The thief comes only to steal and kill and destroy. I came that they may have life and have it abundantly.
>
> *John 10:10 ESV*

> I have said these things to you, that in me you may have peace. In the world you will have tribulation. But take heart; I have overcome the world.
>
> *John 16:33 ESV*

Steal. The Enemy showed up and, by hurting Maria, took a swing and *tried* to steal our beliefs, faith, trust, and hope in the One who came to give life abundantly and overcame the world on the *cross.*

Kill. The Enemy came to kill Maria, and by the world's standards he did. But Jesus came to give her *abundant* life in heaven. We can have peace that our tribulation is evidence that peace can come from the One who ultimately overcomes the world. Maria is alive in heaven.

Destroy. The Thief came to destroy Will Franklin . . . but Jesus gave Will life abundantly. Yes, in this world he will have the tribulation, but Jesus came to give peace in this world and to Will. Will has felt this peace and knows the *One* who has overcome the world.

Maria is alive and Maria is safe.

March 20, 2009

Maria,

You little nugget! We miss you more than it seems we can bear, but we know God has us in His care and we groan in anticipation of what God is doing and will have done when I hold you in my arms again. I love you!

And I kept blogging, because God kept teaching . . .

March 25, 2009

Chin up! That phrase brought on a whole new meaning as I was taking a walk on the beach. I was asking, thinking, talking to God as I was looking down at the ground, mesmerized by the sand and shells I was strolling over.

I guess I was looking for the perfect shell for the girls, or maybe counting my steps in order to just get the walk over. You see, I don't know if I know how to walk to just enjoy the act of walking.

Today was no different. I just wanted to get it done to get on to the next thing. I was laboring away, walking, looking no further than my feet. I'm a "get it done" kind of gal. While I was walking, head down, zoned in to the three feet or less in front of me, I was certain I heard that still small voice of God whispering ever so loudly to my soul . . . *Look up! Chin up!*

Until then, it had been a cloudy, overcast, rainy kind of morning, the sun hidden behind gray clouds.

To my amazement, as I looked up and lifted my chin, I hadn't even noticed that the sun had come out. It had pushed its way through those dreary clouds and was there, bright as could be. The warmth on my face was solid proof that those clouds were gone!

I so desperately long to heal from so much pain . . . missing my sweet Maria. Trying to find the meaning and purpose for how I will live from here on out. But here is what was spoken to my soul this morning:

· If we keep our heads down, either out of defeat or loss or shame or tiredness . . . whatever the reason, we are going to miss the beautiful sun (and Son) that is right there in front of us, shining its warmth on our faces and our souls!

· We need to understand down to the depths of our souls that whether He is quietly behind a storm cloud or blazing obviously in the bright blue sky right in our faces, Jesus, the Son, is always—not sometimes—present. No matter what the circumstance.

· As we walk with chins up, faces directed toward the Son, we won't see or have to deal with the pettiness of life, represented by the hundreds of seashells I was so fixated on. As we focus on Him, the things of life can be stepped over like those shells. (I know, easier said than done. Trust me, I'm trying to preach to the choir here . . . ME!) Is it possible that some of those seashells of life will just go away? I think so!

- As we keep our faces turned toward Him, maybe we won't see life as a walk we feel we just have to get through and cross off our lists of things to get done . . . laboring and counting steps as we go because we just want it to be over. Maybe we can actually start to allow God to direct our lives in the direction that He wants us to go.

- He is going to tell us where to step and when to look down if our faces are on Him. As I was walking and looking up, allowing my face to feel His warm presence, I felt like I was supposed to look down and open my eyes. When I did, I was getting ready to step right on a baby hammerhead shark! It was deceased, but none the less . . . a shark!

- God allows the sharks of life like the hard places of suffering and difficulties. We all have them! But if our faces are turned toward Him, He will tell us when to look and how to survive those times by completely trusting Him. He navigates the steps and takes us where He wants us to go because He loves us and wants us to become more like Him. It is not up to us!

- Today, had that shark been alive, I would have totally freaked . . . heebie-jeebies to the max . . . I could not have handled it! I feel confident that God allowed it to be deceased so that I could at least write this. And besides, I carried it all the way back to the condo where we were staying and became quite the hero to my kids, young and old!

I hope that in some way this has touched or helped you. I hope that my journey will be one that will encourage you to walk . . . *chin up!*

35

Ready or Not

Man of Sorrows! What a name
For the Son of God, who came
Ruined sinners to reclaim
Hallelujah! What a Savior!

Philip Bliss,
"Hallelujah! What a Savior!"

Shattered dreams are never random. They are always a piece in a
larger puzzle, a chapter in a larger story. The Holy Spirit uses the pain
of shattered dreams to help us discover our desire for God, to help
us begin dreaming the highest dream. They are ordained opportunities for the Spirit to awaken, then to satisfy our highest dream.

Larry Crabb

Now it is required that those who have been
given a trust must prove faithful.

1 Corinthians 4:2

April 12, 2009

Easter is here whether I am ready or not. By the time I push the
button to post this blog, it will be officially past midnight and it
will be Easter Sunday.

This year, I didn't do the official Easter shopping outing where the little girls get new dresses, nor did any of the eggs get colored (plastic will do this year, right?). For that matter, the official Chapman Easter baskets were left in the attic and I didn't make it to the store to buy the Easter candy.

Easter just kind of snuck up on me. I knew it was coming, but somehow I thought if I didn't look, it would go right on by without much pain. I think I was mistaken.

Definitely a different Easter. All of us Chapmans spread out and not together. It is mostly different, though, because of one little squinty-eyed girl who made this family complete with her belly giggle and her infectious personality . . . truly a silly, silly goober!

She is painfully missed, and the hole that is left in her absence is one that is the shape of her and her alone. No one else can fill the empty place that Maria left. While I've been reflecting on that, however, I began to think again of Easter and what all it represents.

Until now, Christmas has always been my favorite holiday to celebrate. Why wouldn't it be? Presents to each other, and Christ as a baby—the present to the world so that we could be saved! A beautiful holiday filled with so much joy, expectation, and celebration. Everything we celebrate at Christmas is really in the form of a present, nicely wrapped with a beautiful bow . . . but without Easter, Christmas would be just another day.

Easter has been "colored up" to be a pretty day filled with baskets, candy, gifts, and eggs. But Easter is messy. Easter is the cross. Easter meant suffering. No Christmas without the cross. I hope we as Christians never forget what that symbol of the cross truly means. We have a Savior who put Himself in human form as an infant, fully knowing what the cost would be on the day we celebrate as Easter.

I am thankful in a special way this year.

The suffering of Jesus is comforting to me when I think about Easter without Maria. But even more comforting is that Jesus rose from the dead, walked out of the tomb. People saw Him and touched Him. They knew it was Him, they knew His voice, they touched His scars.

How exciting it is for me to grasp that the risen Lord could be touched, heard, and recognized. Jesus ascended into heaven like that, which tells me that I will see Maria again. I will touch and hug my little cuddle bug in the most physical sense.

I have that hope, not just because of Christmas, but because of what was accomplished on the cross! It is hard to live in this reality most days. It has been hard beyond what I thought I could ever withstand. However, the work on the cross that was done on my behalf, on your behalf, is what I have to hold onto. It has to be what causes me to take steps forward in this life.

Sometimes it is ten steps forward and five steps back, and sometimes it is one step forward and twenty steps back, but I'm moving . . . slowly but surely with my eyes on the prize. Eternity with Christ and a reunion with a chubby little girl that I didn't get near enough hugs and kisses from this side of the veil.

April 23, 2009

Now I find myself sitting in my home all by myself, all dressed up, waiting on my ride to the Grand Ole Opry House where the 40th annual Dove Awards will be. I am excited to be going with my hubby of twenty-four years and am so proud of how he has walked our journey out these last eleven months. He has been so broken but open and humble before God and his family.

The way he has led us through this darkest of valleys has been inspiring to me. I would not be where I am in my grief journey without Steven being right there to catch me when I fall. In my humble opinion, he is husband and father of the year. When the absolute toughest of situations was given to our family to navigate through, God totally knew that Steven was the man to lead all of us through the valley of the shadow of death.

It hasn't been easy, but at every turn or curve in the road, Steven has sought the wisdom of our Father in Heaven to guide us and hold us up. I say this today to simply ask that you all pray for us as we go tonight to the Dove Awards. That we would honor God for the giftings that He has so graciously poured out on Steven. That the entire Chapman family would be a witness to the faithfulness of God. Not that we have it all together and figured out, but that we are clinging to the only hope we have, the One who does have it all together and figured out, Jesus!

May 2, 2009

I am so thankful that Will and his friends were great sports and let us photo-hungry parents do about a half-hour session before they headed off to dinner and then the prom, which was held on a boat this year!

They all ended up at my house later, and had a great time. Prom yesterday, wedding next Sunday—yikes!

My eighteen-year-old going to senior prom and graduating, and my nineteen-year-old getting married and moving into a house! My head is spinning a bit as I try and savor all the emotions and joy that come with these landmark moments in a young adult's life.

And the funny thing right now is that I am sitting here with my nine-year-old watching old *Little House on the Prairie* episodes!

May 3, 2009

Prom, bridal tea! Again, what a mix of emotions! I am so blessed. I would appreciate tons of prayers, as so many events in May do not take away two days that I see staring straight at me: May 13th, sweet Maria's birthday, and as most of you know, May 21st, the first anniversary of losing Maria.

I would give anything to push rewind, but for some reason, God has us walking through glorious and devastating all at the same time. My prayer is that we walk it out with honesty and humility, giving all honor to the One who is walking us through this month of mountaintops and valleys. I won't ever pretend to understand, but I do want to be found offering up the confusion and questions to the Author and Keeper of all things. Love to all and thanks for journeying with me.

May 5, 2009

My son Caleb took me on a "date" last night! A sweet last memory before he takes Julia as his bride this Sunday, Mother's Day. I was going to remind him that when he was a little boy he *always* talked about never leaving me. He used to tell me he would move right down the yard into the tree house and always take care of me.

But before I could remind him of that, he handed me a Mother's Day card. Inside that card was the sweetest note, apologizing that he can't keep his tree house promise!

I would tell him when he was little that someday a sweet young lady would come along and change his mind. He'd wrinkle his nose and say, "No way, Mom!"

Well, that sweet young lady is here—Julia—and this mom and all the Chapmans love her dearly! And they bought a house not five miles from us . . . pretty good considering the whole tree house promise!

May 13, 2009

Maria's birthday. I honestly don't know what to write or what to say. I can think of all the "right" things to say, like, "I'm thankful for the years I had with Maria."

That is a true statement, but I still want more years with her.

I've heard things like, "She wasn't mine to begin with." That is a true statement as well. She belongs to God. He gave her to me so that I could be her mommy. But I still want to be her mommy . . . I wasn't prepared to give her back to the One who gave her to me.

I wish with everything in me that I was spending my night trying to figure out what cake I would make, or what cookies or cupcakes I would be taking to her classroom tomorrow to celebrate her sixth birthday.

But tomorrow will come and go, and Maria won't turn six. At least not here on earth. I'm not sure how it all works in heaven, but I do know that she is complete and whole and happy. But here, this side of the veil, it really just stinks. I miss her and I'd love to have her jump up on my lap with icing all over her and taste her sweet kisses.

Maria was always just a giggle away from a full-on laugh fest. She was the absolute picture of fun and mischief. Our home isn't the same without her, it is much quieter. Our family isn't the same without her, it is like a chunk of our whole body is missing and the wound feels as though it will never heal.

But . . . I will say that I am certain that the world is a better place for knowing who Maria was. I would give anything to have her back . . . to push rewind and go back and have this all be different. But because we can't, we have to point others to the One who is singing "Happy Birthday" to her now.

So as much as we can, we will use our suffering as a place where people see our hope and our faith.

I'm sad. I'm really, really, catastrophically sad. I'm not sure when it will be better. I guess I will get through this but not ever will I get over it! So I will journey on, knowing that this isn't my home, and that when I reach my journey's end, I will be *with* Maria longer than I will have been *without* her.

I can't thank you all enough for the prayers and the support for our family. Please continue to pray for us, but also take time to pray for all families who have suffered loss, that Christ will meet them somewhere in their grief journey and they will encounter *Him*. Bless you today, on this the birthday reminder of my precious Maria Sue. With that said, I guess I will simply name this blog . . . "I Wanted More."

36

Balloons, Lady Bugs, and May 21

Even the saddest things can become, once we have
made peace with them, a source of wisdom and
strength for the journey that still lies ahead.

Frederick Buechner

God is it true that You're thinking of me at this moment?
God is it true that You hear every prayer that I pray?
God is it true every time my heart beats You know it?
Well if it's all true
Then that must be You I hear saying
"Trust Me"

"God Is It True (Trust Me)"
Words and music by Steven Curtis Chapman

May 14, 2009

Steven and I went to school to help Stevey Joy's class remember
Maria. The moms had arranged balloons for the kids to write
notes on and let go in honor of our sweet Maria. We told the class

a few stories and fun memories of Maria, and then everyone wrote their notes.

We then went outside to pray and release our balloons. Steven prayed the sweetest prayer and then, just as God would have it, it was quite windy . . . and we let our balloons go! They blew right up over the church and over the steeple.

Maria loved ladybugs. When we picked out the spot for her shell to be buried, we found a ladybug there. Just about every time we go, a ladybug is there. Maria's sheets in her room were even ladybugs!

At any rate . . . right after the balloons were released and the kids were squealing with excitement, I heard Stevey Joy yell, "Hey, look!"

As I looked down, a ladybug was crawling up her hand. It crawled to the top of her finger and flew away, just like the balloons.

Later that day, family and friends gathered at our barn, had cupcakes, sang "Happy Birthday" to Maria, and did the same thing again! We wrote notes on the balloons and sent them all at once up into the heavens. Part of me couldn't help but want to go right along with the balloons . . . to be gathered up by the wind and be swept to heaven to be with Maria.

I said a silent prayer, asking Jesus to come quickly and to give my Maria a big, tight hug and let her know I love her.

May 21, 2009

Never in a million years would I think I would be sitting here on May 21, 2009. Most of my words will seem empty today because I'm kind of in a surreal place in my heart as I try and express this journey that the Chapman family has been on this past year!

Here is what I *feel* as this day starts out. Sad beyond sad that she isn't here. Angry and mad that this had to happen. Confused and bewildered that it had to involve Maria's big brother, who absolutely adored her. Paralyzing fear that I won't be able to pull through the pain and be able to completely let her go. Speechless to know how to grieve my baby girl, who gave me soooo much laughter and joy, and then turn around and hold tightly to the young man who is walking through this tragedy at eighteen years old . . . Maria's buddy, Will (the bravest young man I know!). And at my darkest place, I wonder . . . God, where are you and why in the world would you choose us to walk this out . . . it isn't fair!

And then, all of a sudden, I hear this other voice in my head that reminds me over and over again of not what I *feel*, but what I *know*.

It might on certain days be buried deep down in my heart and have a hard time computing to my brain, but here is what I know and what I choose to believe, over and over again. I know God loves me and my family. I know God is sovereign and He knows what is best for us. I know He has our days numbered and makes *no* mistakes. I know that He will bring beauty from ashes . . . that is what I cling to in order to make it through another twenty-four hours.

Isaiah 53:3 kept going through my head the day of the accident: "He was . . . a man of sorrows and familiar with suffering."

I said it over and over and over again. He is a Savior who took on the suffering for *all* of us. He knows what it is like to suffer! I love how *The Message* puts Psalm 30:5—"The nights of crying your eyes out give way to days of laughter."

I have to *choose* to believe this right now. I have cried so many tears mixed with the sadness of missing Maria and the joy of remembering her! I think when those tears get all mixed up together and fall, it has to water the dry places of our hearts and begin to slowly start healing us. If not, I would just wither up and die.

I believe that God has not wasted a single bucket of tears that have been cried for this brave little girl who so wanted her brother to put her on the monkey bars that day, and the brave young man who has chosen to allow God to begin to heal him and use him for His glory!

I can only begin to imagine the story and testimony that Will Franklin will have. But please, don't stop praying for him. As with any tragic situation, there are good days and not so good days. We prayed for two miracles one year ago today . . . that Maria's life would be spared and that Will's life would be spared. God chose to bring a spunky little stinker named Maria to Him, while He needed a brave, heroic young man to begin to tell the testimony of how Christ is ministering mercy and peace to him.

There is no doubt in my mind that God will change lives through Will Franklin's walk with Christ . . . so please, please, pray God's protection over him, that he would continue to allow God's healing power to pour over him!

I told someone yesterday that I feel as though I'm not just walking through a desert right now . . . I'm wandering in it with no clear path in front of me. It is a very desperate place to be, and on lots of days I'm strong on the outside but a mess on the inside. But I must hold on to the very real fact that Jesus has gone to prepare a place for me . . . that where He is, I will also be!

That is very, very good news . . . because my Maria is there in that big, big house . . . with lots and lots of rooms and food! I will see her again, and I will be with her then for far longer than I have to be without her now! It stinks on this side of the veil, and at times I've tied a knot on the end of my rope and am just barely hanging on . . . but I'm hanging!

I'm pretty certain that I am still on the journey of making peace with the fact that this tragedy happened to our family. Nonetheless, I'm journeying on. I am trusting that the Giver of life will bestow the wisdom and strength needed to journey faithfully to the end of my time here on earth, where I'll hear and SEE Christ say, "Well done, my good and faithful servant!" And then I will run into the arms of that little Curious George who I'm sure will be standing there in her monkey underwear and nothing else but a big grin that makes it all okay!

I want to thank the thousands of you who have sent comments, emails, cards, letters, memorials. . . . We are completely humbled by your goodness and kindness to continue to lift us up in this way and by continuing to pray for our whole family! We know for certain that those prayers, which we *physically* feel daily, are helping us get up in the mornings and to simply breathe! We love you all so much. Please don't stop!

May 24, 2009

Tonight was the graduation ceremony at Christ Presbyterian Academy, exactly one year to the day that we stood on that very platform to say goodbye to our little girl, Maria Sue.

God is either a truth or a lie. Everything He has said and promised is either 100 percent true, or it is lie after lie after lie. Today, along with many days this year, Satan was crushed, and what the Enemy intended for evil . . . God intended for good, and *great* it was!

Every senior has a blessing written for them and a Scripture verse read over them as they graduate from CPA. The seniors, once again in honor of Maria and our family and the fact that it was the anniversary of the funeral, walked barefooted, symbolizing they were on holy ground!

The speakers both touched on the fact that the graduates of 2009 have grown deeply rooted in their faith because tragedy not only struck once, but three times this year. In May, it was our sweet Maria. In October, a teacher at our school suddenly passed away, leaving a senior daughter to wade the waters of grief. And then in March of 2009, a CPA student took his own life, which rocked the entire community.

This class has been through a lot and they have come through stronger than most, because I believe God has a great plan for the students of the class of 2009.

A day of mourning . . . ashes . . . one year later a place of beauty. The pain is still there . . . most of the time as sharp as ever . . . God allowing the chisel and hammer to do His

Will Franklin Chapman— Courageous, "appointed one," gifted, authentic, and tender; one who has walked with vulnerability and grace through the most trying of times; Will knows what is important and what he values; resourceful, resilient, more than a survivor; a persistent warrior who knows which battles to fight; great sense of humor; excellent musician and great team player; he has walked out the gospel before us; given the gift of faith to carry him through, he is and will be an overcomer and a conqueror . . . steadfast in spirit; he has a radiance and transparency that draw us to Christ.

"Whom have I in heaven but you? And earth has nothing I desire besides you. My flesh and my heart may fail, but God is the strength of my heart and my portion forever" (Psalm 73:25–26 NIV).

Blessing and Scripture for Will Chapman on the occasion of his high school graduation beautiful work in and amongst our friends and family. Maria's death has taken a toll on a lot of us, not just our family. Those closest to us are mourning and grieving her just as deeply as we are, and the toll it has taken on them is as great as ours.

It is just not as fun without Maria. She was the funniest, most stubborn hoot of a little girl ever. We will *always* be different because we knew her . . . we will *always* be different because we lost her.

Could it be that this little girl was simply given to us for a short time so that she would ask Jesus into her heart, and then as simple as that was, leave just two months later to go be with Him?

Hard to fathom, but completely something only God could orchestrate! Lord, I trust you . . . help my unbelief. That is where I am, slowly, slowly wallowing through this complex journey God has set before us Chapmans, who long to show a suffering world that there is hope . . . but only through Him.

37

New Songs

God is always working to make His children aware of a dream that
remains alive beneath the rubble of every shattered dream, a new
dream that when realized will release a new song, sung with tears, till
God wipes them away and we sing with nothing but joy in our hearts.

Larry Crabb

June 7, 2009

I believe God led me to Psalm 40:1–3 today. I'm going to write
it out in the present tense; how I SEE the process of losing Maria
is working itself out in the Chapman family:

> I wait patiently for the LORD; He will turn to me and hear my
> cries. He will lift me out of the slimy pit, out of the mud and
> mire [of loss and grief and anguish of why?]; He will set my
> feet on a rock and give me a firm place to stand. He will and
> is putting a new song in my mouth, a hymn of praise to our
> God. Many will SEE and fear and put their trust in the LORD.

As I write this, I am realizing the changes that are happening
to the Chapmans in these upcoming months.

Tanner and Emily: preparing for a move to Ireland for a year. They will be attending Bible college. May many who meet them SEE Him as they share not only their song of sorrow over the loss of Maria, but the *new* song that He alone is writing on their hearts. God is their Redeemer, the One who is setting their feet back on solid ground and giving them a new song to sing, a story of redemption to tell, so that many will know *Him*!

Caleb, Julia, and Will: Caleb has been writing music for some time now. Julia and Will have been right by his side. Now, Caleb and Will have a testimony to steward well. God has entrusted all of them a new song. It's like the parable of the talents. Caleb and Will can bury theirs or use them for the world to SEE an amazing story of forgiveness and redemption.

Again, a song of sorrow over the loss of Maria, but a new song coming up out of the mud and mire as they tell of a God who will hold them and set them on a solid foundation. (Interesting that our pond is mud and mire, and that is where Caleb held Will the day of the accident and where Caleb ripped Will's shirt off and threw it into that mud.) May many who hear their story SEE only Jesus who can save and do the miracles He has done with my boys.

Julia is an amazing part of all of this, and may she be blessed beyond measure as she supports the process so the new song can be sung!

Shaohannah Hope and Stevey Joy: God has seen fit to leave me with Hope and Joy. My two princesses give me a reason to get up in the mornings and push through the difficult days. God is the God who heals, and I am beginning to SEE a new song in your beautiful Asian eyes!

Many, many days I still hear the song of sorrow being played, but every now and again there are notes of a new song.

Girls, may you make a hopeful and joyful noise unto the Lord as He continues to write your story. I won't ever pretend to understand the why this side of heaven . . . but as your mommy, I vow to help you understand that God is writing a new song in you and He hasn't left you and never will. We'll sing it together, no matter which way the melody goes!

Steven: You sing your songs with a new fervor! There is a new urgency in you. I can see it in how you sing and in how you speak. But as I wait patiently (sometimes not so patiently!) for the new recording to be finished, I know He has written something *new* through you!

It couldn't have been fun, probably mostly painful as you grieved your little girl through the pen as it was poured out with tears into *new songs*. I know this was a different process for you, but please trust me when I say that the world will SEE and hear and many will put their trust in the Lord. Not because of you and your abilities, but because you have been a willing, broken vessel into which you've allowed God to pour Himself. You have set the example for your family on how to allow God to leak out of the broken places of our lives.

Again, I don't like it one bit. I would be just fine with a perfectly unbroken vase, especially one that wasn't broken over the loss of a child. But I'm trusting that God saw fit to entrust us to steward this catastrophic loss well. May He be honored with all us Chapmans as we do our best to let the world SEE that He alone is the Author of our salvation, the Mender of our hearts, the Healer of souls.

38

Maria's Big House of Hope

See, I am doing a new thing! Now it springs up; do you not perceive
it? I am making a way in the desert and streams in the wasteland.

Isaiah 43:19

June 23, 2009

Tonight we celebrated the official name change of Shaohannah's
Hope to Show Hope! We also had the honor of doing a state-
side dedication of Maria's Big House of Hope.

An overwhelming number of our supporters, friends, and
family turned out to support us in the process. We had a packed
house and several key media outlets were on hand to capture
this bittersweet time, dedicating this facility that can serve orphans in China! While I still don't like the fact that Maria isn't
with us in the flesh, I am humbled to have a front row seat to
watch God do a new and amazing thing in her honor.

Here's Show Hope's "official" word on this incredible
ministry:

Location: Luoyang City in the Henan Province, China
Size: 6 floors, 60,000 square feet
Capacity: 128 orphans with special needs
Staff: 190 staff members and nannies at full capacity
Medical Staff: Full time doctor and 5 full time nurses

Maria's Big House of Hope, located in one of the poorest provinces of China, was built by **Show Hope**, a ministry founded by Steven Curtis and Mary Beth Chapman. Show Hope created this beautiful home to give over 120 orphans with special needs the love, shelter, medical care, and hope they so desperately need.

The painful reality facing orphans with special needs is that they don't have the advocacy of a parent or resources of a family . . . so they don't often receive care and life-saving treatment. As a result, many are left to languish alone, and too many die, though their special need might well have been surgically correctable.

Maria's Big House of Hope cares for the least of the least, saving the lives of those we can, and giving the highest level of holistic care to all the children who pass through our doors. This remarkable facility includes floors for children in need of acute care before and after surgery, a floor for those waiting for a forever family, and hospice care for the children who will soon pass away, so they can look to the hope of heaven while being cared for with tender love and attention.

July 2, 2009

Maria's Big House officially opened today! National and local government officials were there to honor Show Hope's efforts to help the special needs orphans of China! We really felt the Spirit of God as we stood there in front of Maria's Big House and dedicated it back to Him and in honor of Maria, who was a special needs orphan herself!

There were several speeches, certificates given to us to commemorate the day, and Steven sang, of all songs, "Yours"—which was so awesome, standing there on a stage saying, *It is all God's!* Right there in China!

July 4, 2009

I wish I had the exact words to describe the emotions and thoughts that were flooding through me as we pulled up to Maria's Big House after all the business and excitement of the grand opening was over and it was just us.

Our group from Tennessee pulled through the gate in the morning with nothing on the agenda but to play, hold, sing, pray, bless, experience this place that has been honored with Maria's name!

There are so far about forty children transitioned into the house, with room for about ninety more. They will transition in groups from mostly the Luoyang city orphanage. Some will come from other areas for surgeries and special care.

We took tons of pictures, cried lots of tears, and sang lots of praise songs through the halls of this special place. We walked into every room, singing praise and worship over the entire place, ending on the roof! We read blessings that Show Hope sponsors had written for the children and prayed that God would do a mighty work in this place.

We ended by going to the Tinker Bell room. We sang "Big House" as loud as we could while the children who are with us started a train through the room.

A pretty special day, but a hard one. I spent some quiet time alone sitting under the mural of the Disney movie *Cars* painted in one of the rooms, which is currently empty. Maria *loved* Mater.

She used to say all the time, "My name is Mater, as in *toe*-Mater except without the toe!"

As I sat there quietly, I tried desperately to hear her sweet voice saying that phrase. She would have loved all the rooms, but the one that would have made her giggle would have been the Mater room, as she would have called it, and the Tinker Bell room. All girl with a little tomboy was my sweet Maria! Oh, to hear that sweet little voice again!

All I heard was silence as I begged God to let me hear her. Nothing.

Then in the distance I began to hear the voices of the little ones living in Maria's Big House of Hope. Whether it was a giggle, cry, or babble, I began to realize that it was up to me to make a choice.

I'm not going to hear Maria's voice again this side of heaven, unless I choose to hear it differently . . . in the voices of these little ones who are going to receive life-giving care in this facility. She is here . . . I have to believe . . . cheering us on because she SEEs fully what we still struggle to SEE. That God is working *all* things together for good for those who love Him. She knows how this story ends and what it will look like when we are all together again.

But until then, her voice will carry on in these precious, broken little people who are in the care of Maria's Big House of Hope!

July 8, 2009

July 8, 2004: Steven, Shaoey, and I were handed the youngest Chapman. "Gotcha Day," for those of you who don't know, is the day that you receive your child in China. Sometimes the official adoption day is the same day, and sometimes it is a few days later.

At any rate, July 8, 2004, was Maria's Gotcha Day. She was adopted a few days later . . . and our lives were changed forever and for the better!

This trip to China, while incredible and good and full of God's love and grace, has also been full of memories of Maria being here, and all of the "what ifs" that the Enemy would like to throw at me. I gotta be honest, I've seen some *hard* things the last couple of days, and the empathy that I could have with these people because of my loss was an incredible gift, for the reason of being able to relate, but I found myself also being so angry at the simple question: "Why, God? Why *so* much suffering in the world? There are so many broken lives everywhere!"

I just would like to say . . . I am so sorry for anyone reading this who is suffering in some form or fashion. Be it health, spouse, child, financial, whatever the reason . . . loss and suffering are hard and very unpredictable. I still trust in the One who gave us Maria to love for such a short time, but I am also a person who trusts while doubting at the same time. I am just being honest. I pray to God that He would build my trust and that my doubting would turn to rejoicing in time.

Maria, you are and will always be my sunshine who makes me happy! I love you, Mommy

July 20, 2009

I was in complete shock when I saw how beautiful our friends had made Maria's memory and Big House look! I have to admit, though, what I remember most about walking in wasn't the beautiful painting as much as it was *their* smiles . . . so badly wanting me to approve and love it!

How could I not *love* it?

I still find myself walking around this place, named after my sweet Maria, begging God to rewind time, to *change* it back to the way it was even as I SEE the amazing things going on here. I know God understands this mama's heart, because He is the One who gave it to me in the first place. But again, as I really stop . . . as I really listen, as I really observe . . . I SEE the good change and the God change that is taking place here.

Miracles happen every day. Some children live and receive life-giving medical care, and others are comforted as they live out their number of days this side of the veil.

In a strange way, I feel Maria closest to me when I spend time with the ones who are in hospice care. I can only imagine it is because these little ones are so close to seeing Jesus, and Maria *is* SEEing Jesus. I picture her there waiting to receive those little ones from MBHOH and usher them into the arms of Jesus!

July 24, 2009

I was standing in the lobby of Maria's Big House looking at the finished artwork, when all of a sudden here they came: two new heart babies through the front door! I immediately reached out my arms and this little guy was placed in my embrace . . . and I fell instantly in love with another little man.

This little guy's diagnosis is not positive and thus he is in palliative care, which is like hospice. My heart is so heavy for him. I spent time making him coo and giggle before rocking him to sleep this morning, and now . . . I find myself thinking of him constantly and praying that God would do a miracle in this little boy.

If not, it's good to know that his care will be compassionate. I told this little guy all about Maria, and I'm quite convinced that when it's time for his life here on earth to be over, he'll be greeted by one sweet little angel—who also knew what it felt like for me to hold her and rock her to sleep.

August 10, 2009

Please continue to pray for us . . . we have so much to process. China was so incredible, and I long to be there more and more. But the girls start school on Monday, which will always be sad with one missing. Emily and Tanner leave for Ireland on September 8. Caleb (with Julia cheering him on) is in meetings about upcoming music opportunities with Will.

So many changes and we have a lot of decisions to make for the rest of 2009 and 2010. Pray that God will lead clearly!

August 22, 2009

This post finds me very saddened, yet grateful over the loss of the precious little guy I told you about from Maria's Big House of Hope just about a month ago.

I was given the privilege of giving him his English name. Hudson, after James Hudson Taylor, an amazing missionary to China!

This little guy's eyes locked onto mine immediately, and I knew I was in trouble. I spent a lot of the rest of my time rocking and singing and snuggling little Hudson. He was born on a 21st, which is the date of Maria's passing, and it happened to be the 21st of July when he arrived at MBHOH.

I was gentle with him as he was fragile and struggling to breathe. Every day I carefully carried him down to the *Cars* room and showed him the murals of Lightning McQueen and Mater. I told Hudson about Maria and what she was like and where she lives now.

One day, while Emily was rocking Hudson, I was leaning over top of him talking silly like mamas do. I was trying to get a first-ever smile out of him.

I wouldn't have believed what happened next if I didn't have Emily as a witness. I was saying in a very silly voice that I was going to pray hard that God would heal him. I told Hudson that I longed to have him healed this side of heaven, but if God chose to take him home early, an amazing little girl named Maria would be waiting for him when he got to heaven!

At the exact moment I said "Maria," Hudson let out his first-ever giggle and smile.

It gave me goose bumps, and I froze. I said, "Emily, please tell me that you saw that!"

She saw it too.

When I left China and came home, I continued to pray for Hudson and all the little ones at MBHOH. I knew that everything was being done that could be done, and I was so grateful that he had found his way to MBHOH. I bought a soft blanket and had his name embroidered on it so that Hudson would have his own snuggly blanket from me. In some way, I hoped that he would sense it was from someone who was really fighting for him on this side of the world.

I received word a couple of days ago that Hudson had taken a turn for the worse. I was really struck again at how short life can be, such a wisp of time and we will be in heaven . . .

Tonight I got a call from my sweet, sweet husband . . . Steven had received the call that little Hudson had passed on, so now he is healed, and he is running in heaven with his new heart with absolutely no problems breathing!

I just know my Maria was waiting for him . . . I am sad, I am heartbroken, but I'm not without hope.

Without hope, Hudson may never have heard the words, "Jesus loves you, this I know," sung to him over and over again. God, who gave us Jesus, knew in His infinite wisdom that for such a time as this, God's people would move and Maria's Big House would be built.

I am so grateful tonight, as I lie here with my two girls, for everyone involved with making this amazing place happen. God can accomplish great things through His people who are willing to act . . . and because of that, this little guy with *big* brown eyes, would be loved, cuddled, and sung to, right up until he was seeing the face of Jesus . . . with an anxious Maria peeking over His shoulder, busting at the seams to meet one of the residents of her namesake.

I am so honored to be a part of MBHOH . . . but to God alone be *all* the glory. May we always be found willing to do what He is asking of us. I'm pretty sure His voice usually isn't loud and clear . . . so get quiet and really listen to that still, small voice. Things might get risky and crazy and break your heart at times, but it is all worth it!

I leave all of you who are hurting or suffering in some way a quote from the man little Hudson was named after, James Hudson Taylor:

> May this be your experience; may you feel that the Hand which inflicts the wound supplies the balm, and that He who has emptied your heart has filled the void with Himself.

Everything, including our pain, is His. I am thankful He will meet me in it.

39

Kissing the Fat

We're not necessarily doubting that God will do the best for us;
we are wondering how painful the best will turn out to be.

C. S. Lewis

September 11, 2009

I went through some of Stevey Joy's and Maria's things today.
I had to get Stevey Joy's desk organized. I've been putting it
off for well over a year now, but it was time to face some more
memories and pain. I was going through old journals. Stevey
Joy has a glittery princess one, and Maria had a green Tinker
Bell one.

While I was thumbing through Maria's journal, I stopped on
a page that brought tears and joy and pain to me all at the same
time. On a page near the back I found a six-petal flower and a
butterfly, completely and brightly colored in by my sweet little
goober of a girl.

This was the same picture she was drawing the day of the terrible accident, except this beautiful picture was finished, colored in! The blue petal that she had colored on May 21 is in the same place on this flower, and the orange center is the same.

I feel as though I got to see the whole picture! God is going to color in the rest of it on *that day* when all the questions won't need to be answered . . . and all our tears will be wiped from our eyes! That little nugget of a girl left me another gift on a day when I have been really struggling with God and the whole suffering journey.

I'm so tired of the "if onlys," and I about drive myself crazy thinking she'll be home the next time I walk in the door. I physically miss her smell, her slobber, and her fat little feet so much that I sometimes feel as though I'm going through some kind of withdrawal.

Emotionally I'm fatigued from wondering what all of this mess and confusion and trauma is doing to Shaoey, Stevey, Will, Caleb, Emily, and Steven. It hurts just typing this because so many people have been affected by the loss of this squinty-eyed, big-smiled little princess who invaded the hearts of many.

I know seeds of hope have been planted . . . and I have even seen some of the sprouting of growth that comes through tragedy, suffering, and what God can accomplish through all of this. But, man, is that ever so hard to embrace on days when it would just feel better to shut down and pull the covers over your head!

But, as Maria's picture so clearly shows me, the bright color is coming. When that foggy glass that we now see through dimly shatters, we will be in the brightly colored, finished picture of heaven where I will hear little Maria say, "SEE, it's everything you said that it would be!" I will hold her and hear her heartbeat again and it will be glorious!

September 19, 2009

You know, it's really cool when we get to SEE when God causes good to come out of such hard times. I was thinking about my sweet friend Lori Mullican, and how weird and awful it is that we both would lose our daughters in accidents. But here's a good thing that came out of Maria's loss.

Ever since the car accident that had killed her sister 10 years earlier, Alex Mullican had struggled with awful feelings of guilt and pain. When she was younger, she never could have put words to it . . . but she felt like it was her fault that her sister had died. In her mind, *she* was the little one who had to go home that night and get in the bed. *She* was the reason that they had to leave the party early.

Lori and Ray had tried to help her every way they could. They'd taken her to therapy and counseling, but nothing had really broken through.

Anyway, Alex is a teenager now. And on the night of Maria's accident, Alex was sitting with one of her friends, crying and praying for us. And then as she was crying out to God to comfort Will, God gave her words she had never uttered before. She began talking about the night of the crash that had robbed her of her sister and her peace. For the first time in 10 years, she verbalized her feelings that *she* was responsible for her sister's death. As she prayed for Will, Alex felt a peace and rest she hadn't known before.

In God's perfect timing, He used my Will's pain as a trigger for Alex's healing. And now she's volunteering at a counseling center, and she's studying for a degree in counseling, so she can help children deal with trauma and brokenness!

September 25, 2009

Today is just one of those days, when it all seems very surreal again, and if I take a nap maybe I'll wake up to life being different, with Maria running up and down the steps a million times like she always did. Maria was loud, as I've told you all before, so her absence is a huge void around here.

For the most part, everyone is adjusting to the new normal—you know the one with a huge elephant in the room that some days you just have to ignore to make it through the day . . . or on other days, you talk it out, cry it out, fight it out, or pray it out of the room.

I've now read so many books on grief that I should have a degree, but you know what? There isn't any one way to do it. My story isn't yours and your story isn't mine. I've come to the conclusion that the only thing people who are suffering and grieving have in common, at least if you believe as I do as a Christian, is the One who suffered for us. And the Father, who grieved for Him going to the cross, understands.

Now, whoever is sitting there saying, "Yeah, sure . . . right," I'm with you! There are days that God is sooooooo quiet that I begin to question Him. I'm just being honest. There seem to be days of silence.

And even with all the seeds sprouting from planting the story of Maria into the hearts of thousands, it still seems quiet when I most need to hear Him. I am still assuming that this is where faith, hope, and trust enter the picture. If I stop believing, then what? Maybe that is what God wants me to learn through all the silence. And some days I'm hopeful.

On other days I'm screaming, "I believe . . . help my unbelief!"

The chronic pain that lives in my heart and my soul wants surgery to fix it . . . get it better quick! But sixteen months into this journey, I'm beginning to realize that God perhaps wants me to heal slowly so that as many things that can be learned about Him are learned. I'm not being a very good student today. Maybe tomorrow my attention will be better!

I am trusting He has the Chapmans' best plan scripted out for us until we are with sweet Maria again. I'm sure it won't be all happy and pain free. I know that suffering is one place where He ministers to us the most. So to think that we've had our quota would be foolish. I am just longing for the day when all the pain stops.

Until then, may we face each struggle with the hope that He is working out His salvation in us, looking to the day when all things will be made new and suffering ends.

I know Maria knows that now. I can't wait until she can give me the VIP tour of heaven! Have a great weekend, and again . . . for those hurting . . . I'm just very, very sorry, and you need to know that God does understand.

October 13, 2009

Twenty-five years ago today this Ohio girl with *big* eighties hair married a Kentucky boy with an impressive mullet! I was nineteen and he was twenty-one. I'm not sure where all the years went . . . but I'm grateful that I have spent them with my best friend!

October 22, 2009

I started this post yesterday . . . I couldn't finish it . . . got frustrated and teary and just walked away.

I had a few things to do, a couple of appointments and errands, and then it happened. I realized that I was all alone. The boys were out of town, the girls were in school, and I had about two or three hours before I needed to pick up Shaoey and take her to trauma counseling. (What a fun extra-curricular activity that is. Some kids play soccer . . . others go to trauma therapy!)

I hate being alone these days, which is ironic because I usually like being alone. But these lonely days leave me open to do nothing but think! Especially on days that happen to be the twenty-first of any month, it is just a little bit harder.

I'm sure as time continues to be a friend and carry us closer to the reality of our true home and inheritance with Christ, it will be . . . well, maybe not easier, but different. Maybe a shift of perspective that life is moving by at a faster and faster pace, and that we really *are* just passing through this land to our permanent home with Christ.

Feeling all this, I did what any sad, grieving mom might do. I went to T.J. Maxx!

You see, I'm not a shopper. I don't like or care about brand names. I avoid the mall unless it is Christmas and I have to purchase gifts for family members. And when I do have to make a retail selection, the bargain hunter in me is unveiled! T.J. Maxx is my friend!

A lot of times I just get a buggy and stroll the aisles, not putting a single thing in my cart. I just stroll, think, and cry as I think of how desperately I miss that chubby-bellied, pigeon-toed, sloppy kisser of a girl.

Yesterday, seventeen months later, I still caught myself bargaining with God to give Maria back to me, to somehow let her be manifested so that I could just see her for a minute, or at least get a small whiff of her sweet, sweaty smell. I would have loved to just feel the sensation of me kissing the fat of her neck and blowing Zerberts until she giggled so hard she could barely speak!

Why? It's been seventeen months! I still think about her that much and miss her that much! I don't know whether I'm stuck . . . stuck in grief . . . or if I'm simply a mom! A mom who knows exactly how many days it's been since she heard, "Mommy,

Well I can't wait to SEE your smile again
The one when your eyes disappear along with all my troubles
And I can't wait to hear you sing a song
Maybe "Jesus Loves Me" or a song you learned up there

Well I can't wait to hear your mama laugh
The way that only you can make her laugh when you get silly
And I can't wait to SEE you in her arms
And know the wound so deep inside her heart is healed for
    good

And I can't wait to dance with you again
Knowing that this time the dance will never have to end

And I can't wait to SEE your sisters play
The way they do when all of you are playing all together
And I can't wait to watch your brother's face
When he can finally SEE with his own eyes
That everything's okay

But I, oh, I just have to wait
'Cause I know that day is coming
So I, oh, I just have to wait

from "Just Have To Wait"
words and music by Steven Curtis Chapman

will you put Cinderella's gloves on for me? Thanks, Mommy, I love you!"

I really hesitate sometimes to write these truest of true thoughts down. I find myself thinking, "Whoever is reading this probably thinks I need to just get over it and move on."

I want you all to know that I am making progress. The waves roll in a little less frequently, but they still roll in. And as far as getting over it, I won't. I'll get through it, not over it.

There is a part of me that will be and is forever changed and different because I buried a child at five years old!

Now, that's not to say I won't ever experience joy. I already have . . . in plenty of ways. I've had two children get married since Maria went to be with Jesus! What joy it was to see my children so in love and happy . . . true joy. Yet, what was forever changed was the fact that I will still go through those joyous times very aware of my brokenness and my sadness.

It's really okay! In fact, God entrusted me with it. Why? Trust *me*? I don't even want to talk about the *why* question. But ultimately, God wanted to use our family to live out this kind of story here on earth.

I only pray that when people see us battling it out and crying our guts out and loving till it hurts, that they know we are doing our best to honor the One who blessed us with Maria for five beautiful years.

Did I want more years? You better believe I did . . . but I also know that Maria didn't live one day longer than she was supposed to. She was never going to learn to ride her bike without training wheels, drive a car, go on a date, or as Shaoey observed, have a senior picture hanging on the senior picture wall.

God knew all of that. He knows all of my pain, and somehow I am trusting that He alone is the One who is going to fix it, heal it, make it right . . . when it is time.

Until then, I'll still be asking God to let me see her, feel her, smell her. And so if you see a woman who is a little disheveled walking the aisles of T.J. Maxx with tears streaming down her face . . . it's probably me!

You see, no matter how much I can tell you it's getting easier, I still end up back where I started. I want so badly to be the strong Christian woman who keeps taking those steps ahead and making that awesome progress.

Yet, when all is said and done, I think I'm going to have to settle for the Little Engine That Could, telling Jesus, "I think I can, I think I can!" and believing it . . . even when I don't!

40

Year Endings and New Beginnings

There is nothing we can do with suffering except to suffer it.

C. S. Lewis

After you have suffered a little while, the God of all grace, who has called you to his eternal glory in Christ, will himself restore, confirm, strengthen, and establish you.

1 Peter 5:10 ESV

The Chapmans' Christmas Letter 2009!

M·E·R·R·Y C·H·R·I·S·T·M·A·S!

M:

May 10, 2009, Steven and I welcomed a new daughter-in-law into the family! Caleb and Julia were married in a quaint ceremony by a lake . . . just like she always dreamed of. She is no newbie around us! Caleb and Julia have been best buddies since elementary school!

God truly showed off bringing these two beautiful people together. Julia's brother David is Willy Frank's best friend . . . and her mom? Only one of my closest buddies in the world! How great is that? Julia works at Show Hope and teaches dance part time, and supports Caleb as he pursues his musical interests and continues all the video work at Show Hope!

E:

Emily and Tanner headed for the beautiful green land o' the Irish in September. They are currently students at Belfast Bible College and are loving the challenge of being in school together, and learning all they can about the Bible and God's love and message for them!

R:

Ruthy and Will are now dating long distance, but for the most part, it has worked out well. Ruthy is finished with school this December and will have a semester break and some summer fun before starting college in the fall. Wherever she ends up going, that university will be lucky to have her! Talk about a smart girl!

R:

Reaching double digits! Shaoey, that is! Shaohannah celebrated her tenth birthday this year! We celebrated with ten of her closest friends and a bunch of family and others back in August. We got her an iPod. That little stinker is so smart. She sold it to her brother Caleb, took the money she made from that, added her birthday money from various grandparents, and headed on over to Best Buy to purchase an iTouch. Now when she is around WiFi, she can text her big sister Emily and her buddy Tanner all the way in Ireland . . . for free . . . thanks to Skype!

Y:

Yelling and yearning: That pretty much sums Mary Beth up. I'm in the second year of grieving one of the six best things to ever be given to me to care for, and now she is in the arms of Jesus, the ultimate Mother and Father!

Perfect forever . . . but that's *there* . . . in heaven. Here on earth, this side of the ever-so-thin veil, it is pretty crappy! No sense hiding it: I've spent a lot of time yelling at God, yelling at myself, yelling to hear myself yell! Wanting so badly for the God who I believe in wholeheartedly to yell back all the answers I long to know . . . which leaves me yearning for the day when all yelling ceases and every question I had will be answered . . . even the questions that I yelled at God! Good news for a loudmouth like me who wants to know and know now!

C:

Caleb and Will Franklin: Are opening for Casting Crowns this spring. The tour is forty cities long. This mom is so proud she can't even stand herself.

With the tragic story God has given Will and Caleb to steward, this is a great place for them to be. Check out www.calebchap man.com for more info!

Can you tell I'm just a tad bit excited for my boys? God is good!

H:

Healing, hoping, and hard have been the themes for all of 2009. A lot of people think that the first year of grieving is the hardest. I'm sure that is true for so many. But for me personally, it's been the second year that has been by far the hardest.

It's as if I am thawing out, waking from a deep freeze, coming back from some out-of-body experience. I am literally missing *huge* chunks of time, and this year, 2009, has me feeling as though I am experiencing some of the "firsts" without Maria, when in reality they are the "seconds."

It just hurts a little more without the numbing effects of adrenaline and denial . . . those places where our minds take us in those unpredictable, panicked moments when all of a sudden we think we can actually go back and change something to make the outcome different . . . and then we realize, "Wait, it's been a year and a half . . . she is not coming back."

We will see her again, and we will spend more time with her than we did without her, but this has been the journey that *no one* would have signed up for.

Good thing for me that *hope* is also in the letter H today. Without that simple word, it would all be a crock! But I have this hope in heaven, in Christ, in the cross, that we will win this battle before us.

R:

Riding a bike! The big news of the year! Yes, Stevey Joy is seven. Yes, maybe she should have learned a little earlier, but she only weighs *38 pounds* at seven years old! I think that was a big part of the problem: she was too light to hold herself up!

But finally, on an warm, fall day, it happened. The wobbles stopped, and the brakes worked when they were supposed to and didn't throw her over the handlebars, and she could turn and come back without going straight forever and ever! The smile was priceless.

Dad, Mom, and Shaoey all witnessed this groundbreaking event live . . . from the driveway. Another day for Mom to wonder if Maria would have learned sooner (she was a little heavier and gutsier) or later (she was the baby of the family). And while I was so proud of Stevey Joy . . . the tears fell as if something was still so terribly wrong!

It sure seemed like there should have been *two* princess bikes outside trying to keep from crashing into each other. Maria would have totally been into demolition derby type of bike riding . . . as a matter of fact, she may have had a *Cars* bike from the boy section of Wal-Mart!

I:

Into the studio Steven went and out he came . . . a very difficult process later . . . with his new project *Beauty Will Rise*. Steven says that they are more of his psalms rather than songs, the journal of his heart as he worked through the grieving of Maria.

S:

Stevey and Shaoey both are currently taking gymnastics and playing basketball . . . along with Stevey doing dance and both girls attempting to keep up with piano and voice!

That makes me tired just typing it.

Stevey is a very gifted gymnast and dancer, while Shaoey loves to flip and flop and make some mean defense happen on the basketball team.

Willy Frank has signed on to help out with Stevey's bball team. It should be a hoot! I'm certain with the Asian genetics, gymnastics is much more in our future! Stevey is on track to compete at some point, while Shaoey just wants to learn impressive skills like her accomplished round off back handspring back tuck.

T:

Travel for Steven, me, and our two little people, heading to Ireland after Christmas. Emily and Tanner have a bit of a break, and we decided for a Christmas present we would cash in some frequent flyer miles, head to the Irish coast, treat Emily and Tanner to a quick visit to London and Paris, and then head back to Dublin and then home. Phew!

M:

Maria's Big House of Hope (MBHOH) officially opened this past summer. Our entire family, along with some close friends, all traveled to China to be a part of the dedication ceremony. It was really, really great, and really, really hard . . . one of those places that God has you walk.

When I left there, I begged God to let me SEE Maria.

I did! I'm convinced that I saw her in every giggle, cry, and child that was being given life-saving medical care there. I heard her in the nannies' voices and I smelled her in the air.

I pray that God would allow me to keep walking in faith to know that *His ways are higher*! Trust, trust, trust! What else do I have?

Believe me, easier said than done. Many days you can find me curled up in my La-Z-Boy crying my eyes out, wishing with everything that she were going to be here to open up Christmas presents with the rest of us this year! I still think I'm dreaming sometimes! Oh, to kiss that little neck of hers!

A:

Answers to all my questions: there have been none. If I had answers . . . then I guess there would be no use for faith and hope! I'm hoping in the unseen. Faith is being sure of what we hope for and certain of what we do not SEE. But one day, my sweet friends . . . we will SEE! I wonder why that was the word she left? Maybe that's an answer!

S:

Speaking. Many of you have asked, so now is the time to address a few things coming up. After much prayer and a huge confirmation from God, we as a family have decided to do some different things next year. Steven will continue to do the Women of Faith conferences, which have been such a blessing to him and the boys.

The wonderful staff of WOF has asked me to be a part of their team and to do a speaking segment at the conference. Yikes!

Do you know what this means? The three things I said I would *never* do:

1. Adopt
2. Homeschool
3. Speak in public

Well, it looks like during the next school year, I'll be taking my *adopted* children out on the road with Steven to *homeschool* them. This is so that I can *speak* to many of you at Women of Faith conferences all over the country!

One thing I've learned, don't tell God what you won't do!

Well, in the Spirit of Maria (who loved to rock out), the Chapmans wish you a *rockin'* Christmas!

February 1, 2010

It doesn't get much better than about five inches of good sledding snow in Tennessee. A rare thing indeed! It has given us a four-day weekend to enjoy the cold, the snow, and some yummy hot chocolate with friends!

Yesterday we ventured onto our neighbors' property (with permission, of course) to find the perfect hill for the little ones, plus some added dangers for the bigger kids in the group!

Our little Maria used to say *all* the time, "I love it when my whole family is together!"

Without Emily and Tanner, who are still studying in Belfast, and of course without that little infectious nugget of a girl who knew how to laugh at all things, while snot and slobber dripped out of every open spot on her face. . . . She must have known in her short time here on earth the importance of that statement—*"I love it when our whole family is together."* I would venture to say that idea isn't just in the physical sense, but in the emotional and spiritual sense as well.

Since May 21, 2008, our whole family being together has been a challenge of the greatest proportions. I'm here to say that this journey is just plain hard. But what do we do?

Just like the silence you hear (or don't) in woods full of snow . . . the insulation it brings from the snow covering everything . . . that's what I feel like I hear on most days . . . *nothing*!

But again, until I die or Jesus comes back, we will do hard. And even when we feel our God is being silent in the pain . . . that is where the truest sense of faith must come into play.

But again, I have hope in how the story ends. I can't wait for the day when I can hear the giggle of that little girl as we lay in the best snow ever and make snow angels like she used to love to do.

In the meantime, I love all of you and consider it a great honor to share my thoughts with you. Here's to faith, trust, and hope . . .

41

Spring Is Coming

春溪

When you *SEE* this, your heart will rejoice and you will flourish
like the grass; the hand of the Lord will be made known.

Isaiah 66:14

Hear the birds start to sing
Feel the life in the breeze
Watch the ice melt away
The kids are coming out to play
Feel the sun on your skin
Growing strong and warm again
Watch the ground
There's something moving
Something is breaking through
New life is breaking through

"Spring Is Coming"
Words and music by
Steven Curtis Chapman

Steven's *Beauty Will Rise* CD is a collection of his psalms about
Maria. For Steven, the raw material of his grieving was like clay

or paint, something to be shaped into art and worship, even if it was rough. He took his pain, his questions, his trust, his love, his fear, and his faith into the recording process.

He didn't want the CD to sound too polished or commercial, so he recorded in foyers, back stage during his "United" tour with Michael W. Smith, on the bus, in locker rooms, in an actual shower stall, and from the road in China in the summer of 2009.

The process was immeasurably hard.

But it was a poignant tribute to life and death, the pain and the comfort that came from saying a temporary goodbye to Maria.

As he was writing what would be the last song on the album, Steven's thoughts returned to the day of Maria's burial. He kept thinking about the words of our pastor, Scotty Smith. At the graveside, Scotty had said that Maria's burial represented a seed being planted into the ground. He talked about what it means to plant a seed and wait—until a seed falls to the ground and dies, it can't come to life.

Because of Jesus' death and resurrection, Maria will also be raised. Not with a weak, natural body, but a powerful, spiritual body. Scotty talked about the promised spring that is coming

> We planted the seed while the tears of our grief soaked the ground
> The sky lost its sun, and the world lost its green to lifeless brown
> Now the chill in the wind has turned the earth hard as stone
> And silent the seed lies beneath ice and snow
> And my heart's heavy now
> But I'm not letting go
> Of this hope I have that tells me
> Spring is coming, Spring is coming
> And all we've been hoping and longing for
> Soon will appear
> Spring is coming, Spring is coming
> It won't be long now,
> It's just about here . . .
>
> "Spring Is Coming"

when all things will be made new. Because the gospel is true, we can wait for that day with real hope . . . the ultimate day when icy winter gives way to the warmth of spring and a permanent, glorious new life will spring forth.

When it came time to record "Spring Is Coming," Steven wanted to do it right at the cemetery where Maria's shell is buried. We had picked her plot because it was in the back of the cemetery and we thought it would be peaceful. We didn't realize that there was an industrial park nearby. With Maria's spunky attitude, she would have loved all the noises that come with traffic and businesses. So it was good for her, so to speak . . . but it just wasn't going to work for recording a CD.

So Steven ended up recording at the home of our dear friends, the Andersons, who had given us respite in the sad days after Maria's departure and where Maria had spent many, many happy days before that.

Steven recorded on the Andersons' dock on their beautiful lake. Here is where Will had cried out so desperately in the days right after the accident, where family and friends had held him and prayed for him.

This was also the same spot that on May 10, 2009, Caleb Stevenson Chapman married Julia Elizabeth Anderson. She had grown up dreaming of getting married on that dock, and we celebrated their union.

So what an appropriate place for Steven to record his haunting, compelling, sweet, powerful song! "Spring Is Coming" became a theme for us all, an emblem of hope in the cold, dark months of grief when our hearts were frozen hard within us.

Then, not long before this book went to press, we found out something we didn't know before.

Emily and Tanner, off at Belfast Bible College, had befriended a Chinese student. One winter evening, Emily was sitting with her new friend, Sophia, and asking her questions about speaking Mandarin, which Emily had studied in college. On a whim she asked Sophia about the English meaning of Maria's Chinese given name. Emily didn't know the Chinese characters for it, just the English phonetic spelling.

"Chun Xi," she told her friend. "It's my little sister's name."

"Oh," Sophia said. "Chun . . . this means 'spring.' And let's see, Xi means 'twilight,' or 'dawn,' like 'spring is on the horizon,' or like 'spring is coming.' Yes, that's it. In English you would say 'spring is coming'!"

Emily couldn't believe it.

Our Maria had been given her Chinese name by an unknown social worker at an orphanage in China soon after she was abandoned at two days old. Because we had met her as "Maria" when she was already with the Hedden family, we didn't think much about researching her Chinese name. We knew it was Chun Xi, but with Maria being Chapman number six, we hadn't taken the time to explore it further.

And now, years later, in the winter of our grief, we were living the poignant title of Steven's song . . . and finding out that her very name meant the exact truth that was sustaining us all: *Spring is coming.*

When Emily called us from Ireland, we were stunned by this amazing story that some might call coincidence. We knew that God had given us another glimpse of the story that He is telling, one He had orchestrated from the beginning of time. He knew what the Chinese social worker in a communist country would name an abandoned orphan . . . and He knew that Steven, grieving his precious daughter's death, would name the last song on his CD the exact meaning of her original name.

Incredible.

We Chapmans are big on due diligence. Emily got a copy of Maria's birth name in its Chinese characters and brought the paper to her Chinese friend.

"Ah, I see," her friend said. "This is very similar, but more specific. The name means 'spring river'!"

We found that name to be even more significant. A spring river results from the melting away of winter's snow. The purest water flows from spring rivers . . . God's means by which formerly frozen ground can soften and bloom again with the life of spring.

So God confirmed this truth yet again: I can choose to SEE His story, or I can miss it. And I know—in the winter of our grieving and the frozen mourning of my plans that will never be and my dreams that have died—the reality is this: God's warm breath is on the move. New life is budding . . . and often where I expected it the least, like right inside of me.

So where better to end this book?

Yes.

Spring *is* coming . . .

Acknowledgments

Where does one who has so many to bless and thank begin? When the accident happened, two years ago at the writing of this, I would never have imagined the journey that I would go through personally. I've come to the conclusion that even if it were just one book that ended up on my bookshelf, the process would have been worth it. The writing of this book has taken me to the depths of my pain that I haven't visited in a long time, and I am grateful for a tender Savior who journeyed with me through some of the darkest places a person can journey. Thank You, Jesus, for shining light in areas that continue to help in the healing process. For where I have been wounded, you are binding me up and turning the winter into spring.

Ellen Vaughn. You are lovely. Not only are you a gifted writer, you were not afraid to step into the messiness and pain of my life. Thank you for coaching me and helping me bring this story from deep within my soul.

The entire gang at Creative Trust. Jim Houser ##., you are the best manager to work for (LOL). You are a brave man for taking on the Chapman clan. Thanks doesn't seem enough for all we've put you through. Dan Raines, Jeanie Kaserman, Kathy Helmers, Meredith Smith, Jenny, Jessica, and the rest: I am grateful for your hard work and diligence in making this book a reality! Thank you for believing. Thanks also to the Chapman web guru, Dale Manning.

To my new family at Revell. Andrea Doering, you are so kind and wise. Twila, Cheryl, Jennifer, Michele, Deonne, Amy, and Mary: I have truly enjoyed learning the process of the book world and am grateful for the hours of work you have done on my behalf. Even when I was driving everyone crazy, I totally felt like you were for me. Thanks for putting up with my idiosyncrasies in trying to deliver the "perfect book." I really tried not to have control issues, but then, something just takes over! You all have been nothing short of stellar in believing in a story of a woman who somehow ended up in a life she didn't plan! God so knew what I needed. Thank you! Please know that handling this story as gently and as carefully as you have does not go unnoticed.

Beth Moore. I have admired your work for many Bible studies. *Breaking Free* changed my life several years ago. Only God in His infinite wisdom would have us connect in the ways that we have. I am flat honored that you shared your precious dream with the reader of this book. My confirmation to move forward and to know in confidence that there is no doubt a wiggly, sticky little girl who goes with me and all is well with her soul. I thank my God for you!

The Women of Faith team. Thanks for the encouragement and for allowing me a place to feel safe while I learn the process of sharing my story.

(Danny) and Melissa, the best Missa in the world. Maria was blessed to know you. I know you miss her, and I'm so sorry for the ache in your heart. Your unwavering belief and reminders to me of where Maria is have kept me breathing on days. She loves you, to infinity and beyond!

David Trask, did you ever know that you're my hero? Thank you for serving the Chapman family as road manager all these years. You're living your own pain-filled life and still have made yourself 100 percent available to us, especially Will.

Grace (amazing), Sydney, Herbie, and Wendy. The people behind the Chapmans. What would we do without you to make Steven and I look like we are half sane. You *all* have been through it with us. Not only walking with us through the pain of loosing Maria, but the pain of watching Steven and me doing our best to allow God to be honored in the story of our lives. Thank you for being the people behind us that we can count on to do the daily "stuff" that keeps us moving forward.

Show Hope—my passion. Steven and I have been blessed to be part of an amazing ministry that all began out of a desire to get children adopted into loving homes and offer care to orphans around the world. The staff as well as the board are the most amazing group of passionate people in the world. God has blessed us beyond measure with our fearless, godly leader, Scott Hasenbalg (when I say Scott, I mean his wife Kerry as well). Scott, you are long-suffering and gentle, always putting others first. You have led Show Hope greatly by being a living example of humility. Charley, Wendy, David, Nick, Kathy, McKensey, Julia, Caleb, Cathy, Melissa, Katie, Brooke, Lindsey, Stacie, Phil and Emily: "I have an idea . . ." jk. I love you dearly. Your commitment to your work and helping the fatherless without voices of their own is inspiring. I appreciate your dedication!

The friends that held us up during the darkest, longest hours of our life:

Reggie, Karen, and the crew. There are no words for what you endured by loving us during this time. You gave us your hearts and your home without hesitation. Saying thank you is simply not enough. Karen, I love you. I've been one tough friend to love through this grief; patience and wisdom are your gifts. David, you are the friend that sticks closer than a brother. Will is blessed by you.

Lori Mullican. I am so sorry it took ten years and more pain for the circle to complete. I knew instinctively to call, and within minutes you were there. I know it brought up so much history and pain, and yet, God was there in the midst of the chaos. The coffee talks have been a balm to my soul. Alex, I'm so proud of you!

Geoff and Jan. We've known you since 1984 when we moved to town. An instant friendship began. When I think about our past together, I look forward with great delight to the future. Thank you for following your heart to China for Anna Grace and Ashley Rose. No words were spoken, but your presence in the room spoke volumes the night of May 21.

Terri and Dan, thank you for stepping way out. It has cost you a lot. I'm so sorry for the hard. You are my adoption heroes. Your example changed the look of our family, and I can't thank you enough. Show Hope was born, in part, as a result of the call on your lives and your faithfulness to follow through. Your heartbeat for orphans is now beating in me.

Mark and Ann, who were the prayer warriors for our whole family. You provided a safe place and sweet Scripture readings over Will Franklin daily. We love you and count it a privilege now to return the favor and intercede on your behalf. Ruthy, you have been an amazing strength for Will. Mature beyond your years. I love you.

Tim, Janie, and Tabby, our new family through Tanner. Thanks for loving us through this time. We all love you, but the girls think you ROCK! Gymnastics and horses—they love it! Tabby, I know you miss her. She loved your aqua hairlights! LOL! You've meant the world to the li'l nuggets . . . especially SJ!

My family is simply amazing. You all have stood with us through much of the good and bad that life has brought our way. Mom, Dad, Jim, Yo, Jeanne, Barry, Herbie, Sherri, Herb Sr., Deniece, Judy, and all the children that go with you. I'm honored to be your daughter, sister, sister-in-law, and daughter-in-law.

The preventative maintenance team: Pastor Scotty Smith, Al Andrews, Lynn Husband, Larry Crabb, and Dan Allendar. Your love, wisdom, insight, and great counsel have proven to be invaluable and a true source of hope when our weary souls couldn't take another step.

Paris Goodyear-Brown and David Thomas. Your expertise and kind hearts have blessed my children. I really don't know what we would have done without the counseling work you walked them through.

Our community at Christ Presbyterian Academy. ALL of you loved on us, brought us food (Tina, I blame you for the extra twenty), wrote us letters, took the girls fun places, on and on its goes. . . . You also entered into Will's pain with him and walked closely beside him his senior year. Thank you! Our family at Christ Community Church . . . ditto. The outpouring of love toward our family was felt in a tangible way.

And finally to you—the one who holds this book in your hand. If you are reading this book, then you more than likely have prayed for me and our family at some point. I can't tell you what it feels like to literally know the world is praying. We felt physically held during the time of losing our Maria, and you were part of the body who cried out on our behalf. Thank you so much. I pray that each word of my story will touch you in a way that gives a blessing back to you for holding us tight during this time. If you are a fellow sufferer, someone who has experienced loss of some kind, I'm so sorry for your pain. All stories of "hard" are different, but pain and suffering are the common ground. I pray for each hurting person that is reading this for some kind of encouragement while life continues on with unrelenting force. Winter comes, that is for sure. But beneath that hard frozen ground is spring, and it most definitely will come.

With love and hugs,

Mary Beth
Hosea 6:1

Mary Beth Chapman is the wife of Grammy and Dove Award winning recording artist Steven Curtis Chapman. Together they began Show Hope, a nonprofit organization dedicated to caring for the world's most vulnerable children by providing financial assistance to families wishing to adopt, as well as increasing awareness of the orphan crisis and funneling resources to orphans domestically and internationally. Mary Beth serves as president of Show Hope and is a speaker for Women of Faith 2010 with her husband. She is also coauthor with Steven of the Shaoey and Dot series of children's picture books. Mary Beth and Steven have six children, Emily, Caleb, Will Franklin, and adopted daughters Shaohannah Hope, Stevey Joy, and Maria Sue, who is now with Jesus. The Chapmans live in Tennessee.

Ellen Vaughn is a *New York Times* bestselling author and inspirational speaker. Her recent books include *Shattered, Lost Boy, Time Peace, Radical Gratitude*, and *It's All About Him*, a *New York Times* bestseller. Former vice president of executive communications for Prison Fellowship, Vaughn collaborated with Chuck Colson on eight nonfiction books and two novels. Vaughn and her husband live in the Washington, D.C. area with their three teenagers.

Permissions

ORPHANS AROUND THE WORLD ARE IN DESPERATE NEED...

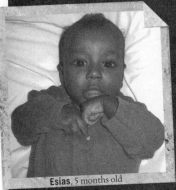

Esias, 5 months old

THIS WAITING ORPHAN LONGED TO BE LOVED

But Esias had no family

WITH THE HELP OF A SHOW HOPE SPONSOR

Esias can have a forever family through the Adoption Aid program

Esias, 16 months old

show HOPE™

A Movement To Care For Orphans

"Religion that is pure and faultless before the Father means that we must care for orphans." —James 1:27

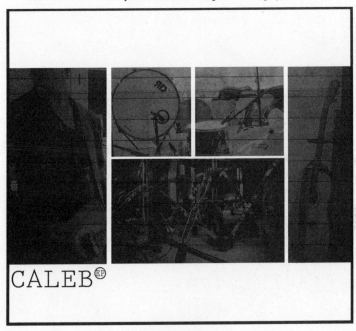